T0214071

Lecture Notes in Computer Science   11878

More information about this series at http://www.springer.com/series/7407

Christophe Debruyne · Hervé Panetto ·
Wided Guédria · Peter Bollen · Ioana Ciuciu ·
George Karabatis · Robert Meersman (Eds.)

On the Move to Meaningful Internet Systems

OTM 2019 Workshops

Confederated International Workshops:
EI2N, FBM, ICSP, Meta4eS and SIAnA 2019
Rhodes, Greece, October 21–25, 2019
Revised Selected Papers

 Springer

Editors
Christophe Debruyne (ID)
Trinity College Dublin
Dublin, Ireland

Wided Guédria
Luxembourg Institute of Science
and Technology
Esch-sur-Alzette, Luxembourg

Ioana Ciuciu (ID)
Babes-Bolyai University
Cluj-Napoca, Romania

Robert Meersman
Graz University of Technology
Graz, Austria

Hervé Panetto (ID)
University of Lorraine
Nancy, France

Peter Bollen
Maastricht University
Maastricht, The Netherlands

George Karabatis
University of Maryland,
Baltimore County (UMBC)
Baltimore, MD, USA

ISSN 0302-9743 ISSN 1611-3349 (electronic)
Lecture Notes in Computer Science
ISBN 978-3-030-40906-7 ISBN 978-3-030-40907-4 (eBook)
https://doi.org/10.1007/978-3-030-40907-4

LNCS Sublibrary: SL1 – Theoretical Computer Science and General Issues

This Springer imprint is published by the registered company Springer Nature Switzerland AG
The registered company address is: Gewerbestrasse 11, 6330 Cham, Switzerland

General Co-chairs and Editors' Message for OnTheMove 2019

The OnTheMove 2019 event held October 21–25 in Rhodes, Greece, further consolidated the importance of the series of annual conferences that was started in 2002 in Irvine, California. It was then moved to Catania (Sicily) in 2003, to Cyprus in 2004 and 2005, Montpellier in 2006, Vilamoura in 2007 and 2009, Monterrey (Mexico) in 2008, Heraklion (Crete) in 2010 and 2011, Rome in 2012, Graz in 2013, Amantea (Italy) in 2014, Rhodes in 2015, 2016, and 2017, and lastly to Valletta in 2018.

This prime event continues to attract a diverse and relevant selection of today's research worldwide on the scientific concepts underlying new computing paradigms, which of necessity must be distributed, heterogeneous, and supporting an environment of resources that are autonomous yet must meaningfully cooperate. Indeed, as such large, complex, and networked intelligent information systems become the focus and norm for computing, there continues to be an acute and even increasing need to address the software, system, and enterprise issues involved and discuss them face to face in an integrated forum that covers methodological, semantic, theoretical, and application issues. As we all realize, e-mail, the Internet, and even video conferences are not by themselves optimal or even sufficient for effective and efficient scientific exchange.

The OnTheMove (OTM) International Federated Conference series has been created precisely to cover the scientific exchange needs of the communities that work in the broad yet closely connected fundamental technological spectrum of Web-based distributed computing. The OTM program every year covers data and Web semantics, distributed objects, Web services, databases, information systems, enterprise workflow and collaboration, ubiquity, interoperability, mobility, as well as grid and high-performance computing.

OnTheMove is proud to give meaning to the "federated" aspect in its full title: it aspires to be a primary scientific meeting place where all aspects of research and development of internet- and intranet-based systems in organizations and for e-business are discussed in a scientifically motivated way, in a forum of interconnected workshops and conferences. This year's 18th edition of the OTM Federated Conferences event therefore once more provided an opportunity for researchers and practitioners to understand, discuss, and publish these developments within the broader context of distributed, ubiquitous computing. To further promote synergy and coherence, the main conferences of OTM 2019 were conceived against a background of their three interlocking global themes:

- Trusted Cloud Computing Infrastructures Emphasizing Security and Privacy
- Technology and Methodology for Data and Knowledge Resources on the (Semantic) Web
- Deployment of Collaborative and Social Computing for and in an Enterprise Context

Originally the federative structure of OTM was formed by the co-location of three related, complementary, and successful main conference series: DOA (Distributed Objects and Applications, held since 1999), covering the relevant infrastructure-enabling technologies, ODBASE (Ontologies, DataBases and Applications of SEmantics, since 2002) covering Web semantics, XML databases, and ontologies, and of course CoopIS (Cooperative Information Systems, held since 1993) which studies the application of these technologies in an enterprise context through, e.g., workflow systems and knowledge management. In the 2011 edition security issues, originally started as topics of the IS workshop in OTM 2006, became the focus of DOA as secure virtual infrastructures, further broadened to cover aspects of trust and privacy in so-called cloud-based systems. As this latter aspect came to dominate agendas in this and overlapping research communities, we decided in 2014 to rename the event as the Cloud and Trusted Computing (C&TC) Conference, and it was originally launched in a workshop format.

These three main conferences specifically seek high-quality contributions of a more mature nature and encourage researchers to treat their respective topics within a framework that simultaneously incorporates (a) theory, (b) conceptual design and development, (c) methodology and pragmatics, and (d) application in particular case studies and industrial solutions.

As in previous years, we again solicited and selected additional quality workshop proposals to complement the more mature and "archival" nature of the main conferences. Our workshops are intended to serve as "incubators" for emergent research results in selected areas related, or becoming related, to the general domain of Web-based distributed computing. We were very glad to see that our earlier successful workshops (EI2N, META4eS, FBM, and SiANA) reappeared in 2019. The Fact Based Modeling (FBM) workshop in 2015 succeeded and expanded the scope of the successful earlier ORM workshop. The Industry Case Studies Program, started in 2011, under the leadership of Hervé Panetto, Wided Guéédria, and Gash Bhullar, further gained momentum and visibility in its ninth edition this year.

The OTM registration format ("one workshop and/or conference buys all workshops and/or conferences") actively intends to promote synergy between related areas in the field of distributed computing and to stimulate workshop audiences to productively mingle with each other and, optionally, with those of the main conferences. In particular, EI2N continues to create and exploit a visible cross-pollination with CoopIS.

As the three main conferences and the associated workshops all share the distributed aspects of modern computing systems, they experience the application pull created by the Internet and by the so-called Semantic Web, in particular developments of big data, increased importance of security issues, and the globalization of mobile-based technologies.

The three conferences seek exclusively original submissions that cover scientific aspects of fundamental theories, methodologies, architectures, and emergent technologies, as well as their adoption and application in enterprises and their impact on societally relevant IT issues.

- CoopIS 2019 (Cooperative Information Systems), our flagship event in its 27th edition since its inception in 1993, invites fundamental contributions on principles and applications of distributed and collaborative computing in the broadest scientific sense in workflows of networked organizations, enterprises, governments, or just communities.
- C&TC 2019 (Cloud and Trusted Computing), is the successor of DOA (Distributed Object Applications) and focuses on critical aspects of virtual infrastructure for cloud computing, specifically spanning issues of trust, reputation, and security.
- ODBASE 2019 (Ontologies, Databases, and Applications of SEmantics) covers the fundamental study of structured and semi-structured data, including linked (open) data and big data, and the meaning of such data as is needed for today's databases, as well as the role of data and semantics in design methodologies and new applications of databases.

As with the earlier OnTheMove editions, the organizers wanted to stimulate this cross-pollination by a program of engaging keynote speakers from academia and industry and shared by all OTM component events. We are quite proud to list for this year:

- Elena Simperl, University of Southampton, UK
- Stefan Thalmann, Karl-Franzens University of Graz, Austria
- Silvie Spreeuwenberg, Lab for Intelligent Business Rules Technology,
  The Netherlands

The general downturn in submissions observed in recent years for almost all conferences in computer science and IT has also affected OnTheMove, but this year the harvest again stabilized at a total of 156 submissions for the three main conferences and over 45 submissions in total for the workshops. Not only may we indeed again claim success in attracting a representative volume of scientific papers, many from the USA and Asia, but these numbers of course allowed the respective Program Committees to again compose a high-quality cross-section of current research in the areas covered by OTM. Acceptance rates vary but the aim was to stay consistently at about one accepted full paper for three submitted, yet as always these rates are subordinated to professional peer assessment of proper scientific quality.

As usual, we separated the proceedings into two volumes with their own titles, one for the main conferences and one for the workshops and posters. But in a different approach to previous years, we decided the latter should appear after the event and so allow workshop authors to eventually improve their peer-reviewed papers based on critiques by the Program Committees and on live interaction at OTM. The resulting additional complexity and effort of editing the proceedings was professionally shouldered by our leading editor, Christophe Debruyne, with the general chairs for the conference volume, and with Hervé Panetto for the workshop volume. We are again most grateful to the Springer LNCS team in Heidelberg for their professional support, suggestions, and meticulous collaboration in producing the files and indexes ready for downloading on the USB sticks. It is a pleasure to work with staff that so deeply understands the scientific context at large and the specific logistics of conference proceedings publication.

The reviewing process by the respective OTM Program Committees was performed to professional quality standards: each paper review in the main conferences was assigned to at least three referees, with arbitrated e-mail discussions in the case of strongly diverging evaluations. It may be worthwhile to emphasize once more that it is an explicit OnTheMove policy that all conference Program Committees and chairs make their selections in a completely sovereign manner, autonomous and independent from any OTM organizational considerations. As in recent years, proceedings in paper form are now only available to be ordered separately.

The general chairs are once more especially grateful to the many people directly or indirectly involved in the setup of these federated conferences. Not everyone realizes the large number of qualified persons that need to be involved, and the huge amount of work, commitment, and financial risk in the uncertain economic and funding climate of 2019, that is entailed by the organization of an event like OTM. Apart from the persons in their aforementioned roles, we wish to thank in particular and explicitly our main conference Program Committee chairs:

- CoopIS 2019: Martin Hepp and Maria Maleshkova
- ODBASE 2019: Dave Lewis and Rob Brennan
- C&TC 2019: Claudio A. Ardagna, Ernesto Damiani, and Athanasios Vasilakos

And similarly we thank the Program Committee (co-)chairs of the 2019 ICSP and Workshops (in their order of appearance on the website): Hervé Panetto, Wided Guédria, Gash Bhullar, Georg Weichhart, Milan Zdravkovic, Peter Bollen, Stijn Hoppenbrouwers, Robert Meersman, Maurice Nijssen, Ioana Ciuciu, Anna Fensel, George Karabatis, and Aryya Gangopadhyay. Together with their many Program Committee members, they performed a superb and professional job in managing the difficult yet vital process of peer review and selection of the best papers from the harvest of submissions. We all also owe a serious debt of gratitude to our supremely competent and experienced conference secretariat and technical admin staff in Guadalajara and Dublin, respectively, Daniel Meersman and Christophe Debruyne. The general conference and workshop co-chairs also thankfully acknowledge the academic freedom, logistic support, and facilities they enjoy from their respective institutions – Technical University of Graz, Austria; University of Lorraine, Nancy, France; Latrobe University, Melbourne, Australia – without which such a project quite simply would not be feasible. Reader, we do hope that the results of this federated scientific enterprise contribute to your research and your place in the scientific network, and we hope to welcome you at next year's event!

September 2019   Hervé Panetto
                                                                  Robert Meersman

Organization

OTM (On The Move) is a federated event involving a series of major international conferences and workshops. These proceedings contain the papers presented at the OTM 2019 Federated Workshops, consisting of the 14th International Workshop on Enterprise Integration, Interoperability and Networking (EI2N 2019), the 5th International Workshop on Fact Based Modeling (FBM 2019), the Industry Case Studies Program 2019 – Industry Day (ICSP 2019), the 8th International Workshop on Methods, Evaluation, Tools and Applications towards a Data-driven e-Society (Meta4eS 2019), and the First International Workshop on Security via Information Analytics and Applications (SIAnA 2019).

OTM Conferences and Workshops General Chairs

Hervé Panetto   University of Lorraine, France
Robert Meersman   TU Graz, Austria

EI2N 2019 PC Co-chairs

Wided Guédria   Luxembourg Institute of Science and Technology,
                             Luxembourg
Georg Weichhart   Profactor GmbH and Johannes Kepler University Linz,
                             Austria
Hervé Panetto   University of Lorraine, France
Milan Zdravkovic   University of Nis, Serbia

FBM 2019 PC Co-chairs

Peter Bollen   Maastricht University, The Netherlands
Stijn Hoppenbrouwers   HAN UAS and Radboud University, The Netherlands
Robert Meersman   TU Graz, Austria
Maurice Nijssen   PNA Group, The Netherlands

ICSP 2019 PC Co-chairs

Hervé Panetto   University of Lorraine, France
Wided Guédria   Luxembourg Institute of Science and Technology,
                             Luxembourg
Gash Bhullar   Control 2K Limited, UK

Meta4eS 2019 PC Co-chairs

Ioana Ciuciu   University Babes-Bolyai Cluj-Napoca, Romania
Anna Fensel   STI Innsbruck, University of Innsbruck, Austria

SIAnA 2019 PC Co-chairs

George Karabatis   University of Maryland, Baltimore County, USA
Aryya Gangopadhyay   University of Maryland, Baltimore County, USA

Publication Chair

Christophe Debruyne   Trinity College Dublin, Ireland

Logistics Team

Daniel Meersman   Mexico
Bernadete Morris   France

EI2N 2019 Program Committee

Rafael Batres   Tecnológico de Monterrey, Mexico
Peter Bernus   Griffith University, Australia
Luis M. Camarinha-Matos   NOVA University of Lisbon, Portugal
Michele Dassisti   Politecnico di Bari, Italy
Andres Garcia   University of Castilla-La Mancha, Spain
Georg Grossmann   University of South Australia, Australia
Sérgio Guerreiro   Instituto Superior Técnico, University of Lisbon,
                            Portugal
Ulrich Jumar   IFAK e.V. Magdeburg, Germany
Udo Kannengiesser   Johannes Kepler University Linz, Germany
Mario Lezoche   University of Lorraine, France
Qing Li   Tsinghua University, China
Eduardo Loures   Pontifical Catholic University of Parana, Brazil
Ivan Luković   University of Novi Sad, Serbia
Julio Cesar Nardi   Federal Institute of Espírito Santo, Brazil
Yannick Naudet   Luxembourg Institute of Science and Technology,
                            Luxembourg
Angel Ortiz   Universitat Politècnica de València, Spain
Raul Poler   Universitat Politècnica de València, Spain
Henderik Proper   Luxembourg Institute of Science and Technology,
                            Luxembourg
David Romero   Tecnológico de Monterrey, Mexico
Richard Soley   Object Management Group, Inc., USA
Nenad Stefanovic   University of Kragujevac, Serbia
Janusz Szpytko   AGH University of Science and Technology, Poland

Miroslav Trajanovic   University of Nis, Serbia
Francois Vernadat   University of Lorraine, France
Marek Wegrzyn   The Jacob of Paradies University, Poland
Esma Yahia   ENSAM Aix-en-Provence, France
Martin Zelm   INTEROP Vlab, Belgium

EI2N 2019 Additional Reviewer

Edson Ruschel   Pontifical Catholic University of Parana, Brazil

FBM 2019 Program Committee

Roel Baardman   Independent Consultant, The Netherlands
John Bulles   PNA Group, The Netherlands
Martijn Evers   I-refact, The Netherlands
Terry Halpin   INTI International University, Australia
Frank Harmsen   Maastricht University, The Netherlands
Hans Mulder   Universiteit Antwerpen, Belgium
Sjir Nijssen   PNA Group, The Netherlands
Jan-Mark Pleijsant   ABN AMRO, The Netherlands
Serge Valera   European Space Agency, The Netherlands
Tom Van Engers   University of Amsterdam, The Netherlands
Bas Van Gils   Strategy Alliance, The Netherlands
Jan Vanthienen   Katholieke Universiteit Leuven, Belgium
Mark von Rosing   Global University Alliance, France
Jos Vos   APG, The Netherlands
Martijn Zoet   Zuyd University of Applied Sciences, The Netherlands

ICSP 2019 Program Committee

Piero De Sabbata   ENEA, Italy
Dennis Brandl   MESA, USA
Christoph Bussler   Oracle Corporation, USA
Luis M. Camarinha-Matos   NOVA University of Lisbon, Portugal
Lawrence E. Whitman   University of Arkansas at Little Rock, USA
Giancarlo Fortino   University of Calabria, Italy
Andres Garcia Higuera   University of Castilla-La Mancha, Spain
Pascal Gendre   AIRBUS SAS, France
Wolfram Kleis   SAP SE, Germany
Mathias Kohler   SAP SE, Germany
Mario Lezoche   University of Lorraine, France
Peter Loos   Saarland University, Germany
Eduardo Loures   Pontifical Catholic University of Parana, Brazil
Richard Martin   Tinwisle Corporation, USA
Arturo Molina   Tecnológico de Monterrey, Mexico

Yannick Naudet	Luxembourg Institute of Science and Technology, Luxembourg
Jean M. Simão	UTFPR, Brazil
Richard Soley	Object Management Group, Inc., USA
Paulo Stadzisz	UTFPR, Brazil
Dimitris Varoutas	National and Kapodistrian University of Athens, Greece
Francois Vernadat	University of Lorraine, France
Milan Zdravković	University of Nis, Serbia
Martin Zelm	INTEROP Vlab, Belgium

ICSP 2019 Additional Reviewer

| Sabine Klein | German Research Center for Artificial Intelligence, Germany |

Meta4eS 2019 Program Committee

Zaenal Akbar	Indonesian Institute of Sciences, Indonesia
Nick Bassiliades	Aristotle University of Thessaloniki, Greece
Josep Domenech	Universitat Politècnica de València, Spain
Kalliopi Kravari	Aristotle University of Thessaloniki, Greece
Andrea Kő	Corvinus University of Budapest, Hungary
Cosmin Lazar	Bosch Automotive Electronics, Romania
Jorge Martinez-Gil	Software Competence Center Hagenberg, Austria
Andras Micsik	SZTAKI, Hungary
Camelia-M. Pintea	Technical University of Cluj-Napoca, Romania
Christophe Roche	Université Savoie Mont Blanc - Condillac, France
Dumitru Roman	University of Oslo, Norway
Dan Mircea Suciu	University Babes-Bolyai Cluj-Napoca, Romania
Özlem Özgöbek	Norwegian University of Science and Technology, Norway

SIAnA 2019 Program Committee

Amrita Anam	University of Maryland, Baltimore County, USA
Iftikhar Sikder	Cleveland State University, USA
Ahmed Aleroud	University of Maryland, Baltimore County, USA
Michael McGuire	Towson University, USA

OTM 2019 Keynotes

Qrowd and the City: Designing People-Centric Smart Cities

Elena Simperl

University of Southampton, UK

Short Bio

Elena Simperl is professor of computer science at the University of Southampton and director of the Southampton Data Science Academy. She is also one of the directors of the Web Science Institute and a Turing Fellow. Before joining Southampton in 2012, she was assistant professor at the Karlsruhe Institute of Technology (KIT), Germany and vice-director of the Semantic Technologies Institute (STI) Innsbruck, Austria. She has contributed to more than twenty research projects, often as principal investigator or project lead. Currently she is the PI on four grants: the EU-funded Data Pitch, which supports SMEs to innovate with data, the EU-funded QROWD, which uses crowd and artificial intelligence to improve smart transportation systems, the EPSRC-funded Data Stories, which works on methods and tools to make data more engaging, and the EU funded ACTION, which develops social computing methods for citizen science. She authored more than 100 papers in sociotechnical systems, knowledge engineering and AI and was programme/general chair of the European and International Semantic Web Conference and of the European Data Forum.

Talk

Smart cities are as much about the needs, expectations and values of the people they serve as they are about the underlying technology. In this talk, I am going to present several areas of system design where human and social factors play a critical role, from fostering participation to augmented intelligence and responsible innovation. I will present ongoing challenges, solutions and opportunities, drawing from recent studies in Qrowd, a Horizon 2020 programme proposing a humane AI approach for transport and mobility.

Managing Knowledge Risks in Data-Centric Collaborations

Stefan Thalmann

Karl-Franzens University of Graz, Austria

Short Bio

Stefan Thalmann is Professor and the Director of the Center for Business Analytics and Data Science of the Karl-Franzens University of Graz, Austria. Prior to that he was with the Graz University of Technology and lead the cognitive decision support group in the application-oriented research center Pro2Future. He managed several industry funded research projects as well as EU funded research projects and worked for universities in Austria, Germany, Italy, Finland and the UK. He holds a diploma in Information Systems from the University of Halle-Wittenberg, a PhD and a habilitation degree in Information Systems from the University of Innsbruck. His research interest includes industrial data analytics, data-driven decision support and the management of knowledge risks in digitized supply chains. Stefan authored more than 50 academic publications and a member of 40 conference and workshop program committees.

Talk

Due to digitization the exchange of data along the supply chain intensified over time and data-centric collaborations emerge. These data sets become more and more comprehensive as cheap sensors, affordable infrastructure and storage capacity intensified the data collection. Based on advanced data analytics it now more likely that supply-chain partners or even competitors discover valuable knowledge out of these data sets. Not sharing is however not an option in most cases and thus a suitable trade-off between sharing and protection needs to be found. Thus data-centric collaborations might be also the source of knowledge risks and need to be considered in an organisational knowledge protection strategy.

In this talk, I will analyze the challenges of data-centric collaborations from a perspective of knowledge risks. I will present examples and insights from current research projects and studies. Further, I will present solutions enabling companies to managing data-centric collaborations by finding a suitable tradeoff between the benefits arising from sharing data in such a collaboration on the one hand and the knowledge risks associated with the sharing of data.

Choose for AI and for Explainability

Silvie Spreeuwenberg

Lab for Intelligent Business Rules Technology – LIBRT,
Amsterdam, The Netherlands

Abstract. As an expert in decision support systems development, I have been promoting transparency and self-explanatory systems to close the plan-do-check-act cycle. AI adoption has tripled in 2018, moving AI towards the Gartner-hype-cycle peak. As AI is getting more mainstream, more conservative companies have good reasons to enter this arena. My impression is that the journey is starting all over again as organizations start using AI technology as black box systems. I think that eventually these companies will also start asking for methods that result in more reliable project outcomes and integrated business systems. The idea that explainable AI is at the expense of accuracy is deeply rooted in the AI community. Unfortunately, this has hampered research into good explainable models and indicates that the human factor in AI is underestimated. Driven by governments asking for transparency, a public asking for unbiased decision making and compliance requirements on business and industry, a new trend and research area is emerging. This talk will explain why explainable artificial intelligence is needed, what makes an explanation good and how ontologies, rule-based systems and knowledge representation may contribute to the research area named XAI.

Contents

Industry Case Studies Program 2019 – Industry Day (ICSP 2019)

8th International Workshop on Methods, Evaluation, Tools and Applications Towards a Data-Driven e-Society (Meta4eS 2019)

1st International Workshop on Security via Information Analytics and Applications (SIAnA 2019)

OTM 2019 Keynote

Choose for AI and for Explainability

Silvie Spreeuwenberg[(✉)]

Lab for Intelligent Business Rules Technology – LIBRT,
Amsterdam, The Netherlands
silvie@librt.com

Abstract. As an expert in decision support systems development, I have been promoting transparency and self-explanatory systems to close the plan-do-check-act cycle. AI adoption has tripled in 2018, moving AI towards the Gartner-hype-cycle peak. As AI is getting more mainstream, more conservative companies have good reasons to enter this arena. My impression is that the journey is starting all over again as organizations start using AI technology as black box systems. I think that eventually these companies will also start asking for methods that result in more reliable project outcomes and integrated business systems. The idea that explainable AI is at the expense of accuracy is deeply rooted in the AI community. Unfortunately, this has hampered research into good explainable models and indicates that the human factor in AI is underestimated. Driven by governments asking for transparency, a public asking for unbiased decision making and compliance requirements on business and industry, a new trend and research area is emerging. This talk will explain why explainable artificial intelligence is needed, what makes an explanation good and how ontologies, rule-based systems and knowledge representation may contribute to the research area named XAI.

1 Extended Abstract

Artificial Intelligence (AI) is increasingly popular in business initiatives in the healthcare and financial services industries, amongst many others, as well as in corporate business functions such as finance and sales. Did you know that startups in AI raise more money? and that, within the next decade, every individual is expected to interact with AI-based technology on a daily basis?

AI is a technology trend covering any development to automate or optimize tasks that traditionally have required human intelligence. Experts in the industry prefer to nuance this broad definition of AI by distinguishing machine learning, statistics, IT and rule-based systems. In this book I will use the term AI to reference all techniques popular today under this name. The availability of huge amounts of data and more processing power - not major technological innovations – make machine learning for better predictions the most popular technique today. However, I will argue in the remainder of this book that the other AI techniques are equally important. While the popularity of AI has triggered me to write this book, most conclusions are applicable to any IT system.

Since the invention of the computer, AI and IT have been closely related. Think of Lady Lovelace, who worked in 1837, together with Charles Babbage, on the first

C. Debruyne et al. (Eds.): OTM 2019 Workshops, LNCS 11878, pp. 3–8, 2020.
https://doi.org/10.1007/978-3-030-40907-4_1

design of a programmable computer. Back then it was known as an 'algebraic machine' and she named it The Analytical Engine.

Lady Lovelace was the daughter of the romantic poet Lord Byron, and was a gifted mathematician and intellectual. When she translated an Italian article on algebraic machines, she supplemented it with extensive notes on such machine's capabilities. These notes, published in 1843, prove that she was the first to record that a machine could be programmed to solve problems of any complexity or even compose music. This formed the inspiration for theories on logic that resulted in the programming languages in use today.

Lovelace died early and the Analytical Engine was not built during her life time. Her soulmate Mr. Babbage did create a trial model of the Analytical Engine that is displayed in the Science Museum in London.

She is regarded as the first computer programmer but was most likely thinking about AI, or what we would call AI today, when she said: "The Analytical Engine has no pretensions whatsoever to originate anything. It can do whatever we know how to order it to perform. It can follow an analysis, but it has no power of anticipating any analytical relations or truth."

Her statement has been debated by Alan Turing, another example of the intertwined relationship between AI and IT in one person. He defined a test of a machine's ability to exhibit intelligent behavior. Turing proposed an experimental setup where someone would judge a conversation without knowing whether the conversation was with a human or a machine. All participants would be separated from one another and aware that one of them was a machine. The Turing test (See Fig. 1) would be successful if none of the participants were able to tell the difference between communicating with the machine and communicating with the (other) human. This test, in many variations, still plays a role in defining AI.

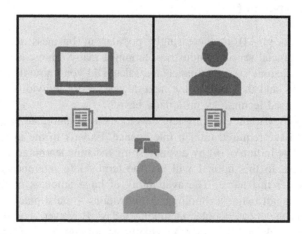

Fig. 1. Setup of the Turing test

At the same time Turing played a crucial role by creating one of the first computers based on the Von Neuman design: a computer that had a stored-program. This marked the beginning of programmable machines, the start of executing the vision of Lady Lovelace and the rise of the software industry.

The consequences of this innovation for humanity have been huge and were, at the time, difficult to oversee. There were pioneers, visionaries, investments and failures needed to get us where we are today. I am so grateful with the result. Every day I use a computer, a smart phone and other technology to provide me travel advise, ways to socialize, recommendations on what to do or buy and help me memorize and acquire new knowledge. Many of these innovations are related to technology developed by researchers in Artificial Intelligence and the full potential has not yet been exploited. *But there are also concerns.*
Artificial intelligence solutions are accepted to be a black box: they provide answers without a motivation, like an oracle.

You may already have seen the results in our society: AI is said to be biased, governments raise concerns about the ethical consequences of AI and regulators require more transparency. Businesses continue to make decisions based on common knowledge, omitting the potential improvements that AI could bring to improve human decision making. As a consequence, you may have become skeptical about AI technology, not only because you may fear losing your job, also because, as a specialist, you are aware of all the uncertainties surrounding your work.

Examples of AI biases: The Allen AI institute demonstrated that some AI systems are gender biased – promoting males for job offers – and ethnicity biased – classifying pictures of black people as gorillas. These biases are a result of the data used to train the algorithms – containing less female job seekers and more pictures of white people. Let's not forget that this data is created and selected by humans who are biased themselves.

Perhaps you need to make choices and guide your company to compete using AI. What approach could you follow without losing the trust of your employees or customers?

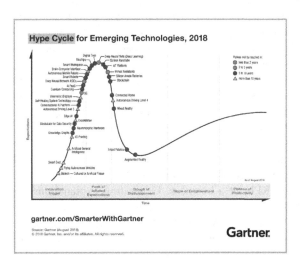

Fig. 2. The 2018 Hype Cycle for Emerging Technologies (from [2]).

Now that AI technology is at the peak in the hype cycle for emerging technologies (see Fig. 2), more conservative businesses want to use the benefits of AI based solutions in their operations. However, they require an answer to some or all of these abovementioned concerns.

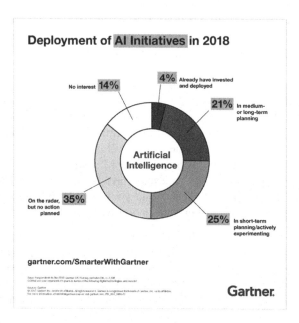

Fig. 3. Deployment of AI initiatives in 2018 (from [1])

To benefit from the potential of AI the resulting decisions must be explainable. For me this is a no-brainer since I have been promoting transparency in decision making using rule-based technology for years. In my vision a decision support system needs to be integrated in the value cycle of an organization. Business stakeholders should really feel responsible for the knowledge and behavior of the system and confident of its outcome. This may sound logical and easy, but everyone with experience in the corporate world knows it is not. The gap between business and IT is filled with misunderstandings, differences in presentation and expectations (Fig. 3).

It takes two to tango. Business, represented by subject matter experts, policy makers, managers, executives and sometimes external stakeholders or operations, should take responsibility using knowledge presentations they understand, and IT should create integrated systems – supporting decision making - directly related to the policies, values and KPIs of a business. Generating explanations for these decisions plays a crucial role.

We should do the same for AI based decisions: Choose AI technology when needed and use explanations to make it a success. That is, explainable AI – known by the acronym 'XAI'.

The five reasons why XAI solutions are more successful than an oracle based on AI, or any black box IT system, are as follows:

1. Decision support systems that explain themselves have a better *return on investment* because explanations close the feedback loop between strategy and operations resulting in timely adaption to changes, longer system lifetime and better integration with business values.
2. Offering explanations *enhances stakeholder trust* because the decisions are credible for your customer and also makes your business accountable towards regulators
3. Decisions with explanations *become better decisions* because the explanations show (unwanted) biases and help to include missing, common sense, knowledge.
4. *It is feasible* to implement AI solutions that generate explanations without a huge drop in performance with the six-step method that I developed, and technology expected from increased research activity.
5. To be *prepared for the increased demand for transparency* based on concerns about the ethics of AI and the effect on the fundamental principles of a democratic society.

The six steps I present are a generalized method and blindly following any method is a recipe for disaster. Understanding the underlying motivation and thinking how to best apply it in a specific situation is a better approach. Furthermore, the steps need not be applied linearly, instead may be revisited as often as needed. So instead of steps that assume a certain linearity, you could call them activities or actions.

The 6 steps that should be in your work cycle to make AI solutions a success and explainable help you all the time to:

1. Get a shared understanding of the domain
2. Understand the task and select the right scope
3. Collect the right data and improve its quality
4. Select AI techniques that deliver results
5. Generate good explanations
6. Evolve the solution over time

Maybe you expected steps such as: write use cases and user stories, create a minimal viable product – MVP, integrate the MVP in IT infrastructure, refine the business process and validate performance. This is the typical terminology used in the AI world today. It aligns well with the "fail early, learn fast" culture, typical for startups (*the "startup way"*) and promoted by venture capitalists. While this way of working is not wrong, we do need a different focus to create an explainable AI solution. Use cases and MVP's focus on the delivery of a product, and of course, that is important too, however, I prefer to focus on integration into the broader context of sustainable business operations and strategy development.

The research on explainable learning algorithms can be divided in three research areas:

1. Change deep learning methods to ensure that only 'features' that are easy to explain are learned. Explainability, next to accuracy and precision, is one of the optimizations criteria in the model.

2. Improve techniques that learn explainable models such as Bayesian networks. An example of a Bayesian network is a well-structured model that shows symptoms and causes with their dependencies and the likelihood of the dependency in a directed graph. These causal models are easier to understand and may therefore be used directly as an explanation.
3. Understand how to use techniques to generate explanations, such as decision tree generation, from black box models. The generated model is used to explain the result of the black box model.

In this research areas there are still unanswered questions that need to be answered and should be on the research agenda, such as:

- How to measure the 'explainability' of a model?
- How to explain the concepts that a trained model learned that we do not have words for?
- How to integrate domain knowledge in machine learning?
- How to create an automated conversation with a user about an explanation?
- What if the user is not familiar with the concepts used in an explanation?
- How can we automatically simplify complex explanations without being biased?

Especially in domains where the costs of false positives are high (for example, when a model incorrectly classifies an applicant as being eligible or a patient as needing treatment), domain experts will be inherently skeptical about AI models. In such domains, explanations should help the domain expert to find the false positives of the AI system before these costly errors are made.

To conclude, an explanation interface should help the expert find outliers in the training data, new trends in the actual data, false positives and ideally act as a mirror, revealing the model's and the expert's decision biases. These biases, false positives, outliers and trends are the fuel for a feedback loop that help to improve the system, resulting in a sustainable solution.

This keynote abstract is based on the book Aix: Artificial Intelligence needs explanation by Silvie Spreeuwenberg, LibRT B.V.

References

1. Goasduff, L.: 2018 Will Mark the Beginning of AI Democratization. Gartner (2018). https://www.gartner.com/smarterwithgartner/2018-will-mark-the-beginning-of-ai-democratization/
2. Walker, M.: Hype Cycle for Emerging Technologies. Gartner (2018). https://www.gartner.com/en/documents/3885468

14th OTM/IFAC/IFIP International Workshop on Enterprise Integration, Interoperability and Networking (EI2N 2019)

OTM/IFAC/IFIP EI2N'2019 Co-chairs Message

In 2019 the 14th edition of the Enterprise Integration, Interoperability and Networking workshop (EI2N'2019) has been organised as part of the On The Move Federated Conferences (OTM'2019). This year's workshop took place in Rhodes, Greece. The workshop has established itself as a major interactive event for researchers exchanging ideas in the context of organisations and information technologies. This is shown by the long list of groups and committees that support this event.

This year, the workshop is co-sponsored by IFAC and supported by IFIP. The main IFAC Technical Committee organising this workshop is TC 5.3 "Enterprise Integration and Networking".

The workshop also received support from IFAC TC 3.1 (Computers for Control), and the IFIP Work Groups TC 5 WG 5.12 on Architectures for Enterprise Integration and TC 5 WG 5.8 on Enterprise Interoperability. Additionally, the SIG INTEROP Grande-Région on "Enterprise Systems Interoperability", the French CNRS National Research Group GDR MACS, and the industrial internet consortium have shown their continuing interest in EI2N.

Today's enterprises have to become S^3 Enterprises: Smart, Sensing and Sustainable Enterprises. These system-of-systems have to adapt in order to be sustainable not only along the environmental but also along economic dimensions. Systems must be able to sense their environment using heterogeneous technologies. The sensed information has to be transferred into knowledge to support smart decisions of systems to adapt. In this context, are enterprise integration, interoperability and networking major disciplines that study how enterprise system-of-systems collaborate, communicate, and coordinate in the most effective way. Enterprise Integration aims at improving synergy within the enterprise so that sustainability is achieved in a more productive and efficient way. Enterprise Interoperability and Networking aims at more adaptability within and across multiple collaborating enterprises. Smartness is required to meet the resulting complexity.

Enterprise modelling, architecture, knowledge management and semantic knowledge formalisation methods (like ontologies) are pillars supporting the S^3 Enterprise.

For EI2N'2019, 8 papers have been received. After a rigorous review process, 5 papers have been accepted. EI2N continuous to show high quality by having an acceptance rate of 62.5%. Accepted papers will be made available in pre-proceedings. After the OTM workshops authors are able to revise their papers and include feedback from the interactive sessions in their work. This improves the quality of the scientific work, and places emphasis on importance of the interaction in scientific workshops.

With respect to interactivity, EI2N will host a highly interactive session called "Workshop Café". This special session is now an integral part of EI2N since many years. The outcomes of these discussions will be reported during a plenary session jointly organized with the CoopIS and the OTM Industry Case Studies Program, in order to share topics and issues for future research with a larger group of experts and scientists. Results will be made available at the IFAC TC 5.3 webpage: http://tc.ifac-control.org/5/3.

We would like to thank the authors, international program committee, sponsors, supporters and our colleagues from the OTM organising team who have together contributed to the continuing success of this workshop.

Wided Guédria
Hervé Panetto
Milan Zdravkovic
Georg Weichhart
The EI2N'2019 Workshop Co-chairs

Design Science as Methodological Approach to Interoperability Engineering in Digital Production

Christian Stary[1]([⊠]), Georg Weichhart[1,2], and Claudia Kaar[1]

[1] Department of Communications Engineering, Johannes Kepler University,
Linz, Austria
{christian.stary,georg.weichhart,claudia.kaar}@jku.at
[2] PROFACTOR Gmbh, Steyr, Austria

Abstract. Interoperability is considered crucial for sustainable digitization of organizations. Interoperability Engineering captures organizational, semantic and technological aspects of production process components, and combines them for operation. In this paper, we present an adaptable methodological development framework stemming from Design Science. It can be used along structured value chains in digital production for aligning various production process components for operation. We demonstrate its applicability for Additive Manufacturing (AM) and its capability to settle organizational, semantic, and technological aspects in the course of a digital production. AM starts with organizational goal setting and structuring requirements for an envisioned solution, which becomes part of an AM project contract. All pre- and post-fabrication steps are framed by design science stages. Their order help structuring interoperability aspects and enable stepwise addressing them along iterative development cycles. Due its openness, the proposed framework can be adapted to various industrial settings.

Keywords: Interoperability · Additive Manufacturing · Design science

1 Introduction

Interoperability has been recognized by political bodies, such as the European Commission, as crucial for the interchange of data and digitization efforts, both for public administration and business operation in various domains (cf. [1–5]). Although several interoperability frameworks have been published, and respective solutions have been presented, a methodologically grounded interoperability framework beyond guidelines for developing solutions for production has not been introduced so far. This is particularly true for adaptive manufacturing solutions like Additive Manufacturing.

In this paper, we introduce a development approach for digital production including organizational, semantic, and technological aspects, taking a design science perspective. We first address the state of the art on enterprise interoperability. We then exemplify cornerstones for working on organizational and semantic interoperability by revealing Additive Manufacturing capabilities and process steps. This is followed by details on interoperability engineering for this type of applications grounded in design

© Springer Nature Switzerland AG 2020
C. Debruyne et al. (Eds.): OTM 2019 Workshops, LNCS 11878, pp. 13–22, 2020.
https://doi.org/10.1007/978-3-030-40907-4_2

science cycles. It promotes stepwise roundtrip engineering, ensuring organizational interoperability through project contracts while focusing on semantic interoperability.

2 Interoperability Engineering

Aspects of interoperability are important in enterprise integration projects. Aiming for interoperability means striving for an infrastructure for organizational, semantic, and technical alignment between multiple systems (cf. [5–8]). Interoperability stresses the idea of a loosely coupled system. Various initiatives and developments have been triggered to identify relevant information elements and their handling in the course of integration and digitalization efforts. The European Interoperability Framework addresses relationships and mechanisms of different aspects required for alignment of governmental systems. Technical interoperability concerns technical systems inter-facing each other. Semantic interoperability needs to be considered between technical systems, between organizational systems, and when humans deal with technology. Organizational interoperability addresses the alignment of services with operation.

Consequently, interoperability engineering has to address technical, semantic, and organizational aspects. On the technical level, among others, message formats, web service protocols, and security issues need to be addressed. For semantic interoper-ability, the meaning of data fields, service calls, rules, and the like need to be aligned. On the organizational level, business process behavior, process coordination and classified information sharing may cause interoperability issues. According to the European Interoperability Framework, semantics seem to be crucial for all dimensions, serving as some kind of glue for fitting solutions in socio technical systems. Hence, interoperability engineering requires a common understanding of meaningful compo-nents and their relations across different interoperability layers.

Interoperability engineering is also a process of adapting to change. Even if alignment has been achieved at a certain point in time, small changes such as software updates require adjustment activities [9]. Interoperability engineering also needs to be considered as a continuous process in a dynamically evolving setting. Even in less complex settings, it may not be possible to predict the impact of a change of one system on others. It is therefore important to consider the organizational dimension, and adjust factors beyond technical interfaces and data exchange. Albeit the high volatility of business operation, sustainable organizational interoperability is one of the challenges in enterprise systems engineering [9, 10].

Early technical interoperability research and solutions were focusing on enterprise application integration, including object broker platforms like OMG's CORBA [11], and distributed simulation for federated enterprise interoperability [12]. Striving for organizational interoperability, MISE 2 provides methodological and tool support for emerging collaborative situations in production systems [13]. Increasingly, emphasis has been put on the dynamic perspective when considering digital production. Applying the concept of Complex Adaptive Systems (CAS), sustainable interoper-ability system architectures consider the relation between functional components from a system-of-systems point of view (cf. [14]). Thereby, agents are systems that contribute to the superordinate system by interacting with other agents [15, 16]. Each agent is a system with properties and its own purpose [17] – cf. Liquid Sensing Enterprise (LSE) [18] and Sensing, Smart and Sustainable Enterprise (S³) [19].

With respect to semantic interoperability, ontologies have turned out to effectively enable capturing conceptual knowledge. For instance, the Ontology of Enterprise Interoperability (OoEI) [7] captures systemic relations based on systems theory. Enriching its core with CAS concepts (OoEICAS), enables agent-based emergence of behavior [16]. Dynamic development support could be achieved through integrating knowledge management facilities [5, 20]. However, often the syntactic formats and business semantics of the systems involved in manufacturing processes are not compatible [21], leading to dedicated ontologies [22] and annotations for data interoperability [23].

Agility and proactivity should be supported through semantic interoperability, addressing information systems within and across organizations [24]. Thereby, evaluation concerning the exchange of information plays a crucial role [25], which requires an operational development framework for aligning organizational with semantic and syntactic development issues.

3 Organizing Process Steps for Additive Production

We ground our contextual approach to interoperability engineering on a capacity building model for Additive Manufacturing (AM). AM is a process of joining materials to produce objects from 3D model data, usually layer upon layer. The introduced process-driven value chain for AM projects helps organizing the workflow of digital production in a semantically coherent way, and thus facilitates incorporating semantical interoperability issues. Implementation details, such as the technological implementation, can be varied according to the availability of resources.

Informed organization of AM projects should include step-by-step direct feedback [26] triggering knowledge creation [27], hands-on experiences, and developer interactions [28, 29], whereby the social, cultural, and physical context matters [30]. Development milestones should comprise strategic planning, goal setting, (self-)evaluation and monitoring, strategic implementation and strategic outcome monitoring [30–32]. They have already been used for staging development [33]. When organizing AM process in a context-sensitive way, three subsequent phases re-occurred (cf. [32]): preparation, performance (or execution), and an appraisal (for adapting strategies). Upfront, specifying the conditions for task accomplishment, goal setting, and planning facilitate AM projects [34, 35], in addition to exploring material and designs [35, 36].

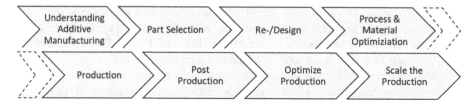

Fig. 1. Stages in additive manufacturing capacity building.

Based on these findings, we suggest eight process steps (see Fig. 1), ranging from preparation (upper part) to (post-)production (lower part).

(1) **Understanding the Production (Process).** To ensure the qualified use of resources and tools, basic concepts of digital production, inputs on printing technologies, materials, and 3D thinking may be required. Producers need to be aware of mutual dependencies, in particular to use proper material and apply appropriate technologies.

(2) **Part Selection.** In some cases, an object may require several parts which need to be combined. In this phase, the basic question about which part can even be printed needs to be discussed. Apart from the high variety of functionalities of 3D printers, not every object makes sense to be printed. Hence, this step requires awareness of the utilized technology and material.

(3) **Re-/Design.** Products or components needs to be designed through modeling, e.g., using 3D software, or 3D scans of an object. For a 3D model a variety of parameters need to be considered, and eventually tested through 3D printing before redesign.

(4) **Process & Material Optimization.** Based on the designed model and specifications, producers need to decide which technology to use. Production sites may provide different 3D printing technologies. The preceding phases should allow the producer to choose the appropriate printer and technology for the project. However, AM can also include finishes for a printed object. Different finishes may lead to a more robust, or water-resistant product. Therefore, this phase serves as last instance to critically think about the product itself, the material used, and the contribution of finishing activities.

(5) **Production.** This phase comprises the actual printing process. The 3D printer will be set up with the chosen material, and the model is transferred to it. While the model is processed by the printer, the producer may need to add material.

(6) **Post Production.** After an object has been printed, the producer should have gained more insight through phase 4 about the finish of the product. Depending on the used technology, objects may need to be cleaned from remains, scaffolds may need to be removed, or, to finalize the polymerization, objects may need to be put into a post-cure chamber.

(7) **Optimize Production.** For organizations, the process does not end with performing post production activities. Each production run provides insights about material and technologies. In addition, process knowledge may need to be

revisited, once organizations want to get insight into processing technologies, eventually requiring prototyping before further production.

(8) **Scale the Production.** The last phase shifts the focus to future developments. Once production industry has explored AM concepts in the proposed bootstrapping way, it could re-design production lines according to the experienced technological capabilities and frame it with a business model. Hence, this stage offers space for further exploration of connected and self-adaptive production.

The presented value chain provides the frame to focus on relevant organizational, semantic and technological interoperability issues. The pre-, post- and production steps can be assigned to two types of design cycles, as demonstrated in the subsequent section.

4   Semantic Interoperability Along Design Science Cycles

Design Science has attracted attention in various domains for the last decade (cf. [37, 38]) due to its nature, equally supporting practical development in a solution-oriented and reflective way. Peffers et al. [39] operationalization allows us to frame the AM production stages as shown in Figs. 2 and 3. Producers, in control of the management and production process, start with a new product ideas or an order for a certain product. In this context the goal, cornerstones of development including interoperability constraints, and required competencies are specified. *Knowing* refers to having knowledge and fundamental understanding, *Applying* empowers a producer for planning and producing an artefact by means of AM; *Innovating* features novel developments by means of AM technologies and novel materials. Then, a project contract needs to be defined. Documentation ensures commitment and transparency. Of particular importance is the set of requirements to be specified before designing the artefact, since they serve as criteria for evaluation in each of the iterated design cycles. They also need to capture interoperability concerns, in order to reduce the number of cycles.

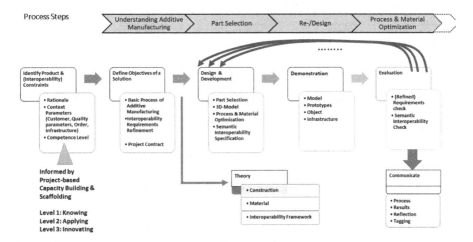

Fig. 2. Framing the pre-production stages.

The separation into two operational parts is given by the fact that pre-production requires to develop and meet a set of requirements that precedes manufacturing. It requires alignment of product properties, part decomposition, and material details including its processing particularities. Consequently, the set of conceptual inputs and theories (construction, material, interoperability framework – semantic issues) differ from those in (post-)production (knowledge and industrial process management, interoperability framework – technological issues). It may even happen that the requirements defined upfront need to be adapted due to semantic and/or technological incompatibilities, as indicated by the wider design science cycle. Interoperability engineering activities are set in design cycle activities within project work as follows.

Semantic Interoperability Management: It includes elaborating the domain-specific, technical content (product data, procedural details, resources) that belongs to the production project. This information is collected and arranged in some process specification(s) in the course of design. Since AM projects require aligning semantically self-contained issues, namely product-specific properties, material adjustment, and machinery for production, design cycles should take into account the corresponding semantic interoperability concerns. Each cycle should help to align system components in a semantically interoperable way (see also Fig. 2): (i) Decomposition of the object to be produced for selecting the parts that can be fabricated in an additive way; (ii) Material selection meeting product requirements while indicating the systems required for production, (iii) Production machinery process(es). Design cycles can be devoted to specific types of requirements (i-iii) or their alignment in the course of AM projects.

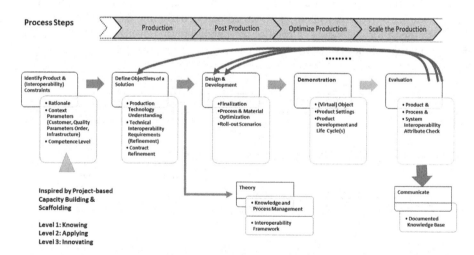

Fig. 3. Framing production and post-production.

The modular Design Science approach allows documenting each design decision in its particular context, including the evaluation results, thus, enabling transparent interoperability engineering. This feature is of particular importance for heterogeneous components often found when digitizing production processes.

Organizational interoperability management: For a production project, organizational interoperability issues are partially encoded in the value chain, e.g., for additive production to select a part design, consider material, and production processes etc. The results of each evaluation may trigger further iterations, e.g., with respect to decomposing an object into printable parts, affecting the design process and requiring adaptations. The Design Science life cycle approach enables aligning evaluation criteria with design results, and later on prototypes and the finally produced object. Moreover, the Design Science step 2 also allows addressing competences required for handling production processes, reflecting a person's profile.

Technical interoperability management starts with technical system support to select parts, material, and produce an object, and ends with producing an object. As indicated in Fig. 3, existing frameworks support this type of interoperability.

The Design Science approach helps structuring interoperability engineering not only in terms of bootstrapping essential steps for informed and transparent results, but also in terms of continuous learning and development of conceptual foundations:

- *Cycle-specific theory grounding and concept recognition*: Each step can be performed in an evidence-based way, namely providing existing knowledge in terms of theories, frameworks, principles, and guidelines, e.g., for basic design and production steps. They may even become part of product or system developments.
- *Knowledge transfer phases*: Each step of a project is documented, and thus may become part of a shared memory, from both a process, and results' perspective. Both can contribute to future designs, and trigger organizational learning processes.

Utilizing this dual nature of design science-based organization of production projects, theoretical concepts and practical guidelines for interoperability engineering co-evolve.

5 Conclusion

Interoperability, being crucial for digitization of production organizations, needs to encompass the organization, semantic process design, and technological aspects. We have introduced a meta-scheme for Additive Manufacturing (AM) stemming from Design Science. A contextual value chain for digital production for the various interoperability aspects has been derived from capacity building approaches. It enables focusing on semantics and the resulting intertwined nature of organizational and technical aspects. The value chain starts interoperability goal setting and refining interoperability requirements for an envisioned solution, which become part of a project contract. The requirements lay ground for artefact evaluations and postproduction activities, following dedicated design science cycles. Bootstrapping for economically viable production in this way provides a contextual and transparent process for bundling resources and optimizing production.

Acknowledgement. This work has been supported by Pro²Future (FFG contract No. 854184). Pro²Future is funded within the COMET Program — Competence Centers for Excellent Technologies - under the auspices of the Austrian Federal Ministry of Transport, Innovation and Technology, the Austrian Federal Ministry for Digital and Economic Affairs and of the Provinces of Upper Austria and Styria. COMET is managed by the Austrian Research Promotion Agency FFG.

References

1. Kalogirou, V., Charalabidis, Y.: The European union landscape on interoperability standardisation: status of European and national interoperability frameworks. In: Popplewell, K., Thoben, K.-D., Knothe, T., Poler, R. (eds.) Enterprise Interoperability VIII. PIC, vol. 9, pp. 359–368. Springer, Cham (2019). https://doi.org/10.1007/978-3-030-13693-2_30

2. McLoughlin, I., Garrety, K., Wilson, R., Yu, P., Dalley, A.: The Digitalization of Healthcare: Electronic Records and the Disruption of Moral Orders. Oxford University Press, Oxford (2017)

3. Salminen, V., Ruohomaa, H., Kantola, J.: Digitalization and big data supporting responsible business co-evolution. In: Kantola, J.I., Barath, T., Nazir, S., Andre, T. (eds.) Advances in Human Factors, Business Management, Training and Education. AISC, vol. 498, pp. 1055–1067. Springer, Cham (2017). https://doi.org/10.1007/978-3-319-42070-7_96

4. Wang, T.-H., Yen, N.Y., Du, Y.-L., Shih, T.K.: Courseware authoring tool for achieving interoperability among various e-learning specifications based on web 2.0 technologies. In: 2007 International Conference on Parallel Processing Workshops (ICPPW 2007), pp. 25–25. IEEE, Xian (2007). https://doi.org/10.1109/ICPPW.2007.32

5. Weichhart, G., Stary, C., Vernadat, F.: Enterprise modelling for interoperable and knowledge-based enterprises. Int. J. Prod. Res. **56**, 2818–2840 (2018). https://doi.org/10.1080/00207543.2017.1406673

6. Ducq, Y., Chen, D., Doumeingts, G.: A contribution of system theory to sustainable enterprise interoperability science base. Comput. Ind. **63**, 844–857 (2012). https://doi.org/10.1016/j.compind.2012.08.005

7. Naudet, Y., Latour, T., Guedria, W., Chen, D.: Towards a systemic formalisation of interoperability. Comput. Ind. **61**, 176–185 (2010). https://doi.org/10.1016/j.compind.2009.10.014

8. Vernadat, F.B.: Interoperable enterprise systems: principles, concepts, and methods. Ann. Rev. Control **31**, 137–145 (2007). https://doi.org/10.1016/j.arcontrol.2007.03.004

9. Agostinho, C., et al.: Towards a sustainable interoperability in networked enterprise information systems: trends of knowledge and model-driven technology. Comput. Ind. **79**, 64–76 (2016). https://doi.org/10.1016/j.compind.2015.07.001

10. Panetto, H., Jardim-Goncalves, R., Molina, A.: Enterprise integration and networking: theory and practice. Ann. Rev. Control **36**, 284–290 (2012). https://doi.org/10.1016/j.arcontrol.2012.09.009

11. Linthicum, D.S.: Enterprise Application Integration. Addison-Wesley, Reading (2000)

12. Tu, Z., Zacharewicz, G., Chen, D.: A federated approach to develop enterprise interoperability. J. Intell. Manuf. **27**, 11–31 (2016). https://doi.org/10.1007/s10845-013-0868-1

13. Benaben, F., Mu, W., Boissel-Dallier, N., Barthe-Delanoe, A.-M., Zribi, S., Pingaud, H.: Supporting interoperability of collaborative networks through engineering of a service-based mediation information system (MISE 2.0). Enterp. Inf. Syst. 1–27 (2014). https://doi.org/10.1080/17517575.2014.928949

14. Stary, C., Wachholder, D.: System-of-systems support—a bigraph approach to interoperability and emergent behavior. Data Knowl. Eng. **105**, 155–172 (2016). https://doi.org/10.1016/j.datak.2015.12.001
15. Gorod, A., White, B.E., Ireland, V., Gandhi, S.J., Sauser, B. (eds.) Case Studies in System of Systems, Enterprise Systems, and Complex Systems Engineering. CRC Press (2014). https://doi.org/10.1201/b17139
16. Weichhart, G., Guédria, W., Naudet, Y.: Supporting interoperability in complex adaptive enterprise systems: a domain specific language approach. Data Knowl. Eng. **105**, 90–106 (2016). https://doi.org/10.1016/j.datak.2016.04.001
17. Holland, J.H.: Complex adaptive systems. Daedalus **121**, 17–30 (1992)
18. Agostinho, C., Jardim-Goncalves, R.: Sustaining interoperability of networked liquid-sensing enterprises: a complex systems perspective. Ann. Rev. Control **39**, 128–143 (2015). https://doi.org/10.1016/j.arcontrol.2015.03.012
19. Weichhart, G., Molina, A., Chen, D., Whitman, L.E., Vernadat, F.: Challenges and current developments for sensing, smart and sustainable enterprise systems. Comput. Ind. **79**, 34–46 (2016). https://doi.org/10.1016/j.compind.2015.07.002
20. Weichhart, G., Stary, C.: A domain specific language for organisational interoperability. In: Ciuciu, I., et al. (eds.) OTM 2015. LNCS, vol. 9416, pp. 117–126. Springer, Cham (2015). https://doi.org/10.1007/978-3-319-26138-6_15
21. Hedberg, T.D., Hartman, N.W., Rosche, P., Fischer, K.: Identified research directions for using manufacturing knowledge earlier in the product life cycle. Int. J. Prod. Res. **55**, 819–827 (2017). https://doi.org/10.1080/00207543.2016.1213453
22. Imran, M., Young, R.I.M.: Reference ontologies for interoperability across multiple assembly systems. Int. J. Prod. Res. **54**, 5381–5403 (2016). https://doi.org/10.1080/00207543.2015.1087654
23. Liao, Y., Lezoche, M., Panetto, H., Boudjlida, N.: Semantic annotations for semantic interoperability in a product lifecycle management context. Int. J. Prod. Res. **54**, 5534–5553 (2016). https://doi.org/10.1080/00207543.2016.1165875
24. Zacharewicz, G., et al.: Model-based approaches for interoperability of next generation enterprise information systems: state of the art and future challenges. Inf. Syst. E-Bus. Manag. **15**, 229–256 (2017). https://doi.org/10.1007/s10257-016-0317-8
25. Vargas, A., Cuenca, L., Boza, A., Sacala, I., Moisescu, M.: Towards the development of the framework for inter sensing enterprise architecture. J. Intell. Manuf. **27**, 55–72 (2016). https://doi.org/10.1007/s10845-014-0901-z
26. Kurti, R.S., Kurti, D.L., Fleming, L.: The philosophy of educational makerspaces: part 1 of making an educational makerspace. Teac. Libr. **41**, 8–11 (2014)
27. Boekaerts, M.: Emotions, emotion regulation, and self-regulation of learning. In: Zimmermann, B.J., Schunk, D.H. (eds.) Handbook of Self-Regulation of Learning and Performance, pp. 408–425. Routledge, New York (2011)
28. Ertmer, P.A., Newby, T.J.: Behaviorism, cognitivism, constructivism: comparing critical features from an instructional design perspective. Perform. Improv. Q. **26**, 43–71 (2013). https://doi.org/10.1002/piq.21143
29. Schcolnik, M., Kol, S., Abarbanel, J.: Constructivism in theory and in practice. Engl. Teach. Forum **44**, 12–20 (2006)
30. Azevedo, R., Behnagh, R.F., Duffy, M., Harley, J.M., Trevors, G.: Metacognition and self-regulated learning in student-centered learning environments. In: Jonassen, D., Land, S. (eds.) Theoretical Foundations of Learning Environments, pp. 171–197. Routledge, New York (2012)

31. Beishuizen, J., Steffens, K.: A conceptual framework for research on self-regulated learning. In: Carneiro, R., Lefrere, P., Steffens, K., Underwood, J. (eds.) Self-Regulated Learning in Technology Enhanced Learning Environments: A European Perspective, pp. 3–19. SensePublishers, Rotterdam (2011). https://doi.org/10.1007/978-94-6091-654-0_1
32. Puustinen, M., Pulkkinen, L.: Models of self-regulated learning: a review. Scand. J. Educ. Res. **45**, 269–286 (2001). https://doi.org/10.1080/00313830120074206
33. Winne, P.H., Hadwin, A.F.: Studying as self-regulated learning. In: Hacker, D.J., Dunlosky, J., Graesser, A.C. (eds.) Metacognition in Educational Theory and Practice, pp. 27–30. Lawrence Erlbaum Associates Publishers, Mahwah (1998)
34. Winne, P.H., Perry, N.E.: Measuring self-regulated learning. In: Handbook of Self-Regulation, pp. 531–566. Elsevier (2000). https://doi.org/10.1016/B978-012109890-2/50045-7
35. Smay, D., Walker, C.: Makerspaces: a creative approach to education. Teach. Libr. **42**, 39–43 (2015)
36. Carulli, M., Bordegoni, M., Bianchini, M., Bolzan, P., Maffei, S.: A Novel Educational Model Based on "Knowing How to Do" Paradigm Implemented in an Academic Makerspace, vol. 34, pp. 7–29 (2017)
37. Hevner, A.: A three cycle view of design science research. Scand. J. Inf. Syst. **19**, 87–92 (2007)
38. Baskerville, R., Baiyere, A., Gergor, S., Hevner, A., Rossi, M.: Design science research contributions: finding a balance between artifact and theory. J. Assoc. Inf. Syst. **19**, 358–376 (2018). https://doi.org/10.17705/1jais.00495
39. Peffers, K., Tuunanen, T., Rothenberger, M.A., Chatterjee, S.: A design science research methodology for information systems research. J. Manag. Inf. Syst. **24**, 45–77 (2007). https://doi.org/10.2753/MIS0742-1222240302

Towards Smart Assessment: A Metamodel Proposal

Marcelo Romero[1,2(✉)], Wided Guédria[1,2], Hervé Panetto[2], and Béatrix Barafort[1]

[1] Luxembourg Institute of Science and Technologie (LIST),
5, Avenue des Hauts-Fourneaux, 4362 Esch-sur-Alzette, Luxembourg
{marcelo.romero,wided.guedria,beatrix.barafort}@list.lu
[2] Université de Lorraine, Centre National de la Recherche Scientifique (CNRS),
Centre de Recherche en Automatique de Nancy (CRAN), Nancy, France
herve.panetto@univ-lorraine.fr

Abstract. Assessment initiatives in organisations are focused on the evaluation of organisational aspects aiming to obtain a critic view of their status. The assessment results are used to lead improvement programs or to serve as base for comparative purposes. Assessment approaches may comprise complex tasks demanding a large amount of time and resources. Moreover, assessment results are highly dependent on the assessment input, which may have a dynamic nature due to the constant evolution of organisations. The assessment results should be adaptable to these changes without much effort whilst being able to provide efficient and reliable results. Therefore, providing smart capabilities to the assessment process or to systems in charge of performing assessments represents a step forward in the search for more efficient appraisal processes. This work proposes a metamodel defining the elements of a Smart Assessment, which is guided by elements related to the smartness concept such as knowledge, learning and reasoning capabilities. The metamodel is further specialised considering a Enterprise Interoperability assessment scenario.

Keywords: Process assessment · Interoperability assessment · Smartness · Smart Assessment · Metamodel

1 Introduction

An assessment is the act of estimating or deciding the amount, value, quality, or importance of a specific entity. In the organisational context, enterprises and the scientific community have pursued to evaluate different aspects such as process performance [1], business processes maturity [2], enterprise interoperability [3], software agility [4], Industry 4.0 readiness [5], enterprise risk management [6], cooperative enterprise information systems interoperability [7], among others. Assessments may serve organisations for descriptive, prescriptive or comparative purposes. The first is based on providing only a current state view of the assessed

© Springer Nature Switzerland AG 2020
C. Debruyne et al. (Eds.): OTM 2019 Workshops, LNCS 11878, pp. 23–32, 2020.
https://doi.org/10.1007/978-3-030-40907-4_3

entity in order to provide an objective vision of the assessed entity to the decision-makers, the second also provides improvement recommendations, and the last one allows to perform bench-marking between industries or regions [8].

Performing assessments could imply the consumption of time and resources, making it expensive for organisations, specially when maturity assessment is performed [9]. Moreover, assessment methods may comprise the performing of highly complex and specialised tasks that must be carried by competent assessors, often relying on the manual gathering of evidence to be used to perform the assessment [10,11], which can lead to errors [12]. On the other hand, since the assessment result is highly dependent on its input, changes in the latter may have direct impact on the former, making necessary to re-carry out some of the assessment activities when there is a change in the input to provide a new result.

The improvement of the assessment process is an open research subject that is addressed in both the scientific community and the industry. Several initiatives from different domains such as business process [13], software engineering process [11,14], enterprise interoperability [15], or organisational agility [16] have been proposed throughout the years in the search for assessment approaches with their activities improved through automation methods so as to provide trustworthy, relevant and adaptable results, and to reduce the time and effort of carrying out the assessment. Due to this tendency towards automation, providing smart capabilities to the assessment process may represent a step closer towards the achievement of more efficient appraisals. Smartness is a concept that has different assumptions depending on the domain that it is treated in. However, common points that are domain-independent include capabilities such as sensing, actuating, learning, and knowledge.

This paper presents an initial formalization of a Smart Assessment process introducing a metamodel for describing its elements and their relationships. We aim at answering the research question: *"What are the elements of an assessment process with smart capabilities?"*. We also present an specialisation of the metamodel presenting a metamodel for Enterprise Interoperability assessment. We rely on the use of a metamodel to explain our view of a smart assessment since metamodels allow to graphically describe general concepts and their relationships [17], providing a clear view of those concepts.

The Design Science Research (DSR) method considering a three cycle view, proposed by [18], is applied to develop the metamodel, which is considered as an artifact within the DSR scope. In the Relevance Cycle, we consider as requirement a set of elements of a smart assessment with their relationships. The research activities of the Design Cycle comprise the design and validation of the model in an iterative cycle. The validation is based on checking if the structure of the model complies with concepts from our source of knowledge (composed of the scientific literature and the international standards) within the Rigour Cycle without discrepancies.

This paper is organised as follows. Section 2 presents the related work. Section 3 details the metamodel for Smart Assessment with a description of its elements. Section 4 describes a specialisation of the metamodel for Enterprise

Interoperability. Finally, Sect. 5 enumerates the conclusions from the work and future research perspectives.

2   Related Work

The search for a better assessment process has been widely addressed in the scientific literature. Some works have pursued the improvement of the assessment process through the automation of some of its activities and, in certain cases, the entire assessment. The work by [14] describes the SEAL of Quality Assessment Tool, which is a software tool for software process assessment. Its main functionality is based on storing the model framework as records in tables of a database. The paper by [19] presents a knowledge-based decision support system for measuring enterprise performance. It is based on a knowledge base that contains a set of rules that are used for inference over a set of weights or scores given by top managers considering key performance dimensions. In [20], an intelligent maturity model assessment tool was proposed. The system has three main properties: a generic data model enabling the use of different maturity models, it is connected to a BPM system allowing to extract part of the information necessary to perform the assessment, and an assistant function that recommends improvement suggestions based on the problems identified during the assessment. In [12], the authors present the Software-mediated Process Assessment (SMPA) to automate the assessment of IT Service Management processes. The tool allows to select the process to be assessed and the data is collected via an online survey. The results are obtained by automatically analyzing the collected data to measure the process capability. The work by [16] presents the AssessAgility software tool that aims at automating and guiding the assessment process based on an exemplar assessment process containing the definitions and guidance to conduct assessments following AgilityMod [4], which is a reference model for performing agility assessment in organisations. The work by [13] describes the development of a Software as a Service tool for carrying out business process assessment projects using the TIPA framework [21]. The latest version of the software (beta) allows to cover almost all activities of an assessment process, from the definition of the assessment to the results presentation activity.

Approaches that rely on ontologies are frequent for improving the assessment process. An ontology is a representation of explicit formalized knowledge that has as main objective the sharing of a common understanding of specific aspects of certain domain and the relationship between its elements [22]. The approach introduced in [10], for instance, is an ontology-based Records Management (RM) evaluation system. It is based on a reasoner that classifies information in a database, containing the baseline and the actual state of the RM system, as asserted individuals in the ontology, which was devised by a knowledge-engineer. The paper by [23] also proposed a system with an ontology at its core, which is based on the association of sustainable manufacturing with concepts of resources, processes, product, and their functions. The approach by [11] is intended to be an enhancement of the CoSEEEK framework introduced by [24]. It focuses on providing automated software engineering process assessment with the capability to support various process assessment reference models defined by standards such as CMMI [25], ISO/IEC 15504 [26], and ISO 9001 [27]. The work by [15] proposed a semi-automated tool for enterprise interoperability assessment that was based on an ontological core in order to automate the Results Calculation phase of an assessment of enterprise interoperability.

A variety of methods discussed in this section are focused on automating single activities, instead of providing means to enhance the entire assessment process through automation methods. Hence, fully automating the assessment process is a research gap addressed by few works. Regarding data collection, there is also a gap related to the tendency to consider only the usage of data originated through asking and deriving strategies (interviews, document reviews, etc.) or data provided by automatic means without considering both paths. Indeed, hybrid data collection approaches are not frequent in the literature. The work by [11] gives a step forward in this direction, since it relies on the use of process mining techniques to automatically extract data from event logs available in information systems [28] and also providing the possibility to manually introduce input data for the assessment. However, the approach is devised specifically for the software process engineering domain. On the other hand, ontologies seem to have emerged as relevant tools for automating the results determination phase of the assessment. Nevertheless, by nature they are highly dependent on human experts that must manually design them. Moreover, depending on the requirements of the application, user-defined rules [29] may also be necessary to provide assessment results. Considering these aspects, a framework to perform assessment in organisations relying on smart capabilities is required to further improve the activities of the assessment process. In this sense, the metamodel introduced in this work is the first step towards the achievement of this objective.

3   The Smart Assessment Metamodel

The concept of smartness is a trending term nowadays. Different initiatives such as Smart Cities [30], Smart Manufacturing [31] and Smart Homes [32] have gained strength in both the industry and the scientific community. Smartness as a concept is associated to some characteristics that may enable improvements of the functioning of certain entities. These characteristics include embedded knowledge, and capabilities such as learning and reasoning. Providing smart characteristics to the assessment process may imply the improvement not only of the result of an assessment but also the diverse activities and sub-activities that are carried during the entire process.

The metamodel for Smart Assessment presented in this work was developed considering the assessment concepts described in the standards ISO 9001 [27], ISO/IEC 33001 [33] and 33002 [34], the Systems Engineering Body of Knowledge [35], and the General System Theory (GST) [36]. On the other hand, considering smart capabilities, we performed a literature review to obtain papers containing definitions of smart entities in order to extract common characteristics. The review was based on a cycle composed of three phases: keywords definition, literature search, and results analysis. Two search strings were defined, both focused on obtaining explicit definitions of smart entities within papers from the literature: "{ *smartness is* }" and "{ *we define smart** } *OR* { *smart* is defined* }". The search was performed on databases including ACM, Scopus, IEEE_Xplore, Taylor & Francis Online, Web of Science, SpringerLink, and Wiley. The obtained papers were filtered considering only those containing explicit definitions and the definitions were manually extracted. Finally, the characteristics were isolated in order to serve as part of the Knowledge Base within the DSR method. A total of 177 definitions were extracted during the literature review, which served to devise the Smart Assessment metamodel in addition to the references mentioned before. The proposed model is shown in Fig. 1, which is represented using the Unified Modelling Language (UML) [37].

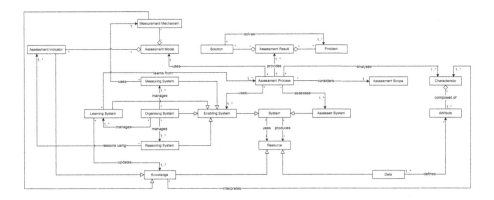

Fig. 1. Conceptual model defining the components of a smart assessment.

The core of the metamodel is the Assessment Process, which assesses an Assessed System considering an Assessment Scope defining the boundaries of the assessment as established by the stakeholders. The Assessment Process uses an Enabling System to properly carry out the assessment activities. An Enabling System is responsible to support a System-of-Interest [35], which is the system of interest of an observer [36]. In our metamodel, the System-of-Interest is the Assessed System. Both systems, Assessed and Enabling, are sub-types of the System element, which is able to use and produce the Resource element. We consider two types of Resources: Knowledge and Data. The Enabling System could be of different types such as Learning System, Reasoning System, and Measuring System. The Learning System is capable of producing or updating Knowledge, whilst the others are focused on using it to provide results. Note that we include an Organising System, able to manage the systems enumerated before. The Assessment Process uses the Assessment Model element, which is an element composed of a set of Assessment Indicators and one or more Measurement Mechanism. The first one is a reflect of the To-Be of the Assessed System whilst the second one defines means to measure the Assessment Result. The Assessment Process analyses some Characteristic of the Assessed System, which subsumes its Attributes. The Data element defines some Attribute to be assessed and it is the input of the Enabling Systems to ultimately define the Assessment Result. In addition, the Knowledge element serves as basis for decision-making regarding the final Assessment Result, which is composed on one or more identified Problems and the proper Solution to solve those problems.

4   Towards a Enterprise Interoperability Smart Assessment

Organisations face different types of challenges and pressures on a daily basis. These challenges include competitiveness, cost reduction, customer satisfaction, innovation, or product quality. Among these issues, organisations also have the necessity to interoperate to share information and achieve objectives [38]. Interoperability is the ability of enterprises to interact, and research in the field is mostly based on removing interoperability barriers [39]. It can occur between the following organisational layers: data, services, processes and businesses [39]. Considering the process layer, interoperability pursuits to make various organisational processes collaboratively work in a standardised manner [39]. Moreover, the literature presents three ways to relate systems in order to interoperate: integrated approach (a common format is defined for models), unified approach (a common format exists but at the meta-level only), and federated approach (there is no common format for models) [40].

In this context, we present a specialisation of the metamodel described in Sect. 3 aiming to explore its capability to adapt to specific needs. The specialised model is focused on Enterprise Interoperability. The objective is to define the Maturity Level of an Enterprise regarding Interoperability. The new elements introduced for the specialised metamodel are defined specifically in the Ontology of Enterprise Interoperability (OoEI) [41], the Maturity Model for Enterprise Interoperability (MMEI) [3], and the standard ISO/IEC 33001 [33] for process assessment concepts and terminology.

The specialisation includes an Enterprise as a type of Assessed System. The Enterprise is assessed considering the Evaluation Criterion element, which is a type of Assessment Indicator for Interoperability. The analysed Characteristic is Interoperability, which is qualified through a Maturity Level provided as a part of the Assessment Result. Moreover, we consider the Interoperability Area as Attribute qualified through an Area Maturity Level. Note that the Maturity Level reflects the global Interoperability Maturity of the Enterprise and it concerns a set of Area Maturity Levels qualifying some Interoperability Area. The element in charge of calculating the maturity levels (for Interoperability Area and Enterprise) is the Measurement Mechanism, which is a schema characterising the methods to provide quantitative measure of Interoperability considering the Maturity Model that is used for the assessment. In addition to the Maturity Level and Area Maturity Level elements, the specialisation includes the Best

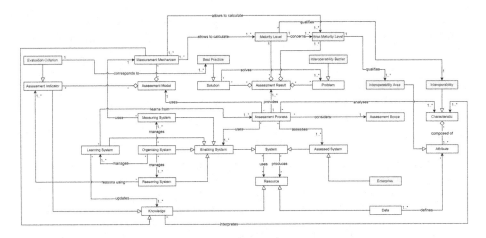

Fig. 2. Smart Assessment specialised for Enterprise Interoperability.

Practice and Interoperability Barrier elements as part of the Assessment Result. The former is a type of Solution to solve the latter, which is a type of Problem. Note that each Evaluation Criterion references one or more Best Practices that allow to remove an Interoperability Barrier. Hence, there is a direct link between an Evaluation Criterion and Interoperability Barriers solved through the Best Practices (Fig. 2).

5   Conclusion

This work presented a metamodel describing a Smart Assessment with its elements and their relationships through a visual diagram. The Design Science Research methodology was applied to develop the metamodel, which is intended to serve as initial artifact in the pursuit of a framework for Smart Assessment able to provide means to enhance the assessment process. The artifact is devised to evolve following an iterative approach by considering the feedback received from the community and experiments consisting of the implementation of instances of the elements defined in the metamodel in real-world scenarios.

The proposed metamodel was specialised for Enterprise Interoperability assessment. For this purpose, we relied on the scientific literature and standard documents addressing interoperability assessment. This specialisation allowed to experiment with the generalisation capability of the model. We consider that it provides the proper structure to be specialised for different domains and assessment approaches. Moreover, we consider that the model could not only applicable for organisational assessment but also to a diverse range of contexts.

We expect that this work will serve as contribution to the development of smarter assessment methods, tools, and artifacts, independently from particularities derived from the assessed system for which the appraisal approach is devised for and the assessment models used to perform it. Future work will aim at refining the artifact by analysing the feedback obtained from the experience of modelling specialised Smart Assessments considering different scenarios. The metamodel will also serve as cornerstone for the development of specific implementations devised for real-world situations, which will be evaluated through case studies. Indeed, this is a natural step forward for the research path introduced in this paper, which will be followed by the authors in the future.

References

1. Van Looy, A., Shafagatova, A.: Business process performance measurement: astructured literature review of indicators, measures and metrics. SpringerPlus **5**(1), 1797 (2016). https://doi.org/10.1186/s40064-016-3498-1
2. Looy, A.V., Backer, M.D., Poels, G.: Defining business process maturity. A journey towards excellence. Total Qual. Manag. Bus. Excell. **22**(11), 1119–1137 (2011). https://doi.org/10.1080/14783363.2011.624779
3. Guédria, W., Naudet, Y., Chen, D.: Maturity model for enterpriseinteroperability. Enterp. Inf. Syst. **9**(1), 1–28 (2015). https://doi.org/10.1080/17517575.2013.805246
4. Ozcan-Top, O., Demirörs, O.: A reference model for software agility assessment: agilitymod. In: Rout, T., O'Connor, R.V., Dorling, A. (eds.) SPICE 2015. CCIS, vol. 526, pp. 145–158. Springer, Cham (2015). https://doi.org/10.1007/978-3-319-19860-6_12
5. Schumacher, A., Erol, S., Sihn, W.: A maturity model for assessing industry 4.0 readiness and maturity of manufacturing enterprises. Procedia Cirp **52**, 161–166 (2016)
6. Oliva, F.L.: A maturity model for enterprise risk management. Int. J. Prod. Econ. **173**, 66–79 (2016)
7. Yahia, E., Aubry, A., Panetto, H.: Formal measures for semantic interoperability assessment in cooperative enterprise information systems. Comput. Ind. **63**(5), 443–457 (2012)
8. De Bruin, T., Freeze, R., Kaulkarni, U., Rosemann, M.: Understanding the main phases of developing a maturity assessment model. In: ACIS 2005 Proceedings (2005)
9. Proença, D., Borbinha, J.: Maturity models for information systems-a state of the art. Procedia Comput. Sci. **100**, 1042–1049 (2016)
10. Alalwan, T.: An ontology-based approach to assessing records management systems. e-Serv. J. **8**(3), 24 (2013). https://doi.org/10.2979/eservicej.8.3.24
11. Grambow, G., Oberhauser, R., Reichert, M.: Automated software engineering process assessment: supporting diverse models using an ontology. Int. J. Adv. Softw. **6**(1 & 2), 213–224 (2013)
12. Cater-Steel, A., Valverde, R., Shrestha, A., Toleman, M.: Decision support systems for IT service management. Int. J. Inf. Decis. Sci. **8**(3), 284 (2016). https://doi.org/10.1504/ijids.2016.078588
13. Barafort, B., Shrestha, A., Cortina, S., Renault, A.: A software artefact to support standard-based process assessment: evolution of the tipa® framework in a design science research project. Comput. Stand. Interfaces **60**, 37–47 (2018)
14. Lok, R.H., Walker, A.J.: Automated tool support for an emerging international software process assessment standard. In: Proceedings of IEEE International Symposium on Software Engineering Standards, pp. 25–35, June 1997. https://doi.org/10.1109/SESS.1997.595563

15. Leal, G.S.S., Guédria, W., Panetto, H., Proper, E.: Towards a semi-automated tool for interoperability assessment: an ontology-based approach. In: Mas, A., Mesquida, A., O'Connor, R.V., Rout, T., Dorling, A. (eds.) SPICE 2017. CCIS, vol. 770, pp. 241–254. Springer, Cham (2017). https://doi.org/10.1007/978-3-319-67383-7_18

16. Adali, O.E., Top, O.O., Demirors, O.: Assessment of agility in software organizations with a web-based agility assessment tool. In: Proceedings - 43rd Euromicro Conference on Software Engineering and Advanced Applications, SEAA 2017, pp. 88–95 (2017). https://doi.org/10.1109/SEAA.2017.61

17. Gascueña, J.M., Navarro, E., Fernández-Caballero, A.: Model-driven engineering techniques for the development of multi-agent systems. Eng. Appl. Artif. Intell. **25**(1), 159–173 (2012)

18. Hevner, A.R.: A three cycle view of design science research. Scand. J. Inf. Syst. **19**(2), 4 (2007)

19. Wen, W., Chen, Y.H., Chen, I.C.: A knowledge-based decision support system for measuring enterprise performance. Knowl. Based Syst. **21**(2), 148–163 (2008). https://doi.org/10.1016/j.knosys.2007.05.009

20. Krivograd, N., Fettke, P., Loos, P.: Development of an intelligent maturity model-tool for business process management. In: Proceedings of the Annual Hawaii International Conference on System Sciences, pp. 3878–3887 (2014). https://doi.org/10.1109/HICSS.2014.481

21. Barafort, B., Rousseau, A., Dubois, E.: How to design an innovative framework for process improvement? The TIPA for ITIL case. In: Barafort, B., O'Connor, R.V., Poth, A., Messnarz, R. (eds.) EuroSPI 2014. CCIS, vol. 425, pp. 48–59. Springer, Heidelberg (2014). https://doi.org/10.1007/978-3-662-43896-1_5

22. Gruber, T.R.: A translation approach to portable ontology specifications. Knowl. Acquis. **5**(2), 199–220 (1993)

23. Giovannini, A., Aubry, A., Panetto, H., Dassisti, M., El Haouzi, H.: Ontology-based system for supporting manufacturing sustainability. Ann. Rev. Control **36**(2), 309–317 (2012). https://doi.org/10.1016/j.arcontrol.2012.09.012

24. Oberhauser, R.: Leveraging semantic web computing for context-aware software engineering environments. In: Semantic Web. IntechOpen (2010)

25. Team, C.P.: CMMI for development, version 1.3. Technical report CMU/SEI-2010-TR-033, Software Engineering Institute, Carnegie Mellon University, Pittsburgh, PA (2010). http://resources.sei.cmu.edu/library/asset-view.cfm?AssetID=9661

26. Secretary, I.C.: ISO/IEC 15504-2: Information technology - process assessment - part 2: Performing an assessment. Standard, International Organization for Standardization (2004)

27. ISO Central Secretary: ISO 9001: Quality management systems - Requirements. Standard, International Organization for Standardization, Geneva, CH, September 2015

28. Van Der Aalst, W.: Process Mining: Discovery, Conformance and Enhancement of Business Processes, vol. 2. Springer, Heidelberg (2011). https://doi.org/10.1007/978-3-642-19345-3

29. Wang, X., Zhang, D., Gu, T., Pung, H.K., et al.: Ontology based context modeling and reasoning using owl. In: PerCom workshops, vol. 18, p. 22. Citeseer (2004)

30. Koutra, S., Becue, V., Ioakimidis, C.S.: Searching for the 'smart' definition through its spatial approach. Energy **169**, 924–936 (2019). https://doi.org/10.1016/j.energy.2018.12.019, http://www.sciencedirect.com/science/article/pii/S0360544218323855

31. Kang, H.S., et al.: Smart manufacturing: past research, present findings, and future directions. Int. J. Precis. Eng. Manuf. Green Technol. **3**(1), 111–128 (2016)

32. Alaa, M., Zaidan, A., Zaidan, B., Talal, M., Kiah, M.L.M.: A review of smart home applications based on internet of things. J. Netw. Comput. Appl. **97**, 48–65 (2017)

33. Secretary, I.C.: ISO33001: Information technology—process assessment—concepts and terminology. Standard, International Organization forStandardization, Geneva, CH, March 2015

34. ISO Central Secretary: ISO33002: Information technology—Processassessment—Requirements for performing process assessment. Standard, International Organization for Standardization, Geneva, CH, March 2015

35. Board, B.E.: The guide to the systems engineering body of knowledge (sebok) (2017)

36. Von Bertalanffy, L.: General system theory. New York **41973**(1968), 40 (1968)

37. Rumbaugh, J., Jacobson, I., Booch, G.: Unified modeling language reference manual, the. Pearson Higher Education (2004)

38. Leal, G.d.S.S., Guédria, W., Panetto, H.: Interoperability assessment: a systematic literature review. Comput. Ind. **106**, 111–132 (2019)

39. Chen, D.: Enterprise interoperability framework. In: EMOI-INTEROP (2006)

40. ISO Central Secretary: ISO 14258: Industrial automation systems - Concepts and rules for enterprise models. Standard, International Organization for Standardization, Geneva, CH, March 1998

41. Naudet, Y., Latour, T., Guedria, W., Chen, D.: Towards a systemic formalisation of interoperability. Comput. Ind. **61**(2), 176–185 (2010). https://doi.org/10.1016/j.compind.2009.10.014, http://www.sciencedirect.com/science/article/pii/S0166361509002073. Integration and Information in Networked Enterprises

General Big Data Architecture and Methodology: An Analysis Focused Framework

Qing Li$^{(\boxtimes)}$, Zhiyong Xu, Hailong Wei, Chao Yu,
and ShuangShuang Wang

Department of Automation, Tsinghua University,
Beijing 100084, People's Republic of China
liqing@tsinghua.edu.cn

Abstract. With the development of information technologies such as cloud computing, the Internet of Things, the mobile Internet, and wireless sensor networks, big data technologies are driving the transformation of information technology and business models. Based on big data technology, data-driven artificial intelligence technology represented by deep learning and reinforcement learning has also been rapidly developed and widely used. But big data technology is also facing a number of challenges. The solution of these problems requires the support of a general big data reference architecture and analytical methodology. Based on the General Architecture Framework (GAF) and the Federal Enterprise Architecture Framework 2.0 (FEAF 2.0), this paper proposes a general big data architecture focusing on big data analysis. Based on GAF and CRISP-DM (cross-industry standard process for data mining), the general methodology and structural approach of big data analysis are proposed.

Keywords: Big data · Architecture framework · Methodology · Modelling

1 Introduction

The typical application scenario of big data technology is to extract value from massive data. Big data has great business prospects, attracting analysts to devote themselves to data mining and machine learning. However, as shown in Table 1, the understanding, analysis and evaluation of big data faces many challenges.

Despite the significant advantages of big data analysis algorithms, human involvement is still a key factor in big data analysis. Big data analysis relies heavily on big data analysts' thinking, technical literacy, and analytical skills. In order to improve the understanding of big data and standardize its analysis and implementation methodology, in parallel with the research of various data analysis algorithms, big data architecture research has always been a hot topic, many research institutes and standardization organizations are advancing research and standardization of big data architectures as discussed in [1].

Although [1] presents a big data analysis architecture and relative reference models, at present, there is no widely accepted and used big data architecture framework,

© Springer Nature Switzerland AG 2020
C. Debruyne et al. (Eds.): OTM 2019 Workshops, LNCS 11878, pp. 33–43, 2020.
https://doi.org/10.1007/978-3-030-40907-4_4

especially the methodology of big data analysis, which provides multi-dimensional and multi-level references for big data analysis.

On the other hand, since the KDD (knowledge discovery in database) process established with the database technology and data mining technology in the 1990s, in the face of the new development of big data technology, there has not been update and improvement. At present, most engineering practices of big data analysis still uses CRISP-DM (cross-industry standard process for data mining) as a structured reference approach.

Table 1. Challenges faced by big data

Aspects	Problems
Cognition	How to systematically understand big data?
	How should analysts participate in big data analysis?
	Does the architecture and methodology of big data exist? Is the model reasonable?
Analysis	How is the big data analysis model built?
	How to avoid the "data lying"?
	How to analyse causality in big data analysis?
	How to overcome the problem of big data analysis in a closed-loop?
Evaluation	How to protect personal privacy and security?
	How to explain big data analysis models and results?
	How to make big data algorithms fair?

CRISP-DM was the main method of KDD and was jointly developed by the EU institutions in 1999 [2]. As shown in Fig. 1, CRISP-DM includes the following data analysis phases.

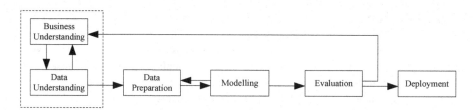

Fig. 1. CRISP-DM

(1) Business Understanding: Understand the requirements and ultimate purpose of the data analysis project from a business perspective and combine these goals with the definition and results of data mining.

(2) Data understanding: Collect raw data, load the data, depict the data, and explore the data characteristics, perform simple feature statistics, and verify the quality of the data, including the integrity and correctness of the data, and the filling of missing values.

(3) Data Preparation: Based on the correlation with the data mining target, data quality and technical limitations, select the data used as the analysis, and further clean the data, construct the derived variables, integrate the data, and format the data according to the requirements of tools.

(4) Modelling: A variety of modelling methods will be selected and used. Typically, there are multiple ways to choose which type of problem to use for the same data mining.

(5) Evaluation: Before proceeding with the final model deployment, it is important to evaluate the model more thoroughly and review each step performed during the build of the model to ensure that the model meet the business goals.

(6) Deployment: Organizing the results and processes of data analysis into readable text. It is important for the customer to understand the activities that need to be performed in order to properly use the built model.

CRISP-DM is a data analysis structural approach developed before data analysis has evolved into big data era. In the face of big data analysis, there are the following shortcomings:

(1) Focusing only on data processing procedures, lack of support for new features formed by the development of big data technology;

(2) Lack of means for business understanding and data understanding;

(3) Lack of integration with systems engineering methodology, without considering big data analysis in a system environment;

(4) Lack of relevance to the architecture and methodology of information technology, and lack of guidance on the construction of big data systems.

Based on the existing enterprise architecture framework (EA), this paper is going to propose a general big data architecture framework, and develops a structural approach and methodology for big data analysis.

2 General Architecture Framework (GAF)

In order to describe, understand, design and improve a complex technology, management and human converged system, plenty of enterprise architectures (EA) are developed, including CIM-OSA, ARIS, PERA, GERAM, FEAF, TOGAF, DoDAF and UAF [3]. The top part of Fig. 2 is the General Architecture Framework (GAF) for complex industrial systems engineering presented by [3].

GAF consists of three dimensions: view, project life cycle, and realization.

(1) View dimension: GAF includes three levels of views: performance, behavior, and structure, which has consistent views classification principles with UML, SysML and FEAF (the Federal Enterprise Architecture Framework).

(2) Project life cycle dimension: Starting from the project definition, after analysis, preliminary design, detailed design, implementation, operation and maintenance.

(3) Realization dimension: From "AS-IS" modelling to "TO-BE" modelling is the key methodology of GAF.

One of the important ideas of GAF is that the system recognition and construction are evolved step by step. In the phase of conceptual definition, it is necessary to define the strategic goal of the enterprise and then confirm the target of the project. Sequentially according to these purposes, we can describe the actuality of an enterprise from the aspects of organization, resource, information, product, function and operating process and then infrastructure and operation mechanism. Under constraints of these descriptions, the system can be analysed with suitable modelling and analysis methods to find its problems and then improve it. Then the target system is constructed and its various views can be formed. This is a specifying and optimizing process. When describing the target system, we can apply other modelling methods besides the method of view description to characterize the system comprehensively. When model-based design is accomplished, it will be transferred into technical specification for constructing system with the help of constructing tool sets and then a real system will be formed. Because the description of the system will still work on while the system operation, it can be used as the operating reference of the real system and then helps to modify and optimize the real system.

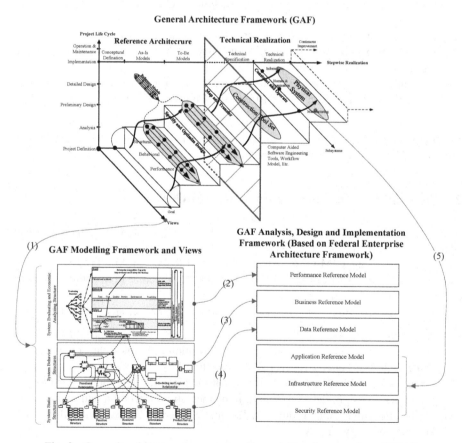

Fig. 2. General architecture framework with modelling framework and FEAF

The left-bottom part of Fig. 2 is the GAF Modelling Framework (GMF), which is consistent with OMG's UML and SysML view classification principles, as well as FEAF 2.0. It is organized into three layers, from top to down that is, system evaluation and economic analysing structure layer, system behaviour/dynamic structure layer and system static structure layer. Models at each layer reflect a particular aspect of an enterprise, and the description of each layer of the framework is given as follows:

(1) System static structure layer: models at which define the static structures of an enterprise including the organizational structure, resource structure, data/information structure, product/service structure and function structure, which define the existence of an enterprise and answer the question of what is the system.
(2) System behaviour/dynamic structure layer: models at which describe logical, sequential and correlative characteristics of the whole system and combine elements defined at the static structure layer together and define the operation mechanism of the enterprise.
(3) System performance structure layer: model at which define the target of the system, the related performance indicators and measurement methods.

The right-bottom part of Fig. 2 is the GAF analysis, design and implementation framework, which has the same construction and framework with FEAF version 2.0 [4]. Arrows in Fig. 2 shows the mapping and transferring relationships among GAF, GMF and FEAF. The top three levels of FEAF have the same ideal with GAF modelling framework. The Bottom three levels of FEAF point out the construction of technical implementation and realization.

3   Construction of General Big Data Architecture and Methodology

Based on GAF, FEAF and GMF, through the reference and mapping of concepts, as shown in Fig. 3, the general big data architecture framework and methodology are constructed. The 16 derivation steps are discussed as follows.

(1) GAF includes view dimensions and involves a complete modelling system and a set of modelling methods and languages. The GMF associated with GAF includes three levels of modelling systems for structure, behaviour, and performance.
(2) GMF's system static structure model includes a series of structural elements such as functional structure, data structure, organization structure, product structure and resource structure. The data reference model included in FEAF is a subset of the GMF static structural model. In general, FEAF's data reference model and GMF's static structural model have the same view partitioning principles and all the solved problems.
(3) GMF's system behaviour structure model mainly describes the behavioural characteristics and operational mechanism of the system through functional relationships and sequential logic relationships, which is consistent with the principles and problems of the FEAF business reference model.

(4) The evaluation model of GMF and the performance reference model of FEAF are consistent in the principle of division and the problem solved.

(5) The GAF views are divided into structure, behaviour, performance/evaluation, and has the same principle and relationship with FEAF data, business and performance reference models. GAF has more connotations in structure, behaviour, and performance than FEAF, and adapts to more different fields and scenarios.

(6) FEAF's six reference models actually cover the two parts of the modelling framework and the information technology infrastructure, namely the two types of architecture defined by ISO15704. Therefore, we can also think that FEAF describes the engineering elements of the actual system in the GAF.

(7) Based on the idea of GMF modelling and analysis, the system modelling and analysis needs to consider three levels of performance, behaviour and structure. The big data analysis architecture should include three levels of modelling and analysis: performance, business and data.

(8) Based on the idea of FEAF modelling and analysis, the big data analysis architecture should include modelling and analysis of performance, business and data. The big data analysis architecture and FEAF's upper three layers of modelling and analysis are highly consistent.

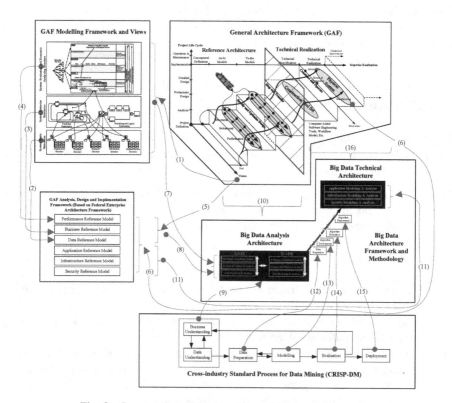

Fig. 3. Construction of the big data architecture framework

(9) The two activities that CRISP-DM initially overlaps repeatedly: business understanding and data understanding, should consider the analysis objectives, performance, evaluation factors, and then become the performance and business in the big data analysis architecture. The understanding of the data, and these understanding activities, is actually the activities of people involved, reflecting the principles and ideas of people in the big data analysis. Enterprise and system modelling tools should be an important means of business understanding and data understanding.

(10) GAF proposes a methodology for analysis and design from AS-IS modelling to TO-BE modelling. This methodology also has important guiding significance for big data modelling and analysis. The process of big data modelling and analysis is to bridge the gap between the AS-IS status and the TO-BE goal, and to complete and solidify/document the process and conclusions of business understanding and data understanding.

(11) With reference to FEAF's application reference model, information technology infrastructure reference model and security reference model, the technical architecture of big data is constructed. From the design point of view, application modelling and analysis, infrastructure modelling and analysis, security modelling and analysis provide a framework and method for the design of the hardware and software infrastructure of big data, and also provide a method for the construction of the basic operating environment of big data.

(12) The core activities in the CRISP-DM process are introduced into the methodology and structured approach of big data analysis, including data preparation.

(13) The modelling activities of CRISP-DM correspond to the algorithm preparation activities of the big data analysis methodology. The modelling here is mainly the algorithm model of mathematical analysis.

(14) The evaluation activities of CRISP-DM correspond to the algorithm evaluation activities of the big data analysis methodology, mainly based on the results of the big data analysis architecture, and evaluate the effectiveness and efficiency of the big data analysis algorithm.

(15) The deployment activities of CRIPS-DM correspond to the algorithm deployment activities of the big data analysis methodology. The code of the algorithm is deployed on the big data analysis technology platform to carry out the processing of big data.

(16) The technical architecture in the big data architecture corresponds to the technical implementation of GAF, focusing on the actual system construction and technical problem solving.

4 Methodology and Structural Approach of Big Data Analysis

Based on the analysis in the previous section, considering that big data modelling and analysis will be repeated and repeated throughout the analysis and processing of big data, the big data architecture framework and methodology proposed in this paper are shown in Fig. 4.

(1) Big data analysis framework

The big data analysis framework mainly provides a framework for modelling and analysis for big data analysts to participate in the analysis and design of big data. The framework includes three levels of modelling and analysis - performance, business, and data - with a layer-by-layer derivation relationship and a mutual iteration in the vertical direction. It includes modelling and analysis of the current situation in the horizontal direction, and on this basis, it compensates for the gap between status que and the goal is to build a model of the target system.

(2) Analysis of AS-IS status

The application of big data technology is to solve problems of enterprises in strategy, business model and data development. Problem-oriented and goal-oriented is that big data analysis needs to be based on the combing and understanding of the status quo. Modelling performance, business and data will improve the standardization and consistency of the whole analysis process.

(3) TO-BE target design

Based on the understanding of the status quo, look for opportunities by big data technology to solve strategic, business and data problems, bridge the gap between the status quo and the target system, and complete the design of the target system.

(4) Performance modelling and analysis

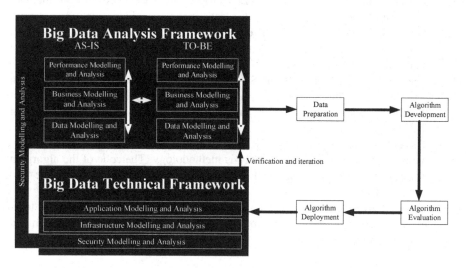

Fig. 4. Big data architecture and methodology

Presenting the needs, goals, and performance considerations of big data projects. Requirements analysis is the starting point for all projects. The determination of goals and performance presents the goal and direction of big data analysis and application, and also the benchmark for the evaluation of algorithms and project effects. Performance modelling can use UML USE-CASE, SysML Requirement, indicator system, AHP/ANP, etc., which can be analysed and determined through comprehensive evaluation methods.

(5) Business modelling and analysis

Understand business models and business logic, present a blend of big data projects and business rules, and support innovation of business mechanisms. The establishment of a business blueprint activity in a large number of consulting methodologies is synonymous with modelling and analysis of big data. The goal of big data business modelling and analysis is to sort out and design the business logic of the business system and present the operating mechanism of the system. Functional modelling and business process modelling methods are applicable to modelling and analysis in this field. Commonly used modelling languages are IDEF0, IDEF3, DFD, system dynamics, ARIS event process chain, BPMN, BPEL, UML sequence diagrams, activities and state machine. Business Process Reengineering (BPR) methods can be used for analysis and optimization of business processes.

(6) Data modelling and analysis

Understand the business logic contained in the data, identify the main entities and relationships, and analyse the more characteristic instances, records and attributes. Compare the target and business logic models, find the combining points, and analyse the integrity and correctness of the data. Common methods of data modelling, such as IDEF1X, entity relationship diagram, UML class diagram, pattern diagram, concept diagram, and knowledge map description method, can be used to understand and build data models.

(7) Bridging the gap between the status quo and the goal

Starting from the current situation modelling and analysis, to the modelling and design of the target system, is the basic methodology of system design. To bridge the gap between the status quo and the goal, it is not a natural process to go beyond the goal. It is necessary to combine the development of new technologies and new management concepts, integrate big data technology into the process of solving strategic and business problems, and creatively develop big data technology, form innovative results of ideas, models and technologies, and achieve the goals of big data analysis projects.

(8) Iteration of performance, business, data modelling and analysis

As with the CRISP-DM process, performance to business to data, and the coupling and iteration of these three levels of modelling and analysis, present an iterative process of business understanding and data understanding. The result is a model and analysis of the three levels of coordination.

(9) Data preparation

The data preparation activities will acquire, organize, supplement, and improve the original data, and through various data cleaning, transformation, mapping, segmentation, aggregation, formatting and other activities, form big data analysis software and hardware platform, so that the algorithm can be stored and processed.

(10) Algorithm preparation and development

According to the types of problems that need to be solved, various algorithms are selected, used, and modified, and the parameters of the algorithm are calibrated to the optimal values through initialization, evaluation, and optimization processes. For the same type of big data analysis and processing problem, it is a common strategy to choose multiple algorithms to deal with the problem.

(11) Algorithm evaluation

Before the algorithm is finally brought online, thorough testing, verification, and evaluation are required to ensure that the algorithm meets the objectives of the project, especially to solve problems that the enterprise has not found and solved in the past, and to make decisions on the results of big data analysis.

(12) Algorithm deployment

Deploy algorithms to the infrastructure of big data analytics to deliver engineering and business applications that create engineering and business value.

(13) Big data technical framework

In order to cope with the complex problems faced by the collection, transmission, storage, processing and display of massive data, software and hardware technologies have been developed. In the case of specific big data analysis projects, it is still necessary to model infrastructure and technical conditions, so as to form the basic hardware and software conditions for the analysis problems and algorithms.

(14) Application modelling and analysis

Build an application software environment for big data analysis, realize interconnection and interoperability between various applications, support the realization of big data analysis algorithms, and complete various functional design of big data analysis.

(15) Infrastructure modelling and analysis

Build hardware and operating system environments for big data analytics, supporting the collection, transmission, storage, and processing of big data on physical mechanisms. The Hadoop-MapReduce system, computer clusters, public clouds, and private cloud environments are typical information technology infrastructures for big data analysis.

(16) Security modelling and analysis

The importance of security issues in the field of big data analysis is becoming more and more important. Privacy protection and information security have become the core issues in the progress of big data business applications. Therefore, the security reference model is placed across all levels of FEAF. Security modelling and analysis is also a key element in big data analysis and technology systems.

(17) Verification and iteration

The modelling and analysis of big data is an iterative process, which continuously summarizes and normalizes the models and algorithms formed during the big data analysis process. It can form a reference model, build a model library, support continuous improvement of analytical techniques, and improve the speed of subsequent projects. As technology and business environment change, analysis strategies and analysis algorithms also need continuous improvement. It is also a process of iterative loop iteration, showing the concept of big data analysis in the ring and people in the ring.

5 Summary and Conclusion

The paper reviews challenges of big data technology and introduces model-based systems engineering into big data analysis project. GAF and FEAF are reviewed and introduced into to construct a model-based general big data architecture framework. Extended from GRISP-DM, a general big data analysis methodology and structural approach is discussed in detailed.

GAF embodies key principles of FEAF, CIM-OSA, GERAM, ToGAF, and so forth, which are widely used generalized enterprise architecture frameworks. GAF also includes key methodology and structural approach for integrated systems design, development, implementation, operation and maintenance, in which integration systems are any systems that relate to industrial technology, information technology and management technology.

The general big data analysis architecture and methodology proposed in the paper can be used as the structural approach for big data analysis projects. It can also be used in wider areas and domains. Any data analysis related project, no matter big or small data, structured or unstructured data, can get support from the architecture and methodology.

The authors applied the general big data analysis architecture and methodology in some actual engineering scenarios, which can be found in [5, 6].

Acknowledgements. This work is sponsored by the National Natural Science Foundation of China No. 61771281, the "New generation artificial intelligence" major project of China No. 2018AAA0101605, the 2018 Industrial Internet innovation and development project, and Tsinghua University initiative Scientific Research Program.

References

1. Li, Q., et al.: Big data architecture and reference models. In: Debruyne, C., Panetto, H., Guédria, W., Bollen, P., Ciuciu, I., Meersman, R. (eds.) OTM 2018. LNCS, vol. 11231, pp. 15–24. Springer, Cham (2019). https://doi.org/10.1007/978-3-030-11683-5_2
2. Wirth, R., Hipp, J.: CRISP-DM: towards a standard process model for data mining. In: Proceedings of the 4th International Conference on the Practical Applications of Knowledge Discovery and Data Mining, pp. 29–39. Citeseer (2000)
3. Li, Q., Chan, I., Tang, Q., Wei, H., Pu, Y.: Rethinking of framework and constructs of enterprise architecture and enterprise modelling standardized by ISO 15704, 19439 and 19440. In: Debruyne, C., Panetto, H., Weichhart, G., Bollen, P., Ciuciu, I., Vidal, M.-E., Meersman, R. (eds.) OTM 2017. LNCS, vol. 10697, pp. 46–55. Springer, Cham (2018). https://doi.org/10.1007/978-3-319-73805-5_5
4. Federal Enterprise Architecture Framework Version 2, 29 January 2013
5. Chan, I.: Big Data Architecture Framework and Data Analytics Modeling. Master degree thesis of Tsinghua University, June 2018
6. Xu, Z.: Big Data Architecture Framework and Modeling Analysis Method. Master degree thesis of Tsinghua University, June 2019

Ensure OPC-UA Interfaces for Digital Plug-and-Produce

Frank-Walter Jaekel[✉], Tobias Wolff, Vincent Happersberger,
and Thomas Knothe

Fraunhofer Institute for Production Systems and Design Technology,
Pascalstr. 8-9, 10587 Berlin, Germany
jaekel@ipk.fraunhofer.de

Abstract. Experiences in industry has illustrated that "**O**pen **P**latform **C**om- munications **U**nified **A**rchitecture" (OPC-UA) as upcoming de-facto standard for Industry 4.0 requires interoperability tests to support a digital plug-and- produce. Existing tools to validate OPC-UA implementations need to be applicable for such validations. Within the German national "**I**nternet **o**f **T**hings **T**est" (IoT-T) project, we developed concepts and software for the validation of interoperability between different cyber physical systems using OPC-UA. The paper focuses on this part of the work and provides insights in the results. The results consists of industrial use cases, requirements, concepts and open source software. It also includes the comparison of the developments in the IoT-T project with the **C**ompliance **T**est **T**ools (CTT) provided by the OPC Founda- tion (OPCF), which checks the conformity of the OPC-UA servers and clients against the OPC-UA specification.

Keywords: CPS · OPC-UA · Plug-and-Produce · Digitalization · Interoperability

1 Motivation and Challenges

In the past, the manufacturing facilities in production were seldom interconnected. Programs were locally adapted to the machines and executed. Plug-in and setup of the facilities referred to physical and logistical parameters of the machines to enable a seamless exchange of equipment within the production process. The digital plug-and- produce and digital components of manufacturing facilities were underestimated in terms of conformance and interoperability. Discussions with industry partners have expressed that the production department is responsible for the shopfloor and the IT department is not be aware of any responsibility for machinery on the shopfloor. This relates to companies, which were part of the discussion within projects in Germany.

The rise of cyber physical systems (CPS), industry 4.0 [1, 2] and industrial internet of things (IIoT) [3] creates a dramatic change. Production facilities are now able to connect to each other but also to enterprise applications, to the intranet and even to the internet [4]. This enables new opportunities in terms of digitalization but also chal- lenges regarding security, performance, robustness and interoperability. It can also

© Springer Nature Switzerland AG 2020
C. Debruyne et al. (Eds.): OTM 2019 Workshops, LNCS 11878, pp. 44–53, 2020.
https://doi.org/10.1007/978-3-030-40907-4_5

create a gap in responsibility between the production department and the IT department, which needs to be covered by the organization.

Enterprises developed their own infrastructures to benefit from the interconnection of manufacturing facilities with enterprise applications. Therefore, the digital-plug-and-produce or the virtual commissioning of control software became important and with IIoT even less local and more flexible than the previous technologies using field buses [5] e.g. with PROFINET [6]. Facilities should be plugged-in and -out without programming effort. This requires conformance regarding the architecture, the protocols, security and the used information model together with the semantic.

Open Platform Communication Unified Architecture (OPC-UA) [7] provides a common infrastructure in terms of combinations of clients and servers. It includes an approach of using communication protocols such as "Transmission Control Protocol" (TCP) or "Message Queuing Telemetry Transport" (MQTT) [8]. However, the specific implementation within an IT infrastructure requires an adequate selection of the communication protocol. Furthermore, OPC-UA provides a concept to build information models (companion specs) and functional semantics regarding conformance units [9]. Therefore, OPC-UA provides a good starting point to deliver interoperability.

Currently standardization organizations and related associations such as the German VDMA work on area specific companion specifications. However, specific semantics of parameters and units are still a challenge even using OPC-UA. For example the unit for temperature might be Celsius defined by a "C" in one companion specification and in another companion specification, Celsius is defined by the whole name or even Kelvin without a unit indication.

This example is quite simple, but describe the problem. It can cause errors and blocking the manufacturing process. Therefore, validations are still required even companion specifications are used. Validation facilities are an opportunity to reduce the risk of mismatching and non-interoperability. The next chapters will give an insight in the consideration and development of test tools to ensure interoperability using OPC-UA for digital plug-and-produce considering also the test facilities of the OPC foundation [10].

The German national IoT-T project developed concepts and software for the validation of interoperability between different cyber physical systems using OPC-UA. The paper will focus on this part of the work and provide insides in the results. The results consist of industrial use cases, requirements, concepts and open source software. The paper will especially focus on the following points:

- Industrial use cases and validation requirements concerning interoperability for digital plug-and-produce,
- CPS ValidationAdapter and CPS Emulation as toolkit for machine provider to check whether their implemented OPC-UA Server and Clients correspond to a companion specification or to a specific information model. In [11] and [12] technical details about these software tools are described.
- The comparison between the compliance test tool from the OPC Foundation (OPCF-CTT) [13] and CPS ValidationAdapter and CPS Emulator to identify benefits and weaknesses as well as future demands.

- The new software developed within the IoT-T project extension to extend inter-operability tests with the possibility to check user specified scenarios.

2 Frameworks and Information Model

In recent years, frameworks concerning Industry 4.0 [2] and industrial IoT became more considered by the public. Well known are "Data Distribution Service" (DDS) [14] and OPC-UA with the focus on the communication between machines, machine controls and monitoring as well as enterprise applications. The industry partners in the IoT-T project choose OPC-UA as technology and framework for the validation of interoperability in the scope of industrial IoT. An initial demand arises from the modular shopfloor IT approach done in the automotive industry [15]. An important feature of the OPC-UA framework is the information model approach to support interoperability between clients and servers.

The OPC foundation (OPCF) invented a common description method of the information model for the OPC-UA framework. An information model in terms of the OPCF consists of a hierarchical network structure of nodes describing an OPC-UA server. Among other features, it contains an address space. A node represents a specific data set. These nodes have attributes such as node ID, names and references. The information model with nodes, type information and attributes is expressed in a XML schema [16]. Currently XML files are used to keep the description of the information model. Depending of the used OPC-UA implementation this description of the information model can be used to configure OPC-UA servers.

Various software suppliers adapted the OPC-UA framework to develop software development kits (SDK) and development tools. More and more machine suppliers implement OPC-UA as a communication interface. In the context of the server and client architecture in OPC-UA machines implements the servers and provide process information, whereas machine executions systems are the clients. To ensure interoperability between servers and clients of different suppliers the IoT-T project develops the CPS ValidationAdapter, which is an OPC-UA client. It validates the information model of an OPC-UA server against a given target information model (Fig. 1).

An initial challenge was the "node ID" in the information model because it is used as a unique ID within the name space of the information model. It depends on the address space of the server and therefore on a specific implementation. In the specification phase of the information model, another approach is necessary if the address space is not known in forehand. The OPC-UA specification provide another way to clearly identify nodes within the address space. Each node provides two names, whereas the browsename (OPC term) is one of them and could be unique, but do not have to.

This allows using the browsename to identify the related nodes between target information model and server information model. Of course, a missing correlation between the specified target information model and the server information model will be indicated as an error within the validation. The validation approach requires that server and client use identical and unique names on both sides. This ensures that the node IDs can be derived from a server within a given IT infrastructure by the validation functionality. Afterwards, further information about the node structure can be checked such as data types and parameter/attribute settings.

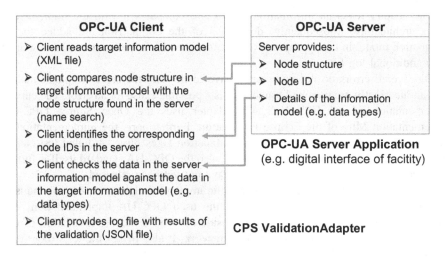

Fig. 1. Use of OPC-UA information model for the validation

The specific checks are provided via a validation configuration file and the results are written into a JSON logfile. The user gets an user interface based on this JSON file providing deviations between the information models and further information such as security or connectivity issues.

3   Architecture

The IoT-T CPS ValidationAdapter provides validation of the conformity of an OPC-UA server against a specification or target information model. A specific target is to provide an easy to use mechanism to test the interoperability between OPC-UA servers and clients. Therefore, the input is an OPC-UA information model and the connection parameters of the server to configure the CPS ValidationAdapter.

Information model and configuration are stored in separated files within the architecture of the CPS ValidationAdapter. Every validation process of the IoT-T CPS ValidationAdapter starts reading a configuration. It contains paths to others files with connection parameters, information models and where the log files are stored in the end of each validation. To establish a connection between client and server the client needs an IP address including port, encryption and a certificate. These information is stored in the test configuration of the CPS ValidationAdapter.

The result is stored in a JSON log file. The logging framework Log4j2 has been used, it offers the output in several formats such as JSON, text files and XML. The implemented logging increases the usability of the CPS ValidationAdapter and allows an error diagnosis in case of an erroneous test run.

However, only information about the test procedure and messages about inconsistencies between specification and server implementation are stored here. A more comprehensive and technical evaluation is provided in addition to logging the test procedure.

The adapter reads an information model and compares it with the implemented server architecture. Subsequently, deviations of the comparison are added to the information model in the appropriate place and the entire information model is written as an additional log file.

Discovered errors do not necessarily have to lie with the server implementation, even an incorrectly programmed framework is a possible cause for an error. The current implementation of the CPS ValidationAdapter uses the Open Source OPC-UA implementation Milo of the Eclipse Foundation. Furthermore, the implementation of the open source framework of the OPC Foundation takes place. A failed test cannot only be caused by an error in the framework, also the OPC-UA standard itself is further developed and the corresponding updates have not yet been released.

To counteract the dependencies on specific implementations and versions industry partners requested an option to exchange the used OPC-UA implementation. The current architecture update (see Fig. 2) considered it by a flexible invocation of different implementations of the OPC-UA framework. It also makes the tests more resilient because different OPC-UA implementation frameworks can apply the same tests.

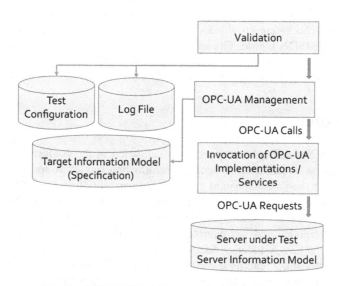

Fig. 2. CPS ValidationAdapter principle architecture

The architecture in OPC-UA consists of servers and clients. To test the CPS ValidationAdapter, which is an OPC-UA client, it needs a remote station. For this purpose, the CPS Emulator has been developed and simulates a CPS in production. The emulator reads in an information model and uses it to set up the server and simulates sensor data that changes in time intervals.

With the CPS ValidationAdapter and the CPS Emulator, two tools are under development to test OPC-UA servers and clients for their conformity to a specification or information model. For system integration, both tools offer the possibility to test interoperability before integration into an IT infrastructure. Both, the IoT-T CPS ValidationAdapter and CPS Emulator are considered as open source software.

4   Comparison of CPS ValidationAdapter and OPCF CTT

The OPC Foundation's (OPCF) Compliance Test Tool (CTT) offers similar test functionalities as described in the previous chapters. The CTT is able to test both servers and clients. When testing servers, the CTT acts as a client, whereas when testing clients, the CTT acts as a kind of proxy in front of the server.

The process of server testing is initially similar for CPS ValidationAdapter and CTT. At first a connection has to be established. The tests then differ in their focus. The validation with the CPS ValidationAdapter concentrates on the application level with the check of the address space of the server. The CTT, on the other hand, checks the conformity of the implementation to the OPC-UA protocol. The OPCF group functionalities of OPC UA in profiles, facets, conformance groups and conformance units. Users of the CTT chose a set of these groups for their own validation:

- Profiles are functionalities that must be supported
- Facets are sets of features
- Conformance groups are logical groupings of conformance units
- Conformance unit is a defined set of properties that can be tested together.

Using these groupings, different test cases can be derived for different applications. Due to the versatile application possibilities of OPC-UA, it is also used in the embedded area. Here the server does not have to support all functionalities of the protocol. The individual test cases are implemented in JavaScript and can be extended independently or even developed by the user.

In addition to server tests, the CTT can also test OPC-UA clients. The CTT is switched as a kind of proxy between server and client. First, the server to which the CTT connects is started. The client can then connect to the CTT again. The client sends a message with a read request or similar to the CTT, which forwards the message to the server and then receives the response from the server.

This is exactly where the CTT intervenes and executes the test cases. The user selects a behavior to be tested. This can be the case with a read request, for example, that the node is not found in the address space. The manipulated message is send to the client, which must then be able to process the error. Therefore, Client tests of the CTT check the error handling of OPC-UA clients. Whereas, the CPS Emulator provides a feature to check clients against their requests to a server regarding a specific information model.

5 Use Case and Requirements

The use case focus on examples from large organizations such as automotive companies. They order new facilities as well as manufacturing lines from machine tool manufacturers and system integrators. In this context, plug-and-produce is already a demand since decades. Now the digital components of the systems require special attention to the IT requirements that exist due to the respective IT infrastructure of the customer [18, 19]. The use case was developed together with the industry partners in the IoT-T project. It has been discussed also across industrial organizations. The derived use case consists of five processes with different scopes for the validation tools. (see Fig. 3). The numbers in the figure correlate with the numbers in the enumeration below:

1. The first step is the development of a company specific standard for interfaces as long as not general standard is available. The user needs to specify the interfaces for the IT infrastructure as well as the specific information models. Conformance units and companion specs can support this. Currently industry starts to develop their own company standards for such interface definitions. In this process, the user checks the feasibility of the interface descriptions using the CPS ValidationAdapter (server tests) and CPS Emulator (client tests) e.g., whether the interface is reasonable for a used MES.

2. In the next step, the user takes the existing company standard and adapted it to specific demands. Adaptation means selection of the required parts of the information model as well as specific extensions. In this process, the test of node configuration takes place with the help of the CPS Emulator and CPS ValidationAdapter to develop an executable specification for the manufacturing system supplier.

3. The manufacturing tool supplier uses the interface specification together with the CPS Emulator and CPS ValidationAdapter in terms of validation environment to ensure the compliance of the digital components to the IT infrastructure of the customer.

4. The user or customer applies the validation tools in the delivery process of new manufacturing systems to support the acceptance tests. This will ensure that the new system can easily plugged into the IT infrastructure.

5. A further challenge is that in the past, after the successful setup of the manufacturing system, it was no more changed. It follows the philosophy: "Do not change a running system". Digital components especially software require continues updates concerning security, bug-fixes and functionality. On the shopfloor it might be a culture change but also the interfaces to enterprise applications are effected. Therefore, the validation tools are also required in the operation process to check the conformance aspects of updates regarding interoperability such as review of adjustments/changes e.g. change in the ERP or MES interface.

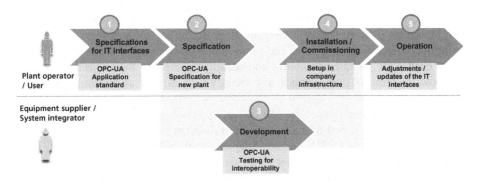

Fig. 3. Use case workflow

It is also relevant for small organizations to have defined interface needs of their IT infrastructures. The challenge for small and medium-sized enterprises (SMEs) might be different, as large enterprises can request specific interfaces from tool manufacturers. This will be more difficult in case of SMEs. They are more bounded to the interfaces provided by the tool providers. In this situation, standardized information models which are accepted by tool vendors are important and a potential solution for SMEs. Therefore, the standard case for SMEs will be to fit to machine tool interfaces but understanding the required information model by the SME can provide information about potential investment costs because of missing conformance.

During the tests of the prototype in industry further requirement were identified from the industry partner related to the reliability of the tests:

- The OPC-UA implementation of the chosen test tools can influence the validation especially if the test tools and the system under test uses different OPC-UA implementations.
- The different OPC-UA test facilities such as the OPCF CTT test tool provides different validation opportunities.
- Validations are currently not dynamic and process related. The validity of changes during the process is required.
- The relatability of the validation needs to be better understood. Is a validation adequate for a system acceptance?

The IoT-T project addresses work on these points until December 2019 especially the substitution of different OPC-UA implementation and the use of different validation functionalities is under consideration.

6   Conclusion

This research and development work was initiated by demands from industry related to interoperability between shopfloor IT and enterprise applications as well as within the shopfloor. The industrial IoT requirements have been identified within a German IoT project considering IoT tests. The tests focus on IoT in general concerning protocols such as MQTT and CoAP [17] for security, interoperability, protocol conformance and performance manner. At the beginning of 2016 industrial IoT was less focused but during the project it became more and more important because of the arising digital-ization challenges for interoperability and security. Therefore, the project results are new tools for protocol conformance and security tests as well as the interoperability validations.

The paper described the results and current approaches regarding these interoper-ability checks and provided an initial insight in different options for supporting tools. The development of the CPS ValidationAdapter and the CPS Emulator has been used to realize initial tests in real industrial scenarios to reduce the risk of missing the digital plug-and-produce. They are also used as a reference to compare with the CTT test facilities that are further developed and updated during the same time by the OPCF. As an outcome of the observations, the discussed software components offer test cases for four different directions:

- CPS ValidationAdapter tests an OPC-UA server at application level.
- CPS Emulator checks OPC-UA clients for interoperability with the OPC-UA server.
- OPCF-CTT Server Test checks the implemented functionalities and properties with regard to the protocol.
- OPCF-CTT Client Test tests the handling of occurring errors.

The demands and possible software support for supporting interoperability has been presented. For the future and especially in the extension of the IoT-T project, the focus will be on the validation via scenario execution, because currently the validations are mostly static, such as checking nodes of the information model. The target is to have a model based automatic scenario validation to support a runtime check of the interop-erability between OPC-UA clients and OPC-UA servers. Initial results are expected until end of December 2019.

Acknowledgement. This research and development is part of the IoT-T project (www.iot-t.de) granted via the smart service world program of the Federal Ministry for Economic Affairs and Energy (BMWi) in Germany.

References

1. Industry 4.0. https://www.plattform-i40.de/PI40/Navigation/EN/Home/home.html. Accessed 31 July 2019
2. Schweichhart, K.: Reference Architectural Model Industrie 4.0 (RAMI 4.0). https://ec. europa.eu/futurium/en/system/files/ged/a2-schweichhart-reference_architectural_model_industrie_4.0_rami_4.0.pdf. Accessed 31 July 2019
3. Industrial Internet Reference Architecture (IIRA). www.iiconsortium.org/IIRA.htm. Acces-sed 31 July 2019
4. Jaekel, F.-W., Torka, J., Eppelein, M., Schliephack, W., Knothe, T.: Model based, modular configuration of cyber physical systems for the information management on shop-floor. In: 2017 International Workshop on Enterprise Integration, Interoperability and Networking (EI2N) 12, Rhodes. OTM Workshops, pp. 16–25 (2017)

5. Pleinevaux, P., Decotignie. J.-D. https://ieeexplore.ieee.org/document/3274. Accessed 31 July 2019. IEEE
6. Feldbusse.de. https://www.feldbusse.de/profinet/profinet.shtml. Accessed 31 July 2019
7. OPC-UA. https://opcfoundation.org/about/opc-technologies/opc-ua/. Accessed 31 July 2019
8. MQTT Version 3.1.1 OASIS Standard 29 October 2014. http://docs.oasis-open.org/mqtt/mqtt/v3.1.1/os/mqtt-v3.1.1-os.html. Accessed 31 July 2019
9. OPC Foundation. https://opcfoundation.org/certification/overview-benefits/. Accessed 31 July 2019
10. OPC Foundation. https://opcfoundation.org/. Accessed 31 July 2019
11. Jäkel, F.-W., Wolff T., Hackel, L. Test services for interoperable and secure shop-floor IT application interfaces in OPC-UA. In: Proceedings 3rd GI/ACM Workshop on Standardization of Industry 4.0 Automation and Control Systems, 24 September 2018, Berlin, Germany
12. Jaekel, F.-W., Torka, J.: Test of the industrial internet of things: opening the black box. In: Zelm, M., Jaekel, F,-W., Doumeingts, G., Wollschlaeger, M.: Enterprise Interoperability: Smart Services and Business Impact of Enterprise Interoperability, 26 October 2018. ISBN: 9781119564034. https://doi.org/10.1002/9781119564034
13. OPC UA Compliance Test Tool (UACTT). https://opcfoundation.org/developer-tools/certification-test-tools/opc-ua-compliance-test-tool-uactt. - last access 31.07.2019
14. Data Distribution Service (DDS) Version 1.4. Object Management Group 2015. www.omg.org/spec/DDS/1.4/PDF/. Accessed 31 July 2019
15. Riedel, O., Margraf, T., Stölzle, S., Knothe, T., Eggers, A., Wintrich, N.: Modellbasierte modulare Shopfloor IT - Integration in die Werkzeuge der Digitalen Fabrik. Study, Electronic Publication 2014. http://publica.fraunhofer.de/eprints/urn_nbn_de_0011-n-3162488.pdf. Accessed 31 July 2019
16. XML Schema. https://opcfoundation.org/UA/schemas/1.04/. Accessed 31 July 2019
17. The Constrained Application Protocol (CoAP). https://tools.ietf.org/html/rfc7252. Accessed 31 July 2019
18. R1.1: IoT-Szenarien im Projekt, Report 25.02.2017. http://www.iot-t.de/wp-content/uploads/sites/11/2017/06/IoT-T_R1.1.pdf. Accessed 01 Sept 2019
19. R1.2:IoT-Prüfanforderungen im Projekt, Report 02.06.2017. http://www.iot-t.de/wp-content/uploads/sites/11/2017/06/IoT-T_R1.2.pdf. Accessed 01 Sept 2019

Predictive Maintenance Model with Dependent Stochastic Degradation Function Components

Janusz Szpytko$^{(\boxtimes)}$ and Yorlandys Salgado Duarte$^{(\boxtimes)}$

AGH University of Science and Technology,
Ave a. Mickiewicza 30, 30-059 Krakow, Poland
{szpytko, salgado}@agh.edu.pl

Abstract. The paper presents an Integrated Maintenance Decision Making Model (IMDMM) concept for cranes under operation with dependent stochastic function into the container type terminals. The target is to improve cranes operational efficiency through minimizing the risk of the Gantry Cranes Inefficiency (GCI) results based on implementation of copula approach model for stochastic degradation function dependency between cranes. In the present study, we investigate the influence of dependent stochastic degradation of multiple cranes on the optimal maintenance decisions. We use copula to model the dependent stochastic degradation of components and we formulate the optimal decision problem based on the minimum GCI expected. We illustrate the developed probabilistic analysis approach and the influence of the dependency of the stochastic degradation on the preferred decisions through numerical examples, and we discuss the close relationship of this approach with interoperability concepts. The crane operation risk is estimated with a sequential Monte Carlo Markov Chain (MCMC) simulation model and the optimization model behind of IMDMM is supported through the Particle Swarm Optimization (PSO) algorithms.

Keywords: Maintenance · Copula approach · Stochastic optimization

1 Introduction

The Institute of Electrical and Electronic Engineers (IEEE) defines *interoperability* as the ability of two or more systems or components to exchange information and use the information exchanged [2, 3]. Some authors understand interoperability as a broad concept with differentiated dimensions. In this sense, we can define *interoperability* as diverse organizations and systems ability to interact with common objectives in order to obtain mutual benefits. The interaction indicates that the organizations involved share information and knowledge through their business processes, through data exchange between their respective systems of information technology and communications.

The electronic administration field has given interoperability great relevance and has driven scientific studies that currently highlight other dimensions over the interoperability technical dimension [3]. It is precisely in this context that interoperability is currently imposed as one of the key elements for electronic administration. In addition

© Springer Nature Switzerland AG 2020
C. Debruyne et al. (Eds.): OTM 2019 Workshops, LNCS 11878, pp. 54–64, 2020.
https://doi.org/10.1007/978-3-030-40907-4_6

to talking about the interoperability governance, interoperability is currently recognized, at least, three well differentiated dimensions, as show the Fig. 1.

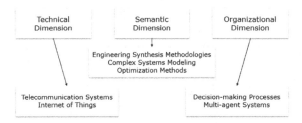

Fig. 1. Interoperability dimensions and study fields.

Interoperability is a critical factor for entities that operate in collaborative/cooperative environments. Performing an interoperability diagnosis based on a reference model allows an organization to know its strengths and prioritize actions, improving performance and maturity.

In this paper, we contribute with an approach that touches the above three dimensions at the same time: technical (we propose a platform concept that use information from data base sources; based on historical data failures in cranes and repair duration structure-time, historical planned process maintenance, it is possible to estimate operational exploitation parameters and maintenance diagnostic), semantic (we use optimization models and complex simulations functions; Monte Carlo Markov Chain simulation and heuristics optimization algorithms to perform the scenarios evaluation) and organizational (we propose an indicator that describe the behavior of the system, and base on this indicator we can improve the decision making process; holistic indicator that describe the system structure, functionality principals targets).

For another hands, multi-disciplinary software interoperability in the Architecture, Engineering, Construction and Operations industry is becoming a new and widely adopted business culture [4]. Technical advances in interoperability architectures, frameworks, methods and standards during the last decade resulted in higher maturity of product and process models. Mature models, in effect, enable data exchange by an increasing number of software applications in the industry. This establishes trust in data exchange and results in the lower cost impact of inefficient interoperability. The negative cost impact increases with advancing lifecycle phase, from planning and design phase to construction phase and to operation and maintenance phase [1].

As we can see, to improve the efficiency of the lifecycle system it is enough to improve any of the processes listed above. In this paper, we focus on the maintenance process. We propose an Integrated Maintenance Decision-Making Model (IMDMM) concept to coordinate the maintenance process in a container terminal, focused on dependent stochastic degradation function of the gantry cranes (critical components in this system). The present paper is a continuous work, almost all data and assumptions considered for us are described previously in the paper [9]. The new considerations in this paper are describe below.

The paper presents an IMDMM concept for cranes under operation with dependent stochastic function into the container type terminals that follow the discussion from the papers [5, 6] but with another approach. The target is to improve cranes operational efficiency through minimizing the risk of the Gantry Cranes Inefficiency (GCI) results based on implementation of copula approach model for stochastic degradation function dependency between cranes. In the present study, we investigate the influence of dependent stochastic degradation of multiple cranes on the optimal maintenance decisions. One of the input variables in the maintenance process proposal model is the cranes random failures, and consequently, when the input variable change, the output change (maintenance scheduling). We use copula to model the dependent stochastic degradation of components and we formulate the optimal decision problem based on the minimum GCI expected like the idea developed in [7]. We illustrate the developed probabilistic analysis approach and the influence of the dependency of the stochastic degradation on the preferred decisions through numerical examples.

The IMDMM concept is generally well known in the literature as CBM (Condition-Based Maintenance) policies and examples conceptual [10] and engineering application [11] show the acceptance of this approach in the industrial maintenance.

The paper is structured in four sections, Introduction, Materials and Methods, Discussions and Results, and Conclusions. In the second one, the stochastics degradation failure historical data dependency is described with the mathematical model t-Copula, as well as the simulation mathematical model of the process, focusing in the gantry cranes operation in the terminal container. In the third section, we discuss the results with previous work, and we match the new results in the Conclusions section.

2 Materials and Methods

In this paper we use the Copula approach in order to simulate fails dependent stochastic degradation function between cranes. The motivation comes because in several systems, such as terminal container, typically we find identical system or components (cranes) working in parallel, with similar operational exploitation parameters and similar maintenance diagnostic and performance process (same manufacturer), therefore, common failures can happen in systems with these characteristics and as a consequence the system (terminal container) come in a critical capacity situation because loss more than one component (cranes) at the same time. For this reason, we propose in this paper to simulate the degradation process (failures) with Copula approach because we want to consider the joint probability of gantry crane failures phenomenon. In addition, the Copula approach resolves the independence between components assumption through the correlation matrix structure of the model. In this section, we introduce the Copula approach (main properties) and we describe the potential application of this approach from the engineering perspective. All the theory described in this section we take from the reference [8], but we adapt the financial concepts approach into a concept approach for technical systems.

2.1   *t*-Copula Approach

An N-dimensional copula is a function C with the following properties:

- Dom $C = \mathbf{I}^N = [0; 1]^N$;
- C is grounded and N-increasing;
- C has margins C_n which satisfy $C_n(u) = C(1; \ldots; 1; u; 1; \ldots; 1) = u$ for all u in $\mathbf{I}$.

A copula corresponds also to a function with several properties. In particular, because of the second and third properties, it follows that $C = \mathbf{I}^N = [0; 1]^N$, and so C is a multivariate uniform distribution. Moreover, it is obvious that if $F_1; \ldots; F_N$ are univariate distribution functions, $C(F_1(x_1); \ldots; F_n(x_n); \ldots; F_N(x_N))$ is a multivariate distribution function with margins $F_1; \ldots; F_N$ because $u_n = F_n(x_n)$ is a uniform random variable. Copula functions are then an adapted tool to construct multivariate distributions.

Theorem 2 (Sklar's theorem). Let F be an N-dimensional distribution function with continuous margins $F_1; \ldots; F_N$ Then F has a unique copula representation:

$$F(x_1, \ldots, x_n, \ldots, x_N) = C(F_1(x_1); \ldots; F_n(x_n); \ldots; F_N(x_N)) \tag{1}$$

The density function c associated to the copula distribution C is given by

$$c(u_1, \ldots, u_n, \ldots u_N) = \frac{\partial C(u_1, \ldots, u_n, \ldots u_N)}{\partial u_1 \ldots \partial u_n \ldots \partial u_N} \tag{2}$$

To obtain the density f of the N-dimensional distribution F, we use the following relationship:

$$f(x_1, \ldots, x_n, \ldots x_N) = c(F_1(x_1), \ldots, F_n(x_n), \ldots, F_N(x_N)) \prod_{n=1}^{N} f_n(x_n) \tag{3}$$

where f_n is the density of the margin F_n.

Copulas are also a powerful tool, because the modeling problem can be appropriate in order to represent the dependence structure in a good manner. This property is relevant in this research because is possible to identify common degradation failures between components with this approach. For this reason, we discuss how measure the dependence, as a measure of concordance. A numeric measure κ of association between two continuous random variables X_1 and X_2 whose copula is C is a measure of concordance if it satisfies the following properties:

- κ is defined for every pair X_1, X_2 of continuous random variables;
- $-1 = \kappa_{X,-X} \leq \cdot \kappa_C \leq \kappa_{X,X} = 1$;
- $\kappa_{X1;X2} = \kappa_{X2;X1}$;
- if X_1 and X_2 are independent, then $\kappa_{X1;X2} = \kappa_C \Leftarrow = 0$;
- $\kappa_{-X1;X2} = \kappa_{X1;-X2} = -\kappa_{X1;X2}$;

- If $C_1 \triangleleft C_2$, then $\leq \cdot \kappa_{C1} \leq \kappa_{C2}$;
- if $(X_{1,\,n}; X_{2,\,n})$ is a sequence of continuous random variables with copulas C_n, and if C_n converges point wise to C, then $\lim_{n \to \infty} \kappa_{Cn} = \kappa_C$.

Another important property of κ comes from the fact the copula function of random variables $(X_1; \ldots; X_n; \ldots; X_N)$ is invariant under strictly increasing transformations:

$$C_{X_1,\ldots,X_n,\ldots X_N} = C_{h_1(X_1),\ldots,h_n(x_n),\ldots,h_N(x_N)} \quad \text{if} \quad \partial_x h_n(x) > 0 \tag{4}$$

Among all the measures of concordance, three famous measures play an important role in non-parametric statistics: the Kendall's tau, the Spearman's rho and the Gini indices. Based on the previous definition, we can say that the correlation matrix is a good measure of concordance. The correlation coefficient of two random variables is a measure of their dependence. The correlation coefficient matrix of two random variables is the matrix of correlation coefficients for each pairwise variable combination. Since X_1 and X_2 are always directly correlated to themselves, the diagonal entries are just 1. If we follow this idea, we can simulate with Copulas random values with the defined dependence from the correlation matrix.

In the analyzed system (terminal container), it is usual to have more than two gantry cranes, so we use the *Copula Multivariate t-Distribution* or *t-Copula* because this model allows us to relate more than two variables, for definition N random variables, being appropriate for the proposal of this paper.

The probability density function of the d-dimensional multivariate Student's t distribution is given by

$$f\left(x. \sum, \upsilon\right) = \frac{1}{\sum^{1/2}} \frac{1}{\sqrt{(\upsilon\pi)^d}} \frac{\Gamma((\upsilon+d)/2)}{\Gamma(\upsilon/2)} \left(1 + \frac{x' \sum^{-1} x}{\upsilon}\right)^{-(\upsilon+d)/2} \tag{5}$$

where x is a 1-by-d vector of random numbers, Σ is a d-by-d symmetric, positive definite matrix, in this case the Pearson correlation matrix, and υ is a positive scalar, in this case the degrees of freedom. While it is possible to define the multivariate Student's t for singular Σ, the density cannot be written as above. For the singular case, only random number generation is supported. This paper is a continuous work, therefor the following section is taken from the paper [9] and at the same time we comment the modifications, also as we declared before, in the end, we describe the proposed simulations.

2.2 Gantry Cranes Modeling

The gantry cranes operation is continuous, eventually fails and is repairable. This random behavior can be described with Markov processes. Considering the operation effectiveness of the container gantry crane, in the paper [9], they fix that the system and its components have two states $z = 0, 1$. In the two-state model, the gantry cranes are considered fully available ($z = 1$) or totally unavailable ($z = 0$). According to the standard systems, each gantry cranes should carry out 25 moves per hour which is equal to 144 s for every movement. To simulate a real operation, the j-th number of movements $C_{GC_{i,j}} \sim N(\mu_{GC_i}, \sigma_{GC_i})$, where μ_{GC_i} is the average move/hour and σ_{GC_i} the standard deviation assumed. The stochastic capacity $U_{GC_{i,j}}(t)$ at the time instant t of a gantry cranes i is determined by the TTF_i (time to failure), TTR_i (time to repair) and $C_{GC_{i,j}}$. The parameters TTF_i, TTR_i and $C_{GC_{i,j}}$ allow to simulate with (2) the behavior of $U_{GC_{i,j}}(t)$ generating k-th independent random numbers.

Previously in the reference [9], they assumed that $TTF_{i,k} \sim W(\alpha_i, \beta_i)$ and $TTR_{i,k} \sim N(\mu_i, \sigma_i)$, where α_i and β_i are the shape and scale parameters of the Weibull distribution function respectively, μ_i is the average time repair and σ_i the standard deviation assumed of the Normal distribution function respectively for each i-th gantry crane.

In the approach [9], they assuming stochastics degradation function independence between cranes because the in the simulation process they used independent random numbers to simulate the operation process in the terminal. It is necessary to know that there may not be any relationship between the degradation process between two or more cranes, but if there is, therefore, the assumption can generate errors in the process simulation. In this paper, we assume that $TTF_{i,k} \sim W(\alpha_i, \beta_i)$, but the random numbers generated to simulate the failure in each gantry cranes are correlated through the correlation matrix Σ, and as a consequence, the failure (degradation) simulation process is implement by t-Copula approach. The main idea is computing random values from the correlation matrix Σ and the degrees of freedom υ using t-Copula. Therefore, we generate a matrix of dependent random values between 0 and 1, inclusive, sampled from a continuous uniform distribution, consequently, the generated data of the Copula has a marginal uniform distribution. When we applied t-Copula, the depended random numbers are generated from the probability density function of the d-dimensional multivariate Student's t distribution (5). Therefore, let ρ be a symmetric, positive definite matrix with diagonal $\rho = 1$ and $T_{p,\upsilon}$ the standardized multivariate Student's t-distribution with υ degrees of freedom and correlation matrix ρ. The multivariate Student's t-Copula is then defined as follows:

$$C(u_1, \ldots, u_n, \ldots u_N; \rho, \upsilon) = T_{\rho,\upsilon}\left(t_\upsilon^{-1}(u_1), \ldots, t_\upsilon^{-1}(u_n), \ldots, t_\upsilon^{-1}(u_N)\right) \qquad (6)$$

with t_υ^{-1} the inverse of the univariate Student's distribution.

The value of the degrees of freedom parameter υ alters the shape of the probability distribution function. As the degrees of freedom υ goes to infinity, the t-distribution approaches the standard normal distribution. The Cauchy distribution is a Student's t-distribution with degrees of freedom υ equal to 1. The Cauchy distribution has an undefined mean and variance. From the previous comments we set the value of the degrees of freedom between 3 and 9 as adequate for this approach to avoid the conditions described above.

From the Eq. (6) we obtain dependent random values between 0 and 1, then with the inverse cumulative Weibull distribution (7) with α_i and β_i parameters, we simulate $TTF_{i,k}$ random values as a follow,

$$TTF_{i,k} = F^{-1}(p|\beta_i, \alpha_i) = -\beta_i[\ln(1 - p)]^{1/\alpha_i} I_{[0,1]}(p) \qquad (7)$$

The model proposed to simulate gantry cranes capacity is defined below:

$$U_{GC_{i,j}}(t) = \begin{cases} C_{GC_{i,j}} & \text{if} \quad t < S_{1_{i,m}} + S_{2_{i,m-1}} \\ 0 & \text{if} \quad S_{1_{i,m}} + S_{2_{i,m-1}} \le t < S_{1_{i,m}} + S_{2_{i,m}} \\ 0 & \text{if} \quad A_{1_{i,n}} + A_{2_{i,n-1}} \le t < A_{1_{i,n}} + A_{2_{i,n}} \end{cases} \tag{8}$$

where: $i = 1, 2, \dots, N_{GC}$; $j = 1, 2, \dots, NH$ (8760 h/year); $S_{1_{i,m}} = \sum_{k=1}^{m} TTF_{i,k}$ for $m = 2, 3, \dots, MN_i$; $S_{2_{i,m}} = \sum_{k=1}^{m} TTR_{i,k}$ for $m = 2, 3, \dots, MN_i$; $A_{1_{i,n}} = \sum_{k=1}^{n} TTM_{i,k}$ for $n = 2, 3, \dots, NK_i$; $A_{2_{i,n}} = \sum_{k=1}^{n} TDM_{i,k}$ for $n = 2, 3, \dots, NK_i$.

The container terminal capacity $TC_n(t)$ defined in Eq. (9) is determined by the j-th gantry cranes total capacity in the container terminal TC_{GC_n} and the time of each vessel in the container terminal $VF_{n-1} \le t < VF_n$:

$$TC_n(t) = \left\{ TC_{GC_n} = \sum_{j=VF_{n-1}}^{VF_n} \sum_{i=1}^{N_{GC}} U_{GC_{i,j}}(t) \quad \text{if} \quad VF_{n-1} \le t < VF_n \right. \tag{9}$$

where $n = 1, 2, \dots, VN$.

The main target of this paper is quantifying the difference of the GCI indicator between the previous work [9] and this paper with the new assumptions. Following this idea, we propose simulate the same system, but in this case, we assume dependent stochastic degradation of components, so we propose simulate the dependence of 0% (previous work), 50% and 85% (correlation matrix), and each scenario with 3 and 9 degrees of freedom and compare the final results. In the next section we evidence the results.

3 Discussions and Results

The information used in the scenarios evaluated in this paper is taken from reference [9]. Usually, the correlation matrix Σ and the degrees of freedom υ are parameters estimated from the real monitoring exploitation parameters data of the gantry crane, but in this research we only intend to show how the maintenance scheduling based on the GCI indicator changes when we set the correlation matrix Σ and the degrees of freedom υ, with the idea of testing the hypothesis that stochastic degradation function dependency between cranes can change the maintenance scheduling.

The model used (t-Copula) to simulate stochastic degradation function dependency between cranes has two parameters. First one, the correlation matrix Σ: Figs. 2, 3 and 4 show, for three different correlation matrix Σ, the simulated failure behavior for two Gantry Cranes, idea that is generalized to all cranes in the scenarios evaluated. Second one, the degrees of freedom υ: this parameter is related with the data, but we used simulation, therefor we fix the value in the simulation, and the Table 1 show the results for each case considered.

Table 1 shows the planning of the simulations and the results of each simulation based on the GCI indicator and Table 2 shows the results of the maintenance scheduling. We can observe that in each scenario the model archives different indicator value (see Table 1), therefore both parameters, correlation matrix Σ and degrees of freedom υ has influence in the results of the maintenance scheduling (see Table 2), however, the differences are more significant when correlation matrix changes. The results of this approach are the evidence that failure data history structure of the gantry cranes is important to consider in the maintenance scheduling process.

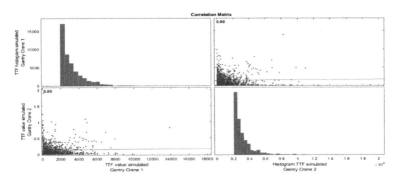

Fig. 2. Full independent simulated failure behavior for two Gantry Cranes (previous work).

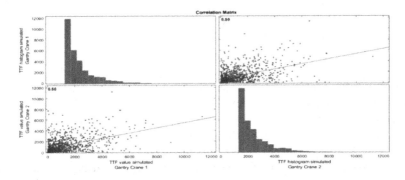

Fig. 3. Simulated failure behavior for two Gantry Cranes with $\kappa = 0.5$.

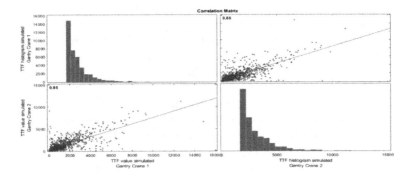

Fig. 4. Simulated failure behavior for two Gantry Cranes with $\kappa = 0.85$.

Table 1. GCI expected value for each scenario evaluated.

Pairwise correlation coefficient	Degrees of freedom	GCI
$\kappa = 0$	–	11.48
$\kappa = 0.5$	$\upsilon = 3$	11.08
$\kappa = 0.85$	$\upsilon = 3$	11.67
$\kappa = 0.5$	$\upsilon = 9$	11.09
$\kappa = 0.85$	$\upsilon = 9$	11.13

Table 2. Maintenance start time (TTM) in hours for each scenario evaluated.

Gantry Crane	$\kappa = 0$	$\kappa = 0.5, \upsilon = 3$	$\kappa = 0.85, \upsilon = 3$	$\kappa = 0.5, \upsilon = 9$	$\kappa = 0.85, \upsilon = 3$
GC1	4602	8045	3256	6173	7241
GC2	7319	8424	6530	3939	3096
GC3	6800	4590	964	3936	2500
GC4	7817	5633	4629	3570	6292
GC5	5009	4138	4077	1761	5700
GC6	6458	4051	2113	6791	7808
GC7	406	1975	4927	6073	1448
GC8	3937	2876	4132	4394	5443
GC9	2224	6466	3657	3473	5733
GC10	6432	2786	2738	6647	5504

Mathematical models based on simulation can model stochastic processes with complex functions, but the time to simulate these processes can be a limitation with the current computing capacity. The research shows the duration time results of ten simulations with a i5 5250U 1.6 GHz CPU; problem solution time in this investigation depends on the samples number (N) necessary to guarantee the error in each simulation and the evaluations number (E) in the objective function to perform the problem solution. According to the results, the problem average solution time is [(2.7580 ± 0. 2542) × $N \times E$] seconds.

The GCI describes the maintenance scheduling behavior and it is useful holistic indicator for the decision-making process in the terminal container because the manager can decide the system risk level and the demand planned frequency and perform a maintenance coordination minimizing catastrophic risks. The new approach proposed is more consistent with the data source (more flexible) and the semantic definition of the problem because considers the data failure historical structure of the cranes degradation. The ending process of the IMDMM concept is an interoperability software application for the manager in the terminal container.

Each methodology has limitations, and this approach isn't the exception. The main issues with the applicability of this approach is the failure data structure. The correlation matrix estimation can be a challenge because is necessary establish the failure monitoring window (each engineering system is different; therefore, the window is different), and only through a window is possible find common failures between the cranes. In this approach, the methodology applicability is related with the data structure and not system, in fact, is possible to extend to another engineering systems.

4 Conclusions

The paper shows that the proposed IMDMM model concept based on risk assessment allows efficiently to schedule the maintenance strategy of gantry cranes under operation in practice considering the failure data history structure of the gantry cranes. In the present study, we evidence the influence of dependent stochastic degradation of multiple cranes on the optimal maintenance decisions using copula approach. We illustrate the developed probabilistic analysis approach and the influence of the dependency of the stochastic degradation on the preferred decisions through numerical examples. The presented model opens the way to extensive simulations under various scenarios and conditions, to detect anomalies and to conduct accurate diagnostics and prognostics of cranes into selected scenarios.

Acknowledgement. The work has been financially supported by the Polish Ministry of Science and Higher Education.

References

1. Terzi, S., Cassina, J., Panetto, H.: Development of a metamodel to foster interoperability along the product lifecycle traceability. In: Konstantas, D., Bourrières, J.P., Léonard, M., Boudjlida, N. (eds.) INTEROP-ESA 2005, pp. 1–11. Springer, London (2006). https://doi.org/10.1007/1-84628-152-0_1

2. Rukanova, B.D., van Slooten, K., Stegwee, R.A.: Business process requirements, modeling technique and standard: how to identify interoperability gaps on a process level. In: Konstantas, D., Bourrières, J.-P., Léonard, M., Boudjlida, N. (eds.) INTEROP-ESA 2005, pp. 13–23. Springer-Verlag, London (2006). https://doi.org/10.1007/1-84628-152-0_2

3. Anicic, N., Ivezic, N., Jones, A.: An architecture for semantic enterprise application integration standards. In: Konstantas, D., Bourrières, J.-P., Léonard, M., Boudjlida, N. (eds.) INTEROP-ESA 2005, pp. 25–34. Springer-Verlag, London (2006). https://doi.org/10.1007/1-84628-152-0_3

4. Davidsson, P., Ramstedt, L., Törnquist, J.: Inter-organization interoperability in transport chains using adapters based on open source freeware. In: Konstantas, D., Bourrières, J.-P., Léonard, M., Boudjlida, N. (eds.) INTEROP-ESA 2005, pp. 35–42. Springer-Verlag, London (2006). https://doi.org/10.1007/1-84628-152-0_4

5. Xi, Z., Jing, R., Wang, P., Huc, C.: A copula-based sampling method for data-driven prognostics. Reliab. Eng. Syst. Saf. **132**, 72–82 (2014)

6. Hong, H.P., Zhou, W., Zhang, S., Ye, W.: Optimal condition-based maintenance decisions for systems with dependent stochastic degradation of components. Reliab. Eng. Syst. Saf. **121**, 276–288 (2014)

7. Li, H., Deloux, E., Dieulle, L.: A condition-based maintenance policy for multi-component systems with Lévy copulas dependence. Reliab. Eng. Syst. Saf. **149**, 44–55 (2016)

8. Mai, J.-F., Scherer, M.: Financial Engineering with Copulas Explained. Palgrave Macmillan, London (2014). 978–1137–32733–8
9. Szpytko, J., Duarte, Y.S.: Digital twins model for cranes operating in container terminal. In: IFAC IMS 2019 Conference Proceedings (2019). https://doi.org/10.1016/j.ifacol.2019.10.014
10. Nguyen, K.T.P., et al.: Joint optimization of monitoring quality and replacement decisions in condition-based maintenance. Reliab. Eng. Syst. Saf. **189**, 177–195 (2019)
11. Besnard, F., et al.: An approach for condition-based maintenance optimization applied to wind turbine blades. IEEE Trans. Sustain. Energy **1**(2), 77–83 (2010)

5th International Workshop on Fact Based Modeling (FBM 2019)

FBM 2019 PC Co-chairs' Message

The FBM 2019 workshop gives insight into the professional application of Fact Based Modeling in government and business practice. Our main theme for this workshop is Conceptual Thinking and Information Modelling at the Core of the Information Economy. For FBM 2019, 8 high quality papers were selected for presentation. We congratulate the authors of these contributions.

FBM 2019 will once again be centered around the presentation of practice reports and theoretical papers on Fact Based Modeling. The focus of this year's workshop will be on Conceptual modelling and data semantics by combining the powerful principles of logic and natural language.

The first session of the workshop will link the concept of data architecture to FBM information modeling.

The second session of the first day of the workshop will be entirely devoted to the concepts of ontologies and how they relate to FBM. The first day of the workshop will be concluded by a paper on a conceptual model of the block chain.

The first presentation session of the 2nd day of the workshop will be on FBM in a legal context.

In the second paper session of the second day, a paper on DMN and FBM will be presented. The second paper in that session is a theoretical paper on the concepts of roles and variables in FBM.

The day will be concluded by an open discussion on the future of Conceptual Modeling chaired by Maurice Nijssen.

October 2019

Peter Bollen
Stijn Hoppenbrouwers
Maurice Nijssen

Word Meaning, Data Semantics, Crowdsourcing, and the BKM/A-Lex Approach

Thomas Nobel[1], Stijn Hoppenbrouwers[1,2(✉)] [iD], Jan Mark Pleijsant[3], and Mats Ouborg[3]

[1] Radboud University, 6525EC Nijmegen, The Netherlands
[2] HAN University of Applied Sciences, 6826CC Arnhem, The Netherlands
stijn.hoppenbrouwers@han.nl
[3] ABN AMRO Bank, 1082MS Amsterdam, The Netherlands

Abstract. The lexical definition of concepts is an integral part of Fact Based Modelling. More in general, structured description of term meaning, in many forms and guises, has since the early days played a role in information systems (data dictionaries, data modelling), data management (business glossaries for data governance), knowledge engineering (applied logic, rule definition and management), and the Semantic Web (RDF). We observe that at the core of many different approaches to lexical meaning lies the combination of semantic networks and textual definitions, and propose to re-appreciate these relatively simple basics as the theoretical but also, and perhaps more so, the practical core of dealing with Data Semantics. We also explore some fundamental concepts from cybernetics, providing some theoretical basis for advocating crowdsourcing as a way of taking up a continuous lexical definition in and across domain communities. We discuss and compare various combined aspects in lexical definition approaches from various relevant fields in view of the A-Lex tool, which supports a crowdsourcing approach to the lexical definition in a data management context: Business Knowledge Mapping. We explain why this approach indeed applies most of the core concepts of "word meaning as a vehicle for dealing with data semantics in and across communities".

Keywords: Data semantics · Semantic networks · Lexical definition · crowdsourcing · Fact Based Modelling · Collaborative modelling

1 Introduction

Lexical definition has been part of Fact Based Modelling (FBM) and Fact Based Thinking (FBT) all the way [8,10]. Since in all practical applications of FBM the combination of linguistic and logical meaning is key, the meaning of terms used in fact based conceptual models is an essential component of their meaning/interpretation [10,13]. In the early days, this aspect was covered by Data

© Springer Nature Switzerland AG 2020
C. Debruyne et al. (Eds.): OTM 2019 Workshops, LNCS 11878, pp. 67–78, 2020.
https://doi.org/10.1007/978-3-030-40907-4_7

Dictionaries [14] in which, among other meta-data, the meaning of at least non-trivial terms was described using natural language descriptions (definitions, glosses). Later, comparable practices have been diversely named and used, typically as auxiliaries to a large and quite varied set of interrelated techniques and representations like data models, data architectures, ontologies, business rule repositories, etcetera. However, despite many differences in details of representation and use, the underlying lexical description practices, related to but still distinct from regular conceptual modelling (which focuses on facts and fact types, not elementary terms), seem to be remarkably similar at the core. They usually take the form of textual definitions of individual items combined with network-like collections of items and the relations between them, involving a limited set of different relation types, and often visualised through graphs.

Though there is some existing work on terminology in FBM (for example, [13]) and Information Systems in general (for example [20]), the lexical aspect seems to be perceived mostly as relatively secondary to (formal) relational structuring in data and knowledge engineering. Most emphasis in dealing with terms and definitions seems to have been on solving ambiguity in the form of synonymy (different terms being used for the same meaning) and, even more so, homonymy (a term being used with various meanings). As elaborately argued in [11], we take a somewhat different stance in that we view lexical diversity, resulting from the pragmatic need to conceptualise differently in various contexts and domains, as a fact of data and information life, and even as something that should in principle be embraced (also see Sect. 2). However, from a different but equally valid perspective, lexical standardisation, basically striving to stamp out synonyms and homonyms, is also a necessary, practical direction to take in many cases. The challenge (not directly addressed in this paper; for discussion, see [11]) is to choose wisely in specific cases/contexts, and effectively deal with the required balance between diversity and standardisation. This issue carries through in fields like data management and data governance, system interoperability, data science, and the Semantic Web.

We believe the above playing fields warrant more extensive research and development in understanding and solving both practical and theoretical issues of dealing with data semantics through lexical semantics. In the current paper, we first discuss some theoretical handholds from Cybernetics concerning language diversity, and social and community factors, relevant to a crowdsourcing approach to continuous lexical definition. We then focus on lexical definition from the perspectives of digital lexicology, semantic (web) technology, and FBM/FBT, and position them in a generic layered model. We refrain from a comprehensive discussion of formal aspects of lexical meaning representation. Instead, we revisit and align the standard basics of approaches to lexical representation. We then summarise how all these aspects relate to a concrete means for data semantic management: the A-Lex tool ("ABN AMRO Lexicon") for crowdsourcing-based lexical definition [22].

A-Lex supports continuous, self-service lexical knowledge description in and across communities, as part of an approach called Business Knowledge Mapping (BKM). Explained in a nutshell, it does this primarily by supporting the systematic creation of a (semantic) network of lexical relations between terms for some specific domain, most prominently specialisation/generalisation, part/whole, object/characteristic. In addition, textual definitions (glosses) can be entered. A-Lex is business-oriented rather than IT-oriented and thus aims at domain-related communities of business people as chief (end)users [22].

2 Second Order Cybernetics: Language Diversity in Organisations

Alan Turing gave us an unambiguous and elaborate computational definition of what a syntax is by stating that syntax is everything which can be captured/accepted by a Turing machine [2]. This, however, does not solve the problem of dealing with lexical semantics, which (as Wittgenstein pointed out) remains largely unfit for practical formalisation. Apart from obviously being neuro-cognitive, language is also (socio-)cultural: a shared and distributed phenomenon [23]. Required language adaption in combination with the complexity of the environment and context in which a domain language is used (see Fig. 1) will result in necessary evolution of its concepts, terms, and semantics, and inevitably leads to diversification among organisational domain languages.

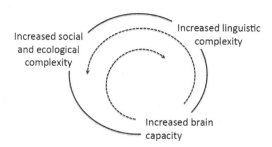

Fig. 1. Language complexity increase, adapted from [23] p3

Cybernetic principles can be applied in researching semantic domain-specific language issues through a theoretical link between information theory (or as Claude Shannon called it, the Theory of Communication) and the evolution of languages [2]. In second-order cybernetics as defined by Niklas Luhmann, the generality of first-order cybernetics is replaced by specificity. Organisations are, in the view of Luhmann, a particular class of social system which continuously conduct "experiments" because the outcome of a decision cannot be determined beforehand.

It is imperative that the set of all possible "complexes of things and processes" which could be produced by a system are reduced to a subset of particular elements which are likely to keep the system (and its internal processes) going. A language element can be rejected because it is not accepted into a system based on the decision premises. This process of creating elements and then rejecting or accepting them keeps repeating during the lifetime of the system [1].

The explanation cybernetics provides for the evolution of (domain-specific) languages and their inherent incessant changing, and adaptive properties entail that organisations should put effort in effective communication, including "linguistic meta-communication", i.e. communication about language [12]. Evolution of languages is a genuine phenomenon in the social systems that are organisations. In data governance (in which data-oriented language elements play a crucial role), language descriptions have to be continuously updated. This is directly related to the continuous development of information systems and emphasises the importance of business-language alignment as part of continuous change management for organisations and their systems.

In sum, there is a fruitful link here between the disciplines of cybernetics, linguistics, information systems, data governance, and organisational change. Without language alignment (or, on the other end of the spectrum, language standardisation), any other kind of alignment or standardisation will be very challenging within a social system such as an organisation. Organisations should, therefore "meta-communicate" (both among themselves and with other domains) and (where relevant) actively decide on the meanings/semantics of their domain terminology, describe and share them in an organised way, and keep this description up to date as the organisation and its systems evolve. This should be part and parcel of Data Governance (and indeed, it increasingly is).

In many of today's organisations, people work in agile and dynamic environments in which many processes, products, etcetera are in a state of continuous improvement and thus propel the specific domain language evolution and diversification. Web 2.0, with all of its technologies and applications, gives rise to many new possibilities for organisations concerning knowledge management [16]. These should be embraced by organisations in order to stay/become innovative and to improve themselves. In Sect. 3.4, we discuss the advantages of the web 2.0 approach and the power of crowds/communities. The BKM/A-Lex approach can assist in this respect by giving organisations a structured, low-threshold way to use the advantages of web 2.0 in order to solve the seemingly inevitable problems emerging from continuous lexical (re)definition due to the evolution and diversification of language in organisations.

3 Describing Word Meaning: Concepts and Lexicons

3.1 Information Systems Context: Closing the Semiotic Gap

A Universe of Discourse ("domain" or "application domain") is the "universe" or "world" we are interested in and/or discoursing about. It can be described using, at the core, concepts and relationships[1]. If one is to model this domain

---

[1] We were tempted to refer to "entities and relationships" here, but decided to stick to the conceptual level of abstraction. Also, we realise one could reasonably claim both entities and relationships are, at a higher level of abstraction, "concepts"; we choose not to do this in the current paper, nor to pursue more detailed discussion, for lack of space and urgency.

comprehensively, then this includes a description of the basic concepts used to describe it. Concepts are mostly labelled by using nouns or nominal phrases, relationships through verbs or verb phrases. Importantly, such labelling typically occurs in and for some specific context, by a specific group of people wielding a UoD-specific language (formally captured at an "information grammar" level in, for example, FBMs).

In Fig. 2 we can see an image of the FRISCO tetrahedron [9]. The theoretical concepts it combines are meant to close the gap between syntax, semantics, and pragmatics in understanding language, (meta-)communication and information in organisations [9,11]. It posits the link between the conception, representation, domain, and actor, with the actor being both interpreter and representer. The "actor" aspect is crucial: it states the subjectiveness of the language used for communicating about the UoD; its origin and existence in the minds of (groups of) individual humans. It implies the viewpoint that social agents involved in communication are also active with regard to the relationship between information and actions. This implies the existence of "Environments of Discourse" (EoD) in which agents, artefacts, vocabularies, media, and various other concepts impact and perform (meta-)communication [11]. Every EoD includes what we can refer to as the "Community of Discourse": the UoD/EoD language community. When two groups communicate, a new EoD emerges with its own conventions and agreements: its UoD.

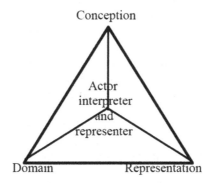

Fig. 2. The FRISCO tetrahedron, [9], p3

The CoD usually engages in linguistic meta-communication (talking about and therefore verifying and fine-tuning "what people mean with particular words") in an ad-hoc fashion, almost implicitly as part of general conversation. However, in some cases (data management as a primary example), it pays off to make such meta-communication explicit, and even organise it. Tools like A-Lex help to do this; in the case of BKM/A-Lex, this is done in line with all major factors we view as valuable.

3.2   Wordnet: Terms and Lexical Relations

The lexical database Wordnet is one of the most widely used and largest in existence [24]. Its purpose is to organise lexical data in such a way that it makes it a better fit for digital use than classical dictionaries. Wordnet links words based on the "senses" (different interpretations) of words. Because Wordnet might seem to resemble a single large thesaurus (there are some important differences) the proximity of different words is crucial. Proximity is used to semantically disambiguate words that are in close proximity to one another in the semantic network. Another interesting feature is that Wordnet gives words semantic relations with other words in the form of "synonym" and "homonym" relations [21]. "Synsets" are sets of cognitive synonyms, each representing a different concept. The synsets to which a word belongs also have conceptual-semantic and lexical relationships with other synsets (for example antonymy, hyponymy, meronymy, troponymy, and entailment relations). It is possible that a word is a member of multiple synsets if it has multiple distinct meanings [18,25].

There is some similarity between how Wordnet structures and defines relationships between different synsets, and how A-Lex structures its lexicons. However, there is also a crucial difference in the way the two approaches handle the description of word meanings: Wordnet aims at describing general national languages (for example, English), whereas BKM/A-Lex aims for the description of UoD "dialects". However, the Wordnet structure and concepts could just as well be used for describing local or domain-specific, just as BKM/A-Lex can also be used for standardised, generic UoDs.

In both Wordnet and classical dictionaries, a definition is given based on an assertion and an empirical description of how a word is typically used: 'Lexical definition' [11]. This is especially interesting in view of digital lexicography and text clustering [5,24]. However, BKM/A-Lex instead focuses on "Stipulative definition", which refers to word meaning purposefully specified for a particular context, with a specific goal, as fits the information systems/data context. However, this then includes the possibility of "Lexical-Stipulative definition", in which the use of a common (lexical) word meaning (Lexical definition) is deliberately adopted and stipulated for a specific context/purpose.

3.3   Textual Definition: Genus and Differentiae

A classic, and still quite useful (and common) principle underlying textual lexical definition (in particular for nominal terms), is to describe their Genus and Differentiae: "the sort of thing they are" (IS-A) and "how they differ from other things of the same type" (relevant properties). For example, a dog can be (very roughly yet effectively) defined as "an animal that barks and wags its tail". Note that an elaborate description of its many other properties, for example "has four legs" and "is a mammal" is not immediately relevant here: the focus is on effective distinguishing features, used for disambiguation. Importantly, such disambiguation is often created for use in a particular context (as, contrary to popular belief, definitions usually are), and therefore, so are the choices of Genus and Differentiae; they depend on the particular UoD and EoD, which set the stage for the specialised linguistic meta-communication that definitions accomplish [11].

Interestingly, the genus-differentiae approach to a definition is also applied if a semantic network (like Wordnet, or A-Lex) is used instead of a text. In fact, verbalisations of network structures can be part of or even constitute definition texts; this is a known practice in FBM, and also in BKM.

3.4   Lexical Definition, Web 2.0, and Crowdsourcing

In the early days of the internet, traffic was mostly one-directional. Users only 'took' and did not 'give' web content. This changed with the dawn of Web 2.0, of which Wikipedia and social media are primary examples. The traffic became bidirectional. This gave rise to new challenges but also to a vast number of possibilities regarding user-created content. The content of Wikipedia, for example, has been created by a vast number of contributors who work voluntarily, without formally checked background or professional qualifications. Errors or gaps are detected by the users (or reviewers) themselves, resulting in edits [6, 16].

Wikipedia and several other internet encyclopedias thus use crowdsourcing of a sort to extend their lemmas, which roughly resemble a lexicon (encyclopedias are not dictionaries in that they focus mostly on more extensive explanation, not underlying semantics and disambiguation). Wikis usually depend on the general public, or some community, to define their content [4]: to create a network of interrelated definitions (and give meaning to them) with the help of a set of pre-described rules. It would be going too far to claim that these rules are actual syntax, but the way these web encyclopedias (and other wiki-like knowledge bases) extend their lemmas, define relations between terms, and use crowdsourcing, is similar to how A-Lex/BKM operates. The similarity extends to many other publicly accessible and editable data sources, ranging from open-source codebases (for example GitHub or a similar software version control platform) to Fandoms (encyclopaedias focused on a specific topic such as science-fiction or gaming) [6].

With the rise of web 2.0, taxonomies of user-created information have emerged: "folksonomies" (a portmanteau of the words "folk" and "taxonomy"). In many articles, blogs, social media pages, and web pages, tags are added, which can be used to compile folksonomies. This allows people to give meaning to terms in information which they share, consume, and generate [7]. The categorisation of content thus becomes a collaborative effort, generating open-ended tags, contrary to professionally developed taxonomies that have a predetermined vocabulary and are inherently 'closed'. Folksonomies can also respond to and initialise changes and innovation rapidly by classifying web content [19].

Now that folksonomies have arisen, giving the social web a serious impulse, there are several Semantic Web technologies which can in principle be applied to the Social Web, such as a formal specification of structured data and reasoning across different data sources. Assertions of tags can be applied in multiple applications. Different semantics may, however, result, entailing that some sort of unified semantics is required across multiple sources: a "tag ontology". This could enable technologies for searching, aggregating and connecting people and their content [7].

3.5   The Semantic Web: Word Meaning on the Internet

In addition to the classic 'web of HTML pages', the World Wide Web Consortium (W3C) initiated the creation of a web of linked data structures called the Semantic Web. It uses formats and techniques like RDF, SPARQL, OWL, and SKOS. We focus on the RDF part of the Semantic Web here, since we are concerned with the basic word meaning component of the Semantic Web and not with the extensive use of hierarchical relations and axioms/rules that constitute, for example, complex ontologies, OWL Style (see Sect. 3.7).

The Semantic Web aims for standardisation of web data/information in such a way that finding, sharing, and reusing data becomes easier. With machine-readable and human-readable information markup such as XML (Extensible Markup Language) it provides an easy way for web data exchange (see Fig. 3). Representing a web page data in a machine-readable way means that machines can search, aggregate, and combine data without human interaction [15], though the intended large-scale application of logic-based AI techniques on this basis seem to lag.

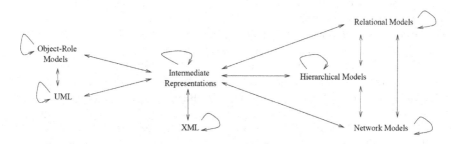

Fig. 3. Transformation of models, in [3] p7

The World Wide Web contains a massive amount of information and in order to effectively use the metadata conventions regarding the syntax, semantics, and structure required, RDF enables the creation and use of meta-data elements, including definitions [17]. Humans are generally quite good at extracting semantic meaning from different syntactic constructs, whereas machines are quite inept for this task. RDF uses a triadic model of resources, property types, and corresponding values to associate resources with specific properties. For example, a resource could be "sprint race" where the corresponding property type would be "won". In order to give meaning to the property type, the corresponding value could be the atomic value "John Johnson". Thus we will get the human-readable sentence "the sprint race is won by John Johnson" [17]. Note that actual definitions (or "descriptions", in RDF and Dublin Core terminology) are created through items identified and accessed through URIs: Uniform Resource Identifiers.

RDF, in combination with URIs, thus provides the means to publish both machine and human processable vocabularies. In this context, vocabularies are sets of properties or a group of metadata elements defined by communities. This form of domain-specific semantics gives rise to semantic modularity because it creates an infrastructure which enables distributed attribute registries which may be reused, extended, and refined to fit domain-specific requirements [17]. The A-Lex developers have expressed their intentions to make A-Lex directly compatible with Semantic Web formats like RDF.

3.6   Fact Based Modelling: Logic and Language

FBM combines terms to form fact types (through describing relationships, most important roles) and describes constraints on fact types (akin to axioms). Formally, it uses arbitrary symbols, not unlike like "$P(x, y)$" for describing logical elements, relations and operators, but in actual models, these symbols are replaced by meaningful terms from natural language, e.g. IsMemberOf(person, department). This is in line with the notion of signature in predicate logic. Crucially, the non-mathematical meaning of elements (terms) carries over to FBM use and practice: 'natural language meaning' combines with 'logical meaning'. This is especially clear and relevant in the case of the creation and use of verbalisations of FBM models. Through the careful use of terminology and extensive verbalisation of facts and fact types, the expressive power of natural language is combined with that of logic. Generally, axioms/constraints are not part of a lexical definition, comparable with the Semantic Web approach in which RDF covers the basic lexical level. FBM does include a dedicated specialisation (IS-A) relation, but this usually applies to fact types, not terms. At the core of fact type description, FBM uses a more open kind of relation which we might call "phrasal": it takes the meaning of a verb or verbal phrase, thus again using lexical meaning as an important building block for more complex semantic description.

3.7   Levels of Description: Comparison

Though the structure and (where available) the formalisation of Wordnet, RDF, URI, and FBM (and, for that matter, other types of conceptual model) are quite different, it still seems both possible and insightful to position parts of them on three related levels: lexical, relational, and constraint level. Focusing on the lexical level, it is important to note that even though relationships can be used to describe the meaning of terms, the networks thus created are strictly speaking not 'data structures' or 'information models': in FBM terms, data structures exist mainly at fact type level, describing how terms are combined into phrases that represent propositions about states of affairs in UoDs. Lexical networks may look very similar, but they serve a different purpose, at a different level of abstraction: that of defining lexical meaning, of elementary terms. This is why Business Knowledge Mapping (and its supporting tool, A-Lex) is an advanced approach for lexical definition, not a replacement for data modelling. As such, it uses several lexical relations, including the phrasal relation, to create lexical networks, in addition to good old textual definitions (as in Wordnet). By adding the possibility of using verbalizations of network relations in textual definitions, it actively combines the textual and the network approaches to the lexical definition.

	Wordnet	Semantic Web	BKM/A-Lex	FBM
Rules & axioms		OWL & axioms		Constraints
Predicates		OWL & RDF		Fact types
Lexical definitions	Network & glosses	Network (IS-A) & URI + glosses	Network & glosses	Network (IS-A object types) & glosses

4   Business Knowledge Mapping: Combining the Perspectives

We wrap up this paper by summarising the links between BKM/A-Lex and the various theoretical aspects and relations discussed in the previous sections. The point of this is to position BKM in the broader theoretical and practical field of lexical definition, as part of practices of conceptual modelling and data management, in a combined social, linguistic, and computational setting.

1. BKM/A-Lex embraces language diversity (in a data management context), while also offering useful support for language standardisation, given that a standard can also be seen as a UoD, with a different social and practical status. Comparison and discussion of local/domain-specific sets of concepts with lexical definitions can be beneficial in creating standards.
2. BKM/A-Lex provides community-based, accessible means of describing local (and also standard) concept sets and their lexical semantics. It uses crowd-sourcing as a concrete way of helping Communities of Discourse, being groups of actors in the sense of Fig. 2, actively engage in lexical definition, in an organised and accessible, self-service manner.
3. BKM/A-Lex explicitly uses both textual definitions (genus-differentiae style), semantic networks (using various lexical relations), and an innovative combi-nation of texts and networks (creating parts of definition texts by verbalising lexical relations). It thereby effectively employs and integrates the two basic techniques of lexical definition.
4. BKM/A-Lex, like Wordnet, supports definition at the lexical (term) level. It complements FBM by specifically addressing this level, complementary to Predicate level (fact types) and Axiom level (constraints). It could also com-plement Semantic Web formats and practices similarly (via RDF) if combined with glosses (descriptions) as identified by URIs.

Further research is required concerning (most in particular) the RDF and URI part of the Semantic Web in relation to FBM and concerning the opportunities for using and integrating A-Lex into a broader set of practices. We expect that well-specified relationships of both OWL/RDF and FBM with A-Lex, concerning axioms and predicates, can be useful to give A-Lex a more solid theoretic foundation and extend the opportunities and applications of the tool. The power of the Semantic Web lies partly in the combination of formats such as OWL, SKOS, and RDF. Future research could investigate whether a similar combination might also benefit A-Lex to such a degree that a broad range of (complex) applications become possible with a solid theoretical foundation.

References

1. Achterbergh, J., Vriens, D.: Organisations: Social Systems Conducting Experiments. Springer, New York (2009). doi: https://doi.org/10.1007/978-3-642-00110-9
2. De Beule, J., Stadler, K.: An evolutionary cybernetics perspective on language and coordination. New Ideas Psychol. **32**, 118–130 (2014). https://doi.org/10.1016/j.newideapsych.2013.03.003
3. van Bommel, P.: Foundations of Informations Systems (2019)
4. Cram, A., Kuswara, A., Richards, D.: Web 2.0 supported collaborative learning activities: towards an affordance perspective. In: Proceedings of the 3rd International LAMS & Learning Design Conference 2008: Perspectives on Learning Design, pp. 70–80. LAMS Foundation, Sydney (2008)
5. Fellbaum, C.: Large-scale lexicography in the digital age. Int. J. Lexicogr. **27**, 378–395 (2014). https://doi.org/10.1093/ijl/ecu018
6. Goodchild, M.: Citizen as voluntary sensors: spatial data infrastructure in the world of Web 2.0. Int. J. Spat. Data Infrastruct. Res. 2, 24–32 (2007)
7. Gruber, J.: Ontology of folksonomy: a mash-up of apples and oranges. Int. J. Semant. Web Inf. Syst. **3**, 1–11 (2007)
8. Halpin, T.: Conceptual Schema and Relational Database Design, 2nd edn. Prentice Hall, New Jersey (1995)
9. Hesse, W., Verrijn-Stuart, A.: Towards a theory of information systems: the FRISCO approach (2000)
10. Hoppenbrouwers, Stijn, Proper, Henderik A., Nijssen, Maurice: Towards Key Principles of Fact Based Thinking. In: Debruyne, Christophe, Panetto, Hervé, Guédria, Wided, Bollen, Peter, Ciuciu, Ioana, Meersman, Robert (eds.) OTM 2018. LNCS, vol. 11231, pp. 77–86. Springer, Cham (2019). https://doi.org/10.1007/978-3-030-11683-5_8
11. Hoppenbrouwers, S.: Freezing language, conceptualisation processes across ICT-supported organisations. Ph.D. thesis, Radboud University, Nijmegen (2003)
12. Hoppenbrouwers, S., Weigand, H.: Meta-communication in the language-action perspective. In: Schoop, M., Quix, C. (eds.) Proceedings of the 5th International Workshop on the Language-Action Perspective on Communication Modelling (LAP 2000), pp. 131–149. RWTH Aachen, Aachen (2000). (AIB Aachener Informatik-Berichte; No. 2000–6)
13. Hoppenbrouwers, J.: Conceptual modelling and the Lexicon. Ph.D. thesis, Tilburg University, Tilburg (1997)
14. IBM: IBM Dictionary of Computing, 10th edn. McGraw-Hill Inc, New York (1993)

15. Jambhulkar, S. V., Karale, S. J.: WordNet: semantic web application generation using Protg tool. In: 2016 Online International Conference on Green Engineering and Technologies (IC-GET), pp. 1–5. IEEE, Piscataway (2016). doi: 10.1109/GET.2016.7916686

16. Levy, M.: WEB 2.0 implications on knowledge management. J. Knowl. Manage. 13, 120–137 (2009). doi: 10.1108/13673270910931215

17. Miller, E.: An introduction to the resource description framework. Bull. Am. Soc. Inf. Sci. Technol. **25**, 15–19 (1998). https://doi.org/10.1002/bult.105

18. Miller, G.: WordNet: a lexical database for English. Commun. ACM **38**, 1–13 (1995). https://doi.org/10.1145/219717.219748

19. Murugesan, S.: Understanding Web 2.0. IT Prof. 9, 34–41 (2007). doi: https://doi.org/10.1109/MITP.2007.78

20. Oude Luttighuis, P., Bodenstaff, L.: The Essence Language, version 2. Essence Project (2013)

21. Peters, I., Stock, W.: Folksonomy and information retrieval. Proc. Am. Soc. Inf. Sci. Technol. **44**, 1–28 (2008). https://doi.org/10.1002/meet.1450440226

22. Pleijsant, Jan Mark: Scale Your Information Modeling Effort Using the Power of the Crowd. In: Debruyne, Christophe, Panetto, Hervé, Guédria, Wided, Bollen, Peter, Ciuciu, Ioana, Meersman, Robert (eds.) OTM 2018. LNCS, vol. 11231, pp. 159–170. Springer, Cham (2019). https://doi.org/10.1007/978-3-030-11683-5_17

23. Steels, L.: Self-organization and selection in cultural language evolution. In: Experiments in Cultural Language Evolution, pp. 1–37. John Benjamins, Amsterdam (2012). doi: 10.1075/ais.3.02ste

24. Wei, T., Lu, Y., Huiyou, C., Zhou, Q., Bao, X.: A semantic approach for text clustering using WordNet and lexical chains. Expert Syst. Appl. **42**, 2264–2275 (2015). https://doi.org/10.1093/ijl/ecu018

25. What is Wordnet? https://wordnet.princeton.edu/. Accessed 6 July 2019

Leveraging Ontologies for Natural Language Processing in Enterprise Applications

Tatiana Erekhinskaya[1], Matthew Morris[1(✉)], Dmitriy Strebkov[2], and Dan Moldovan[1]

[1] Lymba Corporation, Richardson, TX 75080, USA
{tatiana,mmorris,moldovan}@lymba.com
[2] Moscow, Russia
dmitry.strebkov@gmail.com

Abstract. The recent advances in Artificial Intelligence and Deep Learning are widely used in real-world applications. Enterprises create multiple corpora and use them to train machine learning models for various applications. As the adoption becomes more widespread, it raises further concerns in areas such as maintenance, governance and reusability. This paper will explore the ways to leverage ontologies for these tasks in Natural Language Processing. Specifically, we explore the usage of ontologies as a schema, configuration and output format. The approach described in the paper are based on our experience in a number of projects for medical, enterprise and national security domains.

Keywords: Ontology · Natural language processing · Annotation · Configuration · Named entity extractions · Semantic relations

1 Introduction

Although ontologies have been used for knowledge representation and inference for many decades [13], they have mostly been ignored by the data science/NLP community, with a few notable exceptions: [9,15,19,22]. This paper attempts to bridge the gap between ontology-driven and data-driven approaches and explores multiple directions for a beneficial combination of the two.

First of all, an ontology provides a language to describe the labeling schema in a format that is both machine- and human-readable [21]. This helps subject matter experts (SMEs) to agree and formalize category definitions before investing in data annotation. We use the schema to validate manually or automatically created annotations. An ontology helps express restrictions on classes and relations, which can be used to validate annotation or configure a labeling tool to disable invalid labeling.

We blend configuration for AI and NLP tools into our ontologies. This gives more control to SMEs without concerning them with implementation details and shortens the feedback loop.

© Springer Nature Switzerland AG 2020
C. Debruyne et al. (Eds.): OTM 2019 Workshops, LNCS 11878, pp. 79–85, 2020.
https://doi.org/10.1007/978-3-030-40907-4_8

Finally, RDF format is used for the NLP and AI tools output, which can be validated against the main ontology, shared between the tools and used for further inference.

The overall development cycle is depicted in Fig. 1. We start with modeling and creating an ontology that is taken into account in all major steps of the process. During the evaluation phase, the feedback can result in updates for both labeled data and the ontology.

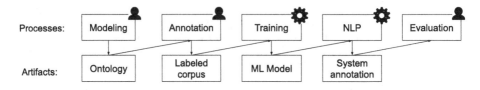

Fig. 1. NLP solution development cycle.

2 Providing Schema for Labeling

We use an ontology to formalize a labeling schema shared between SMEs and NLP tools to gather information about named entity (NE) types, other text span labels and relations between them.

As shown in Fig. 2, a hierarchy of classes is used to derive NE types. The leaf classes are used as named entity types, and higher-level types are inferred from the more specific ones. The class label becomes a named entity label. Individual labels are used as training data and put into the lexicon. One important consideration is to distinguish between mentions of the classes and mentions of the instances. For example, class COUNTRY has an instance "USA". The labels for "country" and "USA" should be something like COUNTRY_CLASS and COUNTRY_INSTANCE respectively.

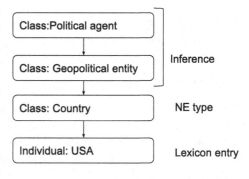

Fig. 2. NLP solution development cycle.

We apply the same logic for labeling any arbitrary text spans for sequence tagging or text fragment classification. We introduce a special super-class, e.g. SECTION_TAG to distinguish classes representing named entities from others.

Labeled relations are critically important as relation types represent the essence of the connection between concepts. For example, between two companies, there might be a HEAD_SUBSIDIARY relation, VENDOR_CLIENT or

COMPETITOR relations among others. The declaration of relation types in ontology include domain and range restrictions as well as properties such as transitivity, etc. that are used for annotation validation and/or inference.

We use ontology to generate annotation configuration of the BRAT tool [17] which is used for named entity and relation annotation so that it is not possible to create annotations that violate the schema.

An additional benefit of ontologies is the opportunity to have multiple layers of representation to streamline the application to similar problems [12]. For instance, an upper ontology can be used for overall domain modeling (e.g. the automotive industry), while manufacturer-specific or dealer-specific information can be expressed on top of the upper ontology as additional files.

3 Modeling for NLP

In the past, the most significant approaches for ontology building were [13] and [20]. From our experience on a number of projects, modeling starts with a brain-storming session that results in an upper-level ontology of 20–30 concepts and 10–20 relation types. The upper ontology is iteratively expanded in a semi-automated manner via mining the unlabeled corpora for additional phrases and relations, which significantly reduces the amount of work for SMEs.

There is a substantial body of literature on data modeling: entity-relationship modeling [6], entity-attribute-value [3], fact-based modeling [7], COMN [10], as well as more NLP-oriented slot-based approaches, such as FrameNet [2] that describes verb arguments. Additionally, there are less formalized domain-specific frameworks, e.g. the PICO model (Patient/population/problem, intervention, comparison, outcome) [16] in health care, which can be transferred to other domains—products and their technical issues, sports teams, companies, etc. All of these framework, together with existing universal ontologies like BFO [1] or domain-specific ontologies like FIBO [4] can be leveraged for a new application.

We summarize below a few recommendations to make ontologies more appropriate for NLP.

1. Labels that are too abstract limit direct usage of the ontology in data-driven approaches. For example, an abstract label "software agent" is unlikely to be mentioned in the text and will require explicit annotation of the training samples, while "software system" may be found in the text and leveraged directly. Similar logic is applicable for relations—the labels closer to the actual text fragments can be more reliably used for weak supervision.
2. Limit the relation types to as compact a set as possible. More specific relations can be further inferred given the argument types, while having fewer types requires less training data.
3. Beware of introducing ambiguity. Consider an example like: "Alice and Barbara are married to Andrew and Bob respectively". It is tempting to label "married" as an event/state and link all four human concepts to it as participants, but that would obscure the pairing expressed in the sentence. The correct way to represent the sentence would be to introduce a relation type MARRIED and use it to connect Alice to Andrew and Barbara to Bob.

4   Configuration of NLP Tools

In addition to classic NLP and Information Extraction tasks that might be augmented with the use of Semantic Web resources [11], ontologies are also used in industrial and IT cases [18]. Recently, ontologies were used to represent ML schema [14].

Currently, the development cycle involves: SMEs providing annotations, data scientists configuring the tools and generating results, then the results being validated by the SMEs, providing more annotations and communicating feedback to the data scientists. This feedback loop can be shortened by adding tool configuration parameters into the ontology and enabling the SMEs to run experiments in a more independent manner.

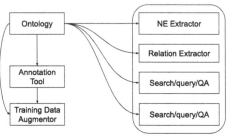

Fig. 3. Integration of ontology, annotation tool and NLP.

While implementation details depend on the actual software used under the hood, the general approach is to augment ontology with additional triples that define software behavior. These triples can be put into a separate file so that the schema itself is not polluted with application-specific triples.

As depicted in Fig. 3, we have successfully used ontologies as a source of:

1. Lexicon entries and their synonyms. These can be manually entered or dumped into ontology formats from other stores.
2. Part-of-speech constraints for candidate named entities, level of character-level fuzziness and allowed case variations in matching.
3. Relation definitions—domain, range and labels—for the automatic generation of relation extraction rules. While imperfect, these rules provide relation candidates and help bootstrap the training data. For example, declaring a relation BOUGHT between COMPANY and COMPANY is enough to generate a simple rule for recognizing this relation in a sentence like "Oracle bought Red Hat".
4. Named entity/class IS-A hierarchy for the relation extraction rules which helps reduce the amount of training data required. For example, dates in contracts can be further specified as a start date, a termination date, as well as various deadlines. Given the hierarchy of date types from the ontology, it is possible to generalize labeled samples such as "Start date is September 1, 2019" to "DATE_TYPE is DATE" using second-order logic, rather than having to provide training samples for each possible combination.
5. Application-focused synonyms and hypernyms for search and question answering for term expansion. While these lists can be automatically learned, for complex domains with little data available, it is a convenient way for SMEs to convey their understanding. For example, "results" can mean particular financial metrics for different applications.

6. Synonyms and hypernyms for paraphrasing and augmentation of training data.

5   RDF Schema

Providing the output in an open standard format can significantly ease chaining and integration of the various tools implemented in different programming languages. The closest analogy is annotations in UIMA [8]; however they are focused on XML/Java implementations, while an RDF representation is implementation-agnostic and allows using multiple tools for visualization and querying.

We use an RDF format [5] to represent an output for each single text (document) processed by the system. While the detailed schema is out of the scope of the current paper, the key elements include: a document and its metadata, sentences, tokens, named entities and relations, as well as text fragment labels.

One consideration is that the output RDF represents mentions of the concepts rather than the concepts themselves. In other words, for "Microsoft bought LinkedIn", we represent Microsoft as a text span and link it to the individual "Microsoft" of type COMPANY from the ontology. This way, it is possible to preserve the origin of each concept and relation as well as its connection to the ontology.

6   Conclusion

Summarizing our experience, we have shown how ontologies can be used together with the most recent NLP methods to help capture domain knowledge, yield more control to SMEs and provide a standard format for tool integration. RDF output provides an open standard supported by numerous open-source and commercial-grade tools which make the integration with NLP tools fairly straightforward.

Other usage scenarios include providing an ontological description for the tools and trained models to facilitate their dissemination within the organization. Furthermore, ontologies can be used to express access level restrictions, which can be used with search and question answering applications.

While the manual creation of ontologies is a labor-intensive process, NLP is successfully used to reduce the effort. After brainstorming the high-level concepts and relations, SMEs can iteratively expand an upper ontology by applying unsupervised NLP techniques of phrase and relation extraction on unlabeled text and reviewing the output.

References

1. Arp, R., Smith, B., Spear, A.D.: Building Ontologies with Basic Formal Ontology. The MIT Press, Cambridge (2015)
2. Baker, C.F., Fillmore, C.J., Lowe, J.B.: The Berkeley FrameNet project. In: Proceedings of the 17th International Conference on Computational Linguistics - Volume 1, COLING 1998, pp. 86–90. Association for Computational Linguistics, Stroudsburg (1998). https://doi.org/10.3115/980451.980860
3. Batra, S., Sachdeva, S., Bhalla, S.: Entity attribute value style modeling approach for archetype based data. Information **9**, 2 (2017)
4. Bennett, M.: The financial industry business ontology: best practice for big data. J. Bank. Regul. **14**(3–4), 255–268 (2013)
5. Brickley, D., Guha, R.: RDF Vocabulary Description Language 1.0: RDF Schema. W3C Recommendation, World Wide Web Consortium (2004). http://www.w3.org/TR/2004/REC-rdf-schema-20040210/
6. Chen, P.P.: The entity-relationship model - toward a unified view of data. ACM Trans. Database Syst. **1**(1), 9–36 (1976)
7. Demey, Y.T.: Adapting the fact-based modeling approach in requirement engineering. In: Meersman, R., et al. (eds.) OTM 2014. LNCS, vol. 8842, pp. 65–69. Springer, Heidelberg (2014). https://doi.org/10.1007/978-3-662-45550-0_9
8. Ferrucci, D., Lally, A., Verspoor, K., Nyberg, E.: Unstructured information management architecture (UIMA) version 1.0. OASIS Standard (2009). https://docs.oasis-open.org/uima/v1.0/uima-v1.0.html
9. Hellmann, S., Lehmann, J., Auer, S., Brümmer, M.: Integrating NLP using linked data. In: Alani, H., et al. (eds.) ISWC 2013. LNCS, pp. 98–113. Springer, Heidelberg (2013). https://doi.org/10.1007/978-3-642-41338-4_7
10. Hills, T.: NoSQL and SQL Data Modeling: Bringing Together Data, Semantics, and Software, 10, vol. 4, 1st edn. Technics Publications, Basking Ridge (2016)
11. Martinez-Rodriguez, J.L., Hogan, A., Lopez-Arevalo, I.: Information extraction meets the semantic web: a survey. Semantic Web, pp. 1–81, October 2018. https://doi.org/10.3233/SW-180333
12. Niles, I., Pease, A.: Towards a standard upper ontology. In: Proceedings of the International Conference on Formal Ontology in Information Systems - Volume 2001. pp. 2–9. FOIS 2001. ACM, New York (2001). https://doi.org/10.1145/505168.505170
13. Noy, N.F., Mcguinness, D.L.: Ontology development 101: a guide to creating your first ontology. Technical report (2001)
14. Publio, G.C., et al.: ML-Schema: exposing the semantics of machine learning with schemas and ontologies. CoRR abs/1807.05351 (2018). http://arxiv.org/abs/1807.05351
15. Rak, R., Ananiadou, S.: Making UIMA truly interoperable with SPARQL. In: Proceedings of the 7th Linguistic Annotation Workshop and Interoperability with Discourse, pp. 89–97. Association for Computational Linguistics, Sofia, August 2013. https://www.aclweb.org/anthology/W13-2311
16. Sackett, D.L., Richardson, W.S., Rosenberg, W., Haynes, R.B.: How to Practice and Teach Evidence-Based Medicine, pp. 118–128. Churchill Livingstone, New York (1997)

17. Stenetorp, P., Pyysalo, S., Topić, G., Ohta, T., Ananiadou, S., Tsujii, J.: BRAT: a web-based tool for NLP-assisted text annotation. In: Proceedings of the Demonstrations at the 13th Conference of the European Chapter of the Association for Computational Linguistics, EACL 2012, pp. 102–107, Association for Computational Linguistics, Stroudsburg (2012). http://dl.acm.org/citation.cfm?id=2380921.2380942

18. Tarasov, V., Seigerroth, U., Sandkuhl, K.: Ontology development strategies in industrial contexts. In: Abramowicz, W., Paschke, A. (eds.) BIS 2018. LNBIP, vol. 339, pp. 156–167. Springer, Cham (2019). https://doi.org/10.1007/978-3-030-04849-5_14

19. Troncy, R., Bruemmer, M.: Nerd meets NIF: Lifting NLP extraction results to the linked data cloud. In: Proceedings of the 5th International Workshop on Linked Data on the Web, LDOW 2012 (2012)

20. Uschold, M., Gruninger, M.: Ontologies: principles, methods and applications. Knowl. Eng. Rev. **11**(2), 93–136 (1996). https://doi.org/10.1017/S0269888900007797

21. Wongthongtham, P., Kasisopha, N., Chang, E., Dillon, T.: A software engineering ontology as software engineering knowledge representation. In: 2008 Third International Conference on Convergence and Hybrid Information Technology. vol. 2, pp. 668–675, November 2008. https://doi.org/10.1109/ICCIT.2008.301

22. Ziad, H., McCrae, J.P., Buitelaar, P.: Teanga: a linked data based platform for natural language processing. In: Proceedings of the Eleventh International Conference on Language Resources and Evaluation, LREC 2018. European Languages Resources Association (ELRA), Miyazaki, Japan, May 2018. https://www.aclweb.org/anthology/L18-1383

Verbalizing Decision Model and Notation

Tomas Cremers$^{(\boxtimes)}$, Maurice Nijssen, and John Bulles

PNA Group, Heerlen, The Netherlands
tomas.cremers@pna-group.com, maurice.nijssen@pna-group.com,
john.bulles@pna-group.com
http://www.pna-group.com

Abstract. The ability to effectively communicate decision rules becomes increasingly important, as the stake of multidisciplinary teams within organizations increases. With Decision Model and Notation (DMN) turning out to become one of the international standards for modelling decision rules, the need for effective communication of decision rules modelled using the standard grows. In order to facilitate this communication we present a structured verbalization for DMN decision tables, using principles of fact based thinking and modelling theory. This verbalization is designed to be fully interpretable by anyone that has knowledge about the described domain. The key to accommodating this interpretability is the use of a structured natural language as the foundation for the verbalization.

Keywords: Decision Model and Notation (DMN) · Verbalization · Structured natural language · Fact based modelling

1 Introduction

The Decision Model and Notation^{TM} or DMN is a standard for modelling decision rules, developed and maintained by the Object Management Group®. Version 1.0 of DMN was released in 2015 [1] and version 1.2, which we will be considering in this paper, in 2019 [2]. DMN consists of two levels, (*i*) a decision requirement level modelling the requirements for a decision and dependencies between different decision and (*ii*) a logic level modelling the logic that is needed for making an individual decision. The logic level is implemented using so called decision tables and this level will be the focus of this paper. Figure 1 depicts a DMN decision table. The main elements of such a table are the input variables (in Fig. 1 input expression), input values (input entry), output variables (output component name), output values (output entry) and the hit policy indicator (hit indicator). Every row in a DMN decision table represents an individual rule and all rules in a decision table use equivalent input variables and output variables.

Note that for the sake of keeping the verbalization understandable for all stakeholders, the Friendly Enough Expression Language (FEEL), as defined in the DMN specifications [2], is kept outside of the scope of this paper. In future work a clear verbalization for FEEL could be made.

© Springer Nature Switzerland AG 2020
C. Debruyne et al. (Eds.): OTM 2019 Workshops, LNCS 11878, pp. 86–94, 2020.
https://doi.org/10.1007/978-3-030-40907-4_9

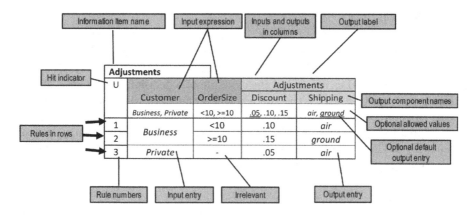

Fig. 1. Overview of a DMN decision table. Source: DMN 1.2 specification [2].

Natural language verbalization for business and decision rules has been around for a while. Languages like SBVR [3] and RuleSpeak [6], for example, define a structured natural language for modelling business and decision rules. But none of these languages seem to have a direct translation to the Decision Modelling Notation (from here on forth also referred to by its acronym DMN), or have the formal structure that DMN allows for. DMN uses a tabular form that can be difficult to interpret when one is not familiar with the meaning of all its elements. Therefore, an effective method to communicate DMN decision tables to the masses becomes desirable. Especially with DMN growing out to be an international standard for modelling decision rules it is apparent that effective communication of these rules to various stakeholders becomes more and more important. This is supported by an initiative of the Dutch government to model decisions regarding public space using a slightly augmented form of DMN [4]. Natural language is a very effective tool to communicate seemingly difficult concepts, such as the meaning of elements in DMN, to a broad range of different people. That is why, in this paper, we make a proposal for a structured verbalization of DMN decision tables. This verbalization will allow for communication to stakeholders using natural language while maintaining the integrity and structure of DMN.

The remainder of the paper is structured as follows. Section 2 will go over the conceptual data model that was made in order to structure the verbalization. Section 3 will discuss general properties and structure of the verbalization. Section 4 will describe the different hit policies defined by DMN. Section 5 will explain how hit policies are introduced into the verbalization with the use of rule groups. Section 6 will give a summary of this paper and touch upon future work.

2   FBM Model

In order to structure the creation of a verbalization, a FBM model of a DMN decision table was created using the cogNIAM methodology [5]. The DMN specifications [2] were used as input and the example of a decision table as was shown in Fig. 1 was used to verify the model. The conceptual data model acted as a basis to create the verbalization. The model defines all the relations between input expressions, output components and rows (or rules). Figure 2 shows a sample Fact Type Diagram which is part of the complete conceptual model. Due to publication space restrictions for this paper, the remainder of the model is not shown.

Decision table input expression allowed value

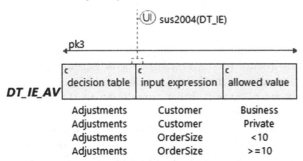

1: The [input expression] <input expression> in the [decision table] <decision table> has the [allowed value] <allowed value>.

1) The [input expression] Customer in the [decision table] Adjustments has the [allowed value] Business.
2) The [input expression] Customer in the [decision table] Adjustments has the [allowed value] Private.
3) The [input expression] OrderSize in the [decision table] Adjustments has the [allowed value] < 10.
4) The [input expression] OrderSize in the [decision table] Adjustments has the [allowed value] >=10.

Fig. 2. Part of the conceptual data model.

3   Verbalization Elements

In a DMN decision table every row describes a single business rule. In order to preserve this inherent structure we will verbalize each row of a decision table separately. To keep the structural grouping of rules that DMN decision tables allow for, rule groups are introduced. Each business rule will always belong to exactly one rule group. Rule groups are also going to prove important for dealing with hit policies.

To distinguish between output and input of a business rule the proposed verbalization splits the rule in two elements. This splitting allows for structure to be created within the verbalization. These two elements are called the result element and the condition element. The result element verbalizes the output labels and output entries of the row in the decision table that the rule corresponds to. The condition element verbalizes the input expressions and the input entries of that row. The order in which the result element and the condition element are presented is not important. This way the modeller can change the order to match their or the readers' preference.

3.1   Result Element

In the result element of the verbalization the output of the business rule is defined. The output variables are defined and next to that the output values. The output variables correspond to the different output labels in the DMN decision table whereas the values are taken from the output entries of the row in the DMN decision table that corresponds to the rule at hand.

Figure 3 shows the verbalization of the result element. When a DMN decision table uses more than one output variable the corresponding verbalization will list these individually as shown in the bottom of Fig. 3.

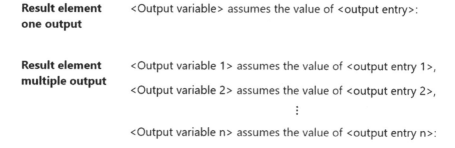

| **Result element one output** | \<Output variable\> assumes the value of \<output entry\>: |

Result element multiple output	\<Output variable 1\> assumes the value of \<output entry 1\>,
	\<Output variable 2\> assumes the value of \<output entry 2\>,
	⋮
	\<Output variable n\> assumes the value of \<output entry n\>:

Fig. 3. Basic template for a verbalization of the result element.

3.2   Condition Element

In the condition element of a verbalization a set of conditions is defined which have to hold in order for the result element to evaluate. The condition element consists of a list of input variables (input expressions in the DMN specification) that are being compared to their corresponding input entries. This comparison is done using a comparison operator. In this paper we consider the following comparison operators:

1. smaller than
2. smaller than or equal to
3. equal to
4. greater than or equal to
5. greater than

6. is
7. is not
8. is within the range of

Figure 4 pictures a generic template for the condition element.

Condition element: If the following conditions are met:

    <Input variable 1> <comparison operator> <input entry 1> and

    <Input variable 2> <comparison operator> <input entry 2> and

    ⋮

    <Input variable 1> <comparison operator> <input entry 1>

Fig. 4. Basic template for a verbalization of the condition element.

In Fig. 5 we have populated the verbalization template for a rule with the rule corresponding to the first row in the decision table as displayed in Fig. 1.

Result element   Discount assumes the value of 0.10,

    Shipping assumes the value of air,

Condition element: If the following conditions are met:

    Customer is equal to Business and

    OrderSize is smaller than 10

Fig. 5. The rule verbalization template populated with the first rule in Fig. 1

4 Hit Policies

In DMN, hit policies are used to define how to handle conflicting or simultaneously firing rules within a decision table. DMN defines two different categories of hit policies and each type is split up into several sub-types. The two categories are single hit policies and multiple hit policies. As a general rule, when no hit policy is defined it is defaulted to 'unique'.

4.1 Single Hit

Single hit policies define a relation over the different rules in a DMN decision table to determine which rule to consider in case multiple rules would give a result. Within a single hit policy a decision table will only produce one output for a given instance of facts.

Unique - In case of a unique hit policy there should be no overlap between the conditions of the rules in the decision table. This means that at all times exactly one rule will give a result.

Any - In case of an any hit policy there may be overlap between the condition of the rules. At any time when multiple rules give a result they should all give the same result.

Priority - In case of a priority hit policy there may be overlap between the conditions of the rules. A priority relation over the possible output values is defined. When multiple rules give a result (which may be different) that output result with the highest priority is the definite result of the decision table.

First - In case of a first priority hit policy there may be overlap between the condition of the rules. A priority relation is defined over the individual rules in a decision table. At any time the result of the rule that is highest in this priority is the definite result of the decision table. In DMN the priority relation is defined by the row numbers, row number 1 being the highest priority, row number 2 the second highest, etc.

4.2   Multiple Hit

Multiple hit policies define a function over output of the different rules in a DMN decision table. Differing from a single hit policy, a multiple hit policy can result in multiple values

Output order - In case of an output order hit policy, a priority relation over the possible output values is defined. The result from the decision table will be an ordered list where output values with a higher priority will be first in the list.

Rule order - In case of a rule order hit policy, a priority relation over the rules is defined. The result from the decision table will be an ordered list where output values of rules with a higher priority will be first in the list.

Collect - A collect hit policy has 4 possible types.

1. Sum - the decision table will return the sum of the output results of rules that returned a result.
2. Min - the decision table will return the minimum output value of all the output values of rules that returned a result.
3. Max - the decision table will return the maximum output value of all the output values of rules that returned a result.
4. Count - the decision table will return the number of rules that returned a result.

5   Rule Groups

To facilitate the use of hit policies, rule groups are introduced to the verbalization. A rule group is an ordered collection of individual rules. This also means that the verbalization of such a rule group will contain all the verbalizations of the rules contained within. All rules originating from the same DMN decision table will be assigned to the same rule group. That rule group will be given the same hit policy as the decision table of origin.

The 'unique' and 'any' hit policies add validation of the output of the collection of rules but they are no, unlike the other hit policies, function of the eventual value of the output variable(s). Since validations are of little importance to the execution of a business rule, they are not necessarily something that needs to be able to be communicated to potential stakeholders. That is why the 'unique' and 'any' hit policies will not be considered in the verbalization for a rule group. Templates for the remaining hit policies can be found in Figs. 6 and 7.

Priority	If multiple different rules return a value, <output variable> has to be set to the value with the highest priority. The priority is defined in the following list:
	1. <output value with priority 1>
	1. <output value with priority 2>
	⋮
	1. <output value with priority n>
First	If multiple different rules return a value, <output variable> has to be set to the value of the rule with the highest priority. The priority is defined in the following list:
	1. <rule priority 1>
	1. <rule priority 2>
	⋮
	1. <rule priority n>

Fig. 6. Basic template for a verbalization of the single hit policies.

6   Summary

In this paper we have proposed a foundation for a structured verbalization for DMN decision tables. As a way of structuring this verbalization a conceptual data model was made using the cogNIAM methodology. We have introduced the concept of a rule group which is a collection of rules with equivalent input variables and output variables. We discussed how to use these rule groups in order to facilitate the different hit policies from DMN.

Furthermore, every rule consists of two elements, a result element and a condition element. The result element deals with the output of a business rule and the condition element handles the input of a rule.

And finally suggestions for templates have been made for the verbalization of rule groups, relevant hit policies and individual rules.

Output order	<output variable> will be set to an ordered list of all the values returned by the rules. The values in the list are ordered according to the following list:

  1. <output value with priority 1>
  1. <output value with priority 2>
       ⋮
  1. <output value with priority n>

Rule order	<output variable> will be set to an ordered list of all the values returned by the rules. The values in the list are ordered according to their corresponding rules in the following list:

  1. <rule priority 1>
  1. <rule priority 2>
       ⋮
  1. <rule priority n>

Collect Sum/ Min/ Max	<output variable> will be set to the sum/minimum/maximum of all the values returned by the rules.

Collect Count	<output variable> will be set to the number of rules that returned a value.

Fig. 7. Basic template for a verbalization of the multiple hit policies.

6.1 Future Work

As mentioned in the introduction of this paper, The 'Friendly Enough Expression Language' was purposefully omitted for clarity and communicability reasons. In future work one could consider to make an understandable verbalization for all or the most commonly used FEEL expressions.

A second topic that warrants future investigation is a verbalization for Decision Requirement Graphs (DRG) or Decision Requirement Diagrams (DRD).

Lastly, in this paper we have considered DMN decision tables in isolation. Imagine when, for example, a data model is coupled with a DMN model. More accurate verbalization would become available. Especially data types would play a big role in this. When, for example, you are dealing with variables with a 'date' data type you could use context specific terms like 'is later than' or 'is earlier than' for the condition operators. As a result the verbalization becomes clearer and thus easier to communicate. In the end there are a lot of different factors that could contribute to the effective communication of decision rules when considering things outside of the isolation. It is interesting to investigate how the bigger picture allows for more complete verbalization.

References

1. Object management group: Decision model and notation version 1.0 (2015). https://www.omg.org/spec/DMN/1.0. Accessed 05 Aug 2019
2. Object management group: Decision model and notation version 1.2 (2019). https://www.omg.org/spec/DMN/1.2. Accessed 05 Aug 2019

3. Object management group: Semantics of business vocabulary and rules version 1.4 (2017). https://www.omg.org/spec/SBVR/About-SBVR/. Accessed 05 Aug 2019
4. Standaard- en informatiemodel toepasbare regels (STTR en IMTR). https://aandeslagmetdeomgevingswet.nl/digitaal-stelsel/technisch-aansluiten/koppelvlakken/toepasbare-regels/standaard/. Accessed 05 Aug 2019
5. Nijssen, G.M.: Kenniskunde 1A. PNA Publishing, Carlisle (2001)
6. Ross, R.: Rulespeak. Business Rule Solutions, LLC (1996)

Fully Traceable Vertical Data Architecture

John Bulles[1(✉)], Rob Arntz[2], and Martijn Evers[2]

[1] PNA, Heerlen, The Netherlands
`john.bulles@pna-group.com`
[2] I-Refact, 's Hertogenbosch, The Netherlands
`{rob.arntz,martijn.evers}@i-refact.com`

Abstract. Data architecture is composed of models, policies, rules or standards that govern which data is collected, and how it is stored, arranged, integrated, and put to use in data systems and organizations [1]. Organizations often use models to describe this data architecture for a domain. But what type of models are needed?

This vertical data architecture approach describes what different models are needed, how these models are interlinked, what the concerns are of certain representation and how an organization can deal with the challenges of keeping these models aligned. This involves the analysis of a Universe of Discourse (UoD), creating conceptual information models (in FBM), transforming these into logical data models and transform these logical models into one or more implementation models. Issues like traceability back to the UoD and impact directly from the UoD to the implementation are main issues which often are hard to tackle.

Keywords: Fact Based Modeling (FBM) · Vertical data architecture · Cognitatie · I-refactory conceptual information model · Logical data model · Model transformation · Traceability

1 Introduction

A lot of organizations fail to align their legal obligations with the implementation of it in their systems. This leads to behavior in the systems which is not in line with the these obligations. Also, determining why a certain rule or data element is needed in a system is hard to establish. Impact analysis of a change in the obligations is often impossible or a least requires a lot of manual work.

The process to implement or enforce regulations through a company's data landscape is supported by data architecture. This data architecture at least addresses the concerns that exists in both vertical and horizontal lineage. Data architecture is about collecting, storing, arranging, integrating and using data in data systems and organizations. Models, policies, rules and standards are used to govern this. In this paper, we will differentiate between horizontal and vertical data architecture. Horizontal data architecture is needed for horizontal data lineage, the journey from source to destination in the physical data. The vertical data architecture supports in vertical data lineage. Vertical data lineage does not look at the lifecycle of the data, but at the origin of the data structures.

© Springer Nature Switzerland AG 2020
C. Debruyne et al. (Eds.): OTM 2019 Workshops, LNCS 11878, pp. 95–105, 2020.
https://doi.org/10.1007/978-3-030-40907-4_10

This textual description of the UoD is understandable for the domain experts, like legal experts. Implementation models can be interpreted by computer systems, but cannot be interpreted by these domain experts. It is needed that the process from textual, understandable business descriptions to computer readable models is supported with all care for validation and verification. Therefore there cannot be this giant leap between these two descriptions of the same UoD. In the described vertical data architecture, we will have multiple small steps, each validated and verified. Also every element of every model must be traceable to its origin in the model above it (vertically). So that in the end, each column in the physical database can be traced back to the text in a document and also determining the impact of a change in a document is only a query on this metadata.

The vertical data architecture described is not only theoretical, it is currently being implemented in one of the largest Dutch governmental organizations. Within this organization, the concept of vertical data architecture is implemented, using multiple tools. In future development we hope that the combination of tools is minimalized to tools working perfectly together. For the first steps Cognitatie is used, followed by PowerDesigner for the logical layer, finally arriving in the i-refactory at implementation level.

The key business drivers for this vertical data architecture are:

- the need for controlled, governed, auditable implementation of in- or external regulations (compliance, control)
- to increase the quality and speed to act upon regulated changes (time to market and efficiency)
- decrease the semantic gap that exists when each department owns its own definition of the regulations without verification (reusability, conformity, exchangeability, integrability)

The vertical data architecture describes the different layers between the origin and the technical implementation in Sect. 2. Section 3 till 6 will describe these layers in more detail. In Sect. 7 we will describe the connection of this vertical data architecture to the horizontal data architecture.

2 Different Layers of Representation

The different representations are needed, to suit all different types of users in their own convenient way. Furthermore, each layer must be validated and verified on correctness of the concerns addressed in that representation and ensure that the validation of the previous layers is maintained. The layers needed for this vertical data architecture are:

1. Document layer
2. Legal analysis model
3. Formal linguistic
4. Logical
5. Implementations

In the first layer all relevant documents that describe the UoD are present. Often these are law and regulation documents, jurisprudence, external and internal policies, etc., but it can also be customer requirements documents, manuals, process descriptions, etc. In the example of this paper, the main concern of this layer is regulation. The representation in this layer is textual. In this vertical data architecture approach, we see this layer as given, we cannot change the content or representation here.

In the second layer, we will go from the textual representation to a more structured representation of these same texts. This involves analysis of the texts from the first layer, classifying part of this text, annotating the text with interpretations and examples and relating these annotations.

The third layer describes the formal linguistic models. The output of the second layer, are classified, annotated and related text elements. In the third layer this input is modelled into a conceptual information model conform FBM. Also rules are conceptually modelled in a formal linguistic rule modelling language. All modeled elements are interlinked with their origin from the second layer, in that way providing traceability.

The next step is transforming the models of the formal linguistic layer into logical models. The FBM model will be transformed into a logical data model, the rule model will be transformed into a corresponding logical rule model. From these logical data models the physical models are created and implemented. Each of these layers and transformations between these layers will be described in more detail.

It is important to realize that there needs to be an overarching definition process that guides and orchestrates the work across these levels of representations. This process is responsible for connecting the different levels of representations together and streamline their work. This is especially important from the regulation to logical levels. Since the logical level represents the cut-off between definition and implementation, this process formally stops here. The Vertical data/information *implementation* process starts at the logical level and defines the implementation levels and their design.

To make the different layers of representation work together in a transparent and consistent fashion transformations between them should be formalized, regulated and automated in a non-destructive and traceable manner. This principle is embodied in the Law of conservation of concerns. This law states that transitions should be both structurally, semantically and algebraically additive. This implies algebraic transformations between levels of representations that preserve structure to relate the levels. This forces alignment between levels and supports a unified process in transitioning between the levels of representations while at the same time allows for lineaging.

3 Analyzing the Universe of Discourse (UoD)

The first layer consists of the (legal) documents that describe the UoD. These are given and must be interpreted by domain experts. In a legal-driven organization, these domain expert are the legal experts. These experts have a lot of knowledge of the UoD and know the intention of the documents. Often these experts are not trained in formalizing this knowledge. A (conceptual) modeler has not this knowledge of the UoD, but is trained in formalizing the knowledge. Therefore, it is necessary to bring these two disciplines together in a multidisciplinary team.

The result is a set of grouped text parts from one or more documents, being the legal context of the UoD, extended with annotations of the domain expert for interpretation and meaning of the (legal) text. Also the result contains a set of validated examples, classification of all knowledge elements within the relevant text parts and relevant concepts and definitions (like defined in the original documents), traceable back to the original text.

For this analysis, a Best Practice for legal analysis is developed, like described in [3]. As supporting tooling, Cognitatie [4] is used. In this paper, an example is used of a regulation of the European Parliament for establishing common rules on compensation and assistance to passengers in the event of denied boarding and of cancellation or long delay of flights (the Flight case). We limit the scope of the example only to the determination whether a certain flight is applicable under this treaty. For results 1, 2 and 3, this is displayed below only for article 1, paragraph 1 (Fig. 1).

Article 1, paragpraph 1 - Subject

1. This Regulation establishes, under the conditions specified herein, minimum rights for passengers when:
    a. they are denied boarding against their will;
    b. their flight is cancelled;
    c. their flight is delayed.

Interpretation:
Cancellation and delay apply to a specific flight, denied boarding for a specific passenger on a specific flight.

Example:
Passenger 123 is denied boarding against his will on flight KL 643 on 12-07-2019.
Flight KL 6020 of 12-07-2019 is cancelled.
Flight KL 641 of 12-07-2019 is delayed.

Fig. 1. Legal context of Flight case

Then the texts in this legal context is analyzed and classified. Such a classification of a piece of text will lead to a concept. This concept is an abstract knowledge element. An annotation is created to link this concept to the words in the document (for traceability). The classification scheme is configurable in Cognitatie. The classification scheme used here is the one described in [3]. Some results of this analysis are presented below as an example.

---

1. This Regulation shall apply:
    a. to passengers departing from an airport located in the territory of a Member State to which the Treaty applies;

Fig. 2. Classified text part

In Fig. 2, the text "Passengers" is classified as a legal entity. "Departing from an airport" is classified as a variable, and "Located in the territory of a Member State to which the Treaty applies" as a condition. In this way, all text of the legal context is analyzed, resulting in a set of concepts. The domain expert will also link some of these concepts to each other using concept relations, for example the mentioned condition will be related to the "Departure airport".

4   Creating the Conceptual Information Model

The result of the second layer is input for the modeler to create a conceptual information model in the formal linguistic layer. In this layer all relevant conceptual models of the UoD are defined. These are:

1. A conceptual information model in FBM, validated with the domain expert and based on the examples of the second layer
2. A conceptual rules model in a formal rule language, validated by the domain expert
3. A concept list with all relevant concepts and definitions within the UoD

A conceptual modeler will take the validated examples as input to set up a fact model (conceptual information model). Also the concepts and concept relations will be taken as input. For example: *Passenger 123 has a reservation for Flight KL 6020 on 12-07-2019.*

In Fact Based Modeling, these examples are generalized to fact types. Such a fact type consists of the roles that are played by object types in the fact type, but also the variables that are populated in the example above. For the fact mentioned above, this fact type is (Fig. 3):

Passenger	Flight		
Passenger number	Airline designator	Flight number	Departure date
123	KL	6020	17-02-2019

Passenger <Passenger number> has a reservation for flight <Airline designator><Flight number> on <Departure date>.

Passenger 123 has a reservation for flight KL6020 on 17-02-2019.

Fig. 3.   Fact type

Because the fact types consist of roles and variables, different FBM-dialect views can be displayed. For the described scope, the complete fact model is presented below in an ORM diagram.

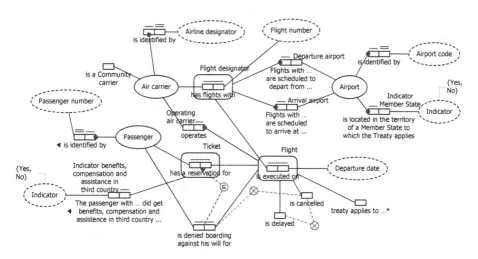

Fig. 4.   Fact model Flight Case

The last representation of the model does not contain the examples and is therefore not suitable to validate the model with the domain expert. Therefore, at all times, the user must be able to see a representation of these fact types containing the examples and thus the variables of the presented roles must be represented as well. A first approach for such a representation is given in [5].

Next to the conceptual information model, the concerned derivation rules must also be described. In the Business Rules Manifesto [2] is stated:

"Rules build on facts, and facts build on concepts as expressed by terms."

The mentioned facts are represented in structure by the fact types of the conceptual information mode. Also the rules will be linked to elements from the analysis in step 2. In this part of the Flight Case, we have a rule which derives whether the Treaty applies for a certain flight, as presented below if a formal natural rule language.

The Treaty applies to a Flight if at least one of the following conditions are met:

- The Indication Member State of the Depart airport of the Flight designator of the Flight is equal to Yes
- All following conditions are met:
  • The Indication Member State of the Arrival airport of the Flight designator of the Flight is equal to Yes
  • The operating air carrier of the Flight is a Community air carrier
  • The Indication benefits, compensation and assistance in third country is equal to no.

5   Transforming to a Logical Data Model

Once we have the conceptual information model, we captured understanding – knowledge – of the Universe of Discourse. Concerns about the semantics of the required information are addressed. Considerations on the *structure* of the information is not yet addressed in this model.

When addressing the structure of the required data, we enter the logical data model arena. According to [6] a logical data model (LDM) is "an entity-relationship data model including attributes that represents the inherent properties of the data, including names, definitions, structure, and integrity rules, independent of software, hardware, volume metrics, frequency of use, or performance considerations".

This definition gives some guidance on how a logical model looks like; "an entity-relationship data model". Although we could use other modeling paradigms to express logical data models, the fast majority of LDMs are expressed as entity-relationship diagrams (ERDs). The definition also shows that it should contain "attributes that represents the inherent properties of the data". All these attributes should already be described in the fact model.

Often ERDs are used to do business validation of models. However ERDs are not very suitable for this task as the notation used is not known to most business experts (it's not their language) and misses the concrete examples and verbalizations to help to express the semantics of the model. In the vertical data lineage approach the validation is already done at the formal linguistic layer. We must propagate this acquired validation towards the logical model by ensuring that all information of the formal linguistic layer is reflected in the logical domain model.

Main concern of a logical domain model is to be able to verify data models to ensure that they are well-formed. For example, we must be able to verify whether model is in a desired normal form [7] or the adherence to the principle of orthogonal design [8].

Another form of verification is to check internal consistency of constraints. Constraints that can be derived from other constraints should be detected. To be able to detected this redundancy in constraints, we have to formulate the constraints in a formal way. First order logic and set theory can be used to express constraints. Based on these formal – literally logical – expressed constraints, automated constraint verification can be executed.

Algorithms to transform from a fact model to an ER logical model have been described in e.g. [9]. These algorithms are implemented in FBM case tools. In order to obey to the principles or vertical data architecture, we have to ensure that these algorithms are non-destructive as we would miss out metadata required for the vertical lineage.

These types of algorithms transform the information from a fact model into ER structures, while retaining the semantics as much as possible.

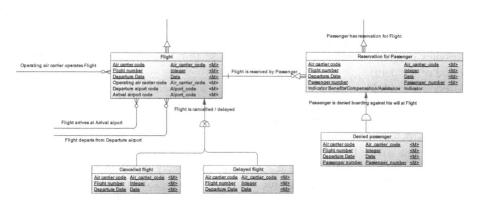

Fig. 5. Part of the logical model Flight case

In Fig. 5 a part of the LDM is shown that represents the Flight case as ERD, using SAP PowerDesigner. It contains all information of the fact model in Fig. 4. The names of attributes and entities are inherited from the fact model. Also the semantics of the inheritance and cardinality relationships can be easily transformed from the fact model towards the LDM.

The transformation can be automated to an high extend, however some choices in structure transformation will need human intervention. For instance, in the Flight case we have two fact types: "<Passenger> has reservation for <Flight>." And "<Passenger> is denied boarding against his will for <Flight>.". In the logical model we could have expressed these fact types as two n:m relationships. However the subset constraint expressing that a Passenger can only be denied boarding from a Flight for which the Passenger holds a reservation, can be modelled more explicit using a subtype.

In order to ensure vertical lineage, every entity, attribute, relationship and constraints in a LDM, is linked to a fact type or rule in the conceptual information model. This link is maintained as additional metadata on top of the metadata to store the metadata of the ERD itself.

Another concern that needs to be addressed in logical models is related to the way timelines in the data are handled. Some functional timelines are given by the fact model, like "<Flight designator> is executed on <Departure date>." The departure date brings a notion of time to the model. However there might be more time aspects to the model not addressed in the fact model; for instance when the data entered the system (a so called technical timeline) or the version that is being used (a so called functional timeline). These timelines will cause the primary identifiers of entities to change as they refine the granularity of these entities. Bringing these timelines in the fact models would create awkward long fact type expressions as the validity dates are mentioned for every object. Those long sentences hamper proper validation, the main reason to use fact modeling in the first place. There are ways to overcome this linguistic hurdle in fact models, like annotating fact types as proposed in [10]. When doing so, we are overloading logical concerns into the linguistic modeling layer. These concerns are properly addressed in the logical layer.

Like with the addition of time, other aspects of the data may require a standard way of handling, which can be expressed in the logical model. Aspects like privacy by design and life cycle management aspects can be covered. For example we could add attributes to store information on the retention security classification or the retention period of the data.

For a greenfield situation in which the goal is to implement a new system the next step is to transform the logical model into implementation models. However if the information need has to be obtained using existing data sources, we have to take a deviating route.

Each data source bring its own 'data reality': a realm in which facts are valid. It is almost a given that a source data reality does not entirely match the desired logical target model. Therefore we create for each source a logical source model. Such a logical model is a projection of the target model on the structure and constraints that are valid for the given data source. These models form the basis for the formal agreements with the supplying sources, which are laid down in a data delivery agreement.

One Universe in Discourse has one logical target model and can have one or more logical source models. All these models (and hence realities) have to be aligned in order to be able to create a data flow from source to target. This alignment is described in a so called logical integration model.

In a logical integration model the way of integrating entities based on their keys is modelled. Also the derivation rules of the integrated attributes is described in integration rules. These integration rules need business validation. This validation can be hard as it requires both domain knowledge of the Universe of Discourse as well as system knowledge on the implementation in the different source systems. Quite often this knowledge is shared across different persons. It is one of the major tasks of the logical modeler to bring this knowledge together and to capture it in the logical integration model.

To ensure full lineage it is necessary to maintain the metadata for the linkage between logical source models and the logical integration models and the logical integration model towards the logical target model.

6 Arriving at the Implementation Models

The vertical data lineage is all about a transforming knowledge of an Universe of Discourse into a form that can be used to obtain and retrieve data. The representation of the logical models for a given implementation platform is ensured by implementation models. One logical model may be implemented on different (database) platforms and hence have multiple implementation models. Once more, metadata ensures the lineage between the different models.

The last step to achieve our goal is to transform the logical models to structures that can be implemented. This transformation is not trivial. Especially because every implementation platform has its own possibilities and limitations.

One strategy is to apply a horizontal data architecture in which validation, historized storage and access of data are separated. For each of these functions an implementation model has to be created. These models are interlinked to ensure horizontal lineage. These implementation models are derived from the logical model, taking in consideration the functional and physical aspects for that part of the implementation.

Keeping all these implementation models in synch is a hard job, that can be performed in 3 ways:

1. Procedural: Using a procedural approach in which it is prescribed how a data engineer – responsible for creating and maintaining implementation models – should enforce both horizontal and vertical lineage. This will be very hard in practice and requires a lot of verification;
2. Model driven data fabric: Using a tool-supported guided approach for model creation in which models for the basis for generating a configurable data flow;
3. LDM driven data fabric: Like the model driven data fabric, where all implementation models are directly derived from the logical data models.

An example of a model driven data fabric is the i-refactory [11]. This is a data management solution that extracts, integrates and provides data in a fully auditable and traceable manner. The solution is fully based on models; no programming is required as all logic – including data transformations – is captured in models.

The i-refactory supports a multi-layer horizontal architecture coming from source to target. Each layer has its own model artifacts:

- Technical Staging layer: layer to capture the information from a source. Model is equal to the source system's technical format;
- Logical Validation layer: layer to verify that information from a source is in accordance with the structure of the logical source model (fully normalized model);

- Central Fact Persistency layer: layer in which source facts and facts from the integration model are stored and historized. Base for this layer are the source **and** the integration models. This layer is modelled using Unified Anchor Modelling, a modelling technique that combines Fact Based Modelling with Anchor Style modeling. This modeling technique is especially designed for vertical lineage be ensuring non-destructive transformation for all modeling patterns used in fact and logical models;
- Generic Data Access layer: layer for extracting the data from the data platform. Structured for all data realities. This is the layer in which the data reality in the target model comes to live.

All these layers deal with their own concerns. All implementation models are linked to the corresponding logical models.

7   Connection to Horizontal Data Architecture

As can be seen in the i-refactory implementation, the data flows from source to target via different layers. The layers form decoupling points in the data logistics. The functionality of the layers are described in the horizontal data architecture.

Key to full lineage is to connect the horizontal lineage on "How flows data from A to B?" to the vertical lineage that should be able to provide information on the what the data actually represents in the Universe of Discourse. The i-refactory has a metadata repository to cater for the full horizontal lineage. Combined with the metadata of vertical lineage from Universe of Discourse to the implementation models, all descriptive, structural and administrative is available to obtain full lineage.

8   Summary

Data architecture involves horizontal lineage but also vertical lineage. To be able to provide this vertical lineage, different layers of representation are introduced. The most business-like representation layer concerns the actual text documents, like laws and policies. From there, using different methods and techniques, the Universe of Discourse is analyzed to a conceptual information model, using FBM. Also derivation rules are conceptually described. Main concerns of this layer are the validation of these models with the domain expert and the linkage between the textual documents and the models.

Next step is the transformation of these conceptual models into logical models in which models are verified using formal methods and concerns like data historization, data life cycle management and privacy by design are addressed.

When data has to be obtained from different sources, there will be more data realities to handle; those from the sources and the one for the target which is derived from the fact model. To encompass the deviations between logical source models and the logical target a integration model has to be created.

By models alone data won't flow. To ensure data can flow we need to implement a horizontal data architecture describing how data is obtained, enriched, stored and accessed. All layers within the horizontal data architecture have to be created using implementation models.

As all models are upon each other and their metadata is interlinked there is a model-to-model lineage possible from a fact model towards the implementation models.

In the end, this provides a fully traceable vertical data architecture in which the lineage between the origin in for example a law and any part in the implementation. With this lineage the possibility is there to ask for a particular element in the implementation why it exists, who can access the data, when the data is entered etc. But also the other way around; if a certain text part in a law changes, what is the impact on the underlying implementations.

References

1. Wikipedia Data architecture (2019). https://en.wikipedia.org/wiki/Data_architecture. Accessed 3 July 2019
2. Business Rules Group: Business Rules Manifesto version 2.0 (2003). http://www.businessrulesgroup.org/brmanifesto.htm. Accessed 17 July 2019
3. Bulles, J., Bouwmeester, H., Ausems, A.: A best practice for the analysis of legal documents. In: On the Move to Meaningful Internet Systems 2019 Workshops, Rhodes, October 2019 (2019)
4. PNA Group: Cognitatie (2019). http://www.cognitatie.nl. Accessed 10 July 2019
5. Saton, J., Koster, J.P.: Roles and variables, two sides of the same coin. In: On the Move to Meaningful Internet Systems 2019 Workshops, Rhodes, October 2019 (2019)
6. The Data Management Association: The DAMA Dictionary of Data Management, 2nd edn. Technics Publications, Basking Ridge (2011)
7. Codd, E.F.: Recent investigations into relational data base systems. In: Proceedings of IFIP Congress, Stockholm (1974)
8. Date, C.: The Principle of Orthogonal Design Part 1, Database Programming & Design 7, No. 6, June 1994 (1994)
9. Manoku, E.: Repositories and transformations - FCO-IM to ERM (2014). http://www.fco-im.nl/pdfFiles/Repositories_and_Transformation.pdf. Accessed 29 Aug 2019
10. CaseTalk: Temporal & Transitional Modeling (2019). https://casetalk.com/news/blog/267-temporal-transitional-modeling. Accessed 22 July 2019
11. I-Refact: Datafabriek, het datamodel vormt de basis (Dutch) (2019). https://www.i-refact.com/i-refactory/. Accessed 19 July 2019

A Best Practice for the Analysis
of Legal Documents

John Bulles[1]([✉]), Hennie Bouwmeester[1], and Anouschka Ausems[2]

[1] PNA, Heerlen, The Netherlands
{john.bulles,hennie.bouwmeester}@pna-group.com
[2] Belastingdienst, Apeldoorn, The Netherlands
a.ausems@belastingdienst.nl

Abstract. Organisations deal with a large set of source documents, often concerning law and regulation, that they need to comply to or bring to execution. In the past, a team of legal specialists analysed these documents and wrote new documents containing informal preliminary specifications which are hard to validate. Another group of experts translates these documents to specifications for IT-systems.

The Best Practice as described in this paper, takes another approach. In a multidisciplinary team of experts, combining the knowledge of legal specialists with the modelling competences of knowledge modelers. It describes how legal experts will analyse legal documents, add interpretations and classifications (model elements) and how knowledge modelers assist in creating extended conceptual information models.

The result is a validated and extended conceptual information model, in which all knowledge elements are traceable to the original legal text. This happens with fewer translation steps compared to the approach mentioned above.

Keywords: Fact based modeling (FBM) · Legal analysis · Cognitatie · Conceptual data model · Rule model · Traceability · Multidisciplinary teamwork

1 Introduction

This document focuses on the transformation, performed by a multidisciplinary team, of the original legal text into a structured and validated conceptual model of that original legal text. In that transformation all explicit and implicit knowledge (concepts, data structures, rules, rights and so on) in that original legal text is taken into account and is stored in a structured and validated conceptual model. We call this transformation process 'legal analysis', resulting in a scalable model of the original text.

Essential to the Best Practise is multidisciplinary teamwork, legal analysts and knowledge modelers work together in an iterative way of constructing the structured and validated conceptual model. A central part in this approach is played by Fact Based Modeling, including input and output example facts of each rule. The use of concrete examples as early as possible in the process is very important. The Best Practice will

© Springer Nature Switzerland AG 2020
C. Debruyne et al. (Eds.): OTM 2019 Workshops, LNCS 11878, pp. 106–116, 2020.
https://doi.org/10.1007/978-3-030-40907-4_11

integrate data, rules, processes and semantics. In the current version of the approach, processes are not yet included. This will be subject of further development in the upcoming year.

A goal of the Best Practise is to maximize the explicitation of the semantics of the origin legal text. All implicit knowledge must be externalized. Another goal is to be able to review the analysis process on the basis of the stored intermediate results and the concrete validated examples. It is essential that the results of the legal analysis are developed once and are reused by multiple different roles inside or outside the organisation.

2 Why Is a Best Practice Needed

In the current situation, government agencies in the Netherlands implement legislation by using IT-systems. This requires traceable IT-specifications for the software build with a crystal clear interpretation. The past has shown many difficulties when translating legislation into IT-specification [2, 4]. The most important ones are:

a. Legislation and associated policies are not traceable to specifications and vice versa. The origin of the IT-specifications are not or insufficiently recorded in business documents. Legislation and policy knowledge and interpretations are hidden in design documentation and the IT-systems itself. This results in government agencies loosing time and flexibility in the management of their IT-specifications. For example on determining the impact of legislative change. Also the knowledge is not easily accessible for business.
b. The translation is implicitly done without recording intermediate steps. The interpretation takes place inside the heads of the legal specialists or process experts. If it is recorded, this often happens in word documents (no structure and no relation to the origin) with the result that no validation or re-use is possible. The steps taken in the translation are not clear, making management of a correct translation difficult. Validation and traceability are keys in high-quality IT-specifications.
c. In government organizations just a small group of people have thorough knowledge of certain legislation and policies. Knowledge transfer is more difficult because interpretations and intermediate steps in the translation are not recorded in a structured manner. This makes an organisation vulnerable in terms of knowledge management. Due to the increasing aging of the population of employees within the government agencies, it is becoming increasingly important to make legal and policy knowledge explicit and recorded for the purpose of drawing up and testing IT-specifications.
d. At present, legal specialists make daily interpretations of the same legislation. Duplication of work and different interpretations of the same original text result in the loss of worktime and the risk of incorrect interpretations. This detracts from the desired unity of policy and implementation.
e. At present, many government agencies cannot yet provide insight into their logic and the link to the underlying legislation [1]. Citizens and companies can hardly check the legality of the automated decisions of government agencies. On the basis of the General Data Protection Regulation government agency's must, upon

request, provide citizens or companies with insight into the logic underlying the automated processing of their data and legislation. A Law model, that can be accessed automatically, generate different views and has a direct relationship with the IT-specifications, could provide for this.

f. The analysis of legislation with the aim of resulting into IT-specifications, is carried out by different people at different stages of production. Knowledge and specific skills are fragmented. This detracts from the quality of the analysis, the manner of recording and the way of sharing the results of the analysis (the knowledge needed for good IT-specifications).

These aspects have led to the developing of a Best Practice for the Analysis of Legal Documents at a Dutch government agency. This Best Practice yields in more knowledge retention and overview (continuity) with less risk of errors in specifications (fiscal accuracy) and feedback loop between IT-specifications and legislator, without loss of speed in production. Furthermore it yields improved specifications that are readable and linked to the origins and systems, so traceable. This will result in shorter impact assessment and more efficient specification because the results of law analysis and specifications based on it can be re-used for other services.

What are the most important starting points for this?

A. **Methodical analysis of legislation**

Improving the analysis of legislation starts with a more methodical analysis in which the significance of legislation and policies is made as explicit as possible with the help of modeling techniques. The validation and structural recording of the results (including validation cases) takes place in a legible and maintainable Law model. This Law model can be presented in different views and can therefore be consulted by everyone (legal, business and IT-specialists). It provides insight into the explanation and application of every relevant piece of legislation. It requires properly and thoroughly analyzing the meaning of legislation and policies in one go. Everyone must be able to become acquainted with the results and to follow the underlying analysis steps and test them. They do not have to perform an analysis again. This makes legal and policies knowledge explicit and re-usable.

B. **Multidisciplinary working**

In addition to professionalising, it is also necessary that analysis of legislation takes place on a multidisciplinary basis. In today's world with a multitude of rules, data and processes, a legal specialist can no longer do this alone. In addition, most legal specialists are not trained with knowledge of modeling, and modeling is necessary to document the results of the analysis in a structured and methodical way. Good analysis of legislation therefore requires a multidisciplinary approach.

C. **Automated support**

To support all this and also to reduce the number of manual steps, adequate tooling is needed for a professional analysis of legislation. Adequate tools are essential for capturing, mass sharing and managing the results of the analysis. The translation into unambiguous, complete and explainable IT-specifications for IT production can then be made easier. Fewer manual steps are required, and the results of the law analysis can be shown in different views from within the Law model.

3 The Analysis Process

The Best Practise process consists of the following steps:

1. Agree on the end result of the job to be done
2. Gather the initially pointed out relevant (legal) texts
3. In an iterative way:
   a. Determine (next) (ultimate) decision as result of this legal analysis process
   b. Determine (first) next text part that will be analysed
   c. Analyse that text
   d. Validate the results of the text analysis by means of concrete examples
   e. Construct all aspects of the conceptual model related to that text
   f. Construct all requested views of the conceptual model related to that text

In this chapter, a concrete example of a part of a non-official translation from the Dutch Law Income 2001 Act with a validity date of December 31th 2018, concerning own home (principle residences) is used. The result of the job to be done, as described as step 1 above, is defining all rules concerning home ownership in this legislation.

The second step is the gathering of relevant text parts. This is often an initial gathering, in step 3 text parts that were not initially pointed out can be added to the relevant text parts. For the example we will keep it simple for now, and only add Article 3.110 of this law as relevant text part.

For the example, we will take the calculation of the taxable revenues from own home as starting point of step 3a and the text part of 3b will be Article 3.110

"Article 3.110. Taxable revenues from own home (principle residence) Taxable revenues from own home are the financial advantages from own home reduced by the deductible costs charged at that financial advantages from own home (article 3.120)."

In step 3c, we will start by classifying and annotating the text. Classifying is the process that is performed during the law analysis Best Practice to assign parts of text to a certain class from the Law model. A classification scheme indicates from which classes one can choose when assigning a piece of text from a source to a class in the Law model. The used classification scheme is a further development of the work done in [3]. Annotating is connecting (providing back and forth traceability) an element in the Law model with the original text. For displaying the example, the tool Cognitatie [7] is used to display the annotations and classifications as well for the conceptual modelling diagrams.

The following classifications and annotations are made in this text:

1. As derivation rule

Article 3.110. Taxable revenues from own home (principle residence)

Taxable revenues from own home are the financial advantages from own home reduced by the deductible costs charged at that financial advantages from own home (article 3.120).

For a derivation rule, also the output and input variables and the derivation prescription must be determined and if possible classified and annotated.

2. In the first smaller part of the text, a variable is classified

Article 3.110. Taxable revenues from own home (principle residence)

Taxable revenues from own home are the financial advantages from own home reduced by the deductible costs charged at that financial advantages from own home (article 3.120).

3. This variable (Taxable revenues from own home) will be linked to a concept. A concept is a more general element to which multiple classified text phrases can reference (possibly with different texts and in different documents). For a variable, directly after classifying the text, is determined:

   a. What person, thing or case this variable belongs to in the context of this law (in FBM wording, to what entity type it belongs) In this case: *Domestic tax duty owner with own home*

   b. What kind of time frame is relevant for the variable In this case: *whole year*

   c. What are concrete examples of the variable, represented as verbalized facts of the variable and the related entity type and time frame

   d. In this case:

      i. *Domestic tax duty owner with own home **444** has as taxable revenues from own home **1130** euros in tax year **2018**.*

      ii. *Domestic tax duty owner with own home **555** has as taxable revenues from own home **2260** euros in tax year **2018**.*

This will lead to a fact type (and if not yet present entity and value types) in the conceptual data model, for which directly the uniqueness constraints are determined (Fig. 1).

Domestic taks duty owner has Taxable revenues from own home in Tax year

Domestic tax duty owner with own home	Tax year	Amount (VT)
ID	Year number	Taxable revenues from own home
444	2018	1130
555	2018	2260

1:   Domestic tax duty owner with own home <ID> has as taxable revenues from own home <Taxable revenues from own home> euros in tax year <Year number>.

Fig. 1. Fact type

3. The next text part ("are"), is classified as an assignment operator

Article 3.110. Taxable revenues from own home (principle residence)

Taxable revenues from own home are the financial advantages from own home reduced by the deductible costs charged at that financial advantages from own home (article 3.120).

4. The sequentially following text part, is also classified as a variable

Article 3.110. Taxable revenues from own home (principle residence)

Taxable revenues from own home are the financial advantages from own home reduced by the deductible costs charged at that financial advantages from own home (article 3.120).

The same steps as earlier are performed for this variable
a. The variable also belongs to *Domestic tax duty owner with own home*
b. With a time frame of *whole year*
c. And concrete examples:
  i. *Domestic tax duty owner with own home **444** has as financial advantages from own home **1430** euros in tax year **2018**.*
  ii. *Domestic tax duty owner with own home **555** has as financial advantages from own home **2960** euros in tax year **2018**.*

This will also lead to a fact type which is not displayed in this document.

5. The next text phrase, is classified as an arithmetical operator

Article 3.110. Taxable revenues from own home (principle residence)

Taxable revenues from own home are the financial advantages from own home reduced by the deductible costs charged at that financial advantages from own home (article 3.120).

This arithmetical operator classification points to the arithmetical operator "Substract"
6. The following text part, is again classified as a variable

Article 3.110. Taxable revenues from own home (principle residence)

Taxable revenues from own home are the financial advantages from own home reduced by the deductible costs charged at that financial advantages from own home (article 3.120).

The same steps as earlier are performed for this variable:
a. The variable also belongs to *Domestic tax duty owner with own home*
b. With a time frame of *whole year*
c. And concrete examples:
  i. *Domestic tax duty owner with own home **444** has as Deductible costs charged from own home **300** euros in tax year **2018**.*
  ii. *Domestic tax duty owner with own home **555** has as Deductible costs charged from own home **700** euros in tax year **2018**.*
  Again, this leads to a fact type which is not displayed in this document.

7. The last text part, is classified as a explicit reference

Article 3.110. Taxable revenues from own home (principle residence)

Taxable revenues from own home are the financial advantages from own home reduced by the deductible costs charged at that financial advantages from own home (article 3.120).

The reference leads to an other article, which in, more detail, describes the Deductible costs charged at that financial advantages from own home. For this referenced text part, it is needed to decide whether it is in scope of the currently described service or not. If so, the article will be added to the relevant text parts and analysed similar as this text part. Also explicit references to this article must be scoped. For example in chapter 10 (article 10bis.3) of the same law an explicit reference to this article is made. Finally, a lot of implicit references appear in law texts as well. Here the knowledge of the legal expert is essential in pointing out the references and again scoping these to the currently described service.

After classifying and annotating this text, the different created concepts will be related as well, for example defining what variables are input and output of the derivation rule. All these concepts must be defined semantically, leading to concept definitions of these concepts, the terms to express the concepts and all references between the concepts.

After this, the next step performed is the determination of the prescription of the derivation rule. First the modeler will determine the construction of the rule. Then the exact rule pattern will be selected. From there on the exact rule prescription text will be defined. This will result in:

The taxable revenues from own home of a domestic tax duty owner with own home
is calculated as
his financial advantages from own home minus
his deductible costs charged at that financial advantages from own home.

Step 3d is all about validation. The examples added in step 3c for the fact types is already a first validation, but we also need to validate the derivation rule. For this, a Law Validation Integration Diagram is introduced, showing:

1. the law and regulation texts, including citations
2. the derivation rule, expressed in a formal rule representation like RegelSpraak (developed at the Dutch Tax and Customs Administration)
3. (concrete example) facts that are used as input by the derivation rule
4. (concrete example) facts that are derived as output by the derivation rule (Fig. 2)

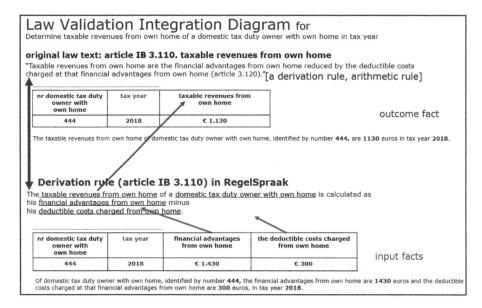

Fig. 2. Law Validation Integration Diagram

After the analysis and validation of the text part, parts of the conceptual model are already defined. In step 3e, the knowledge modeler will proceed with this work. This involves:

1. Make the set of relevant validation scenarios complete
2. Describe the relevant concept definitions
3. Determine the other relevant conceptual constraints of the relevant fact types
4. Link all elements (where not yet done in the earlier steps of constructing the conceptual model) to the elements of the Law model for traceability and impact analysis.

And then, in step 3f all requested views of the conceptual model are created (or when possible generated). Some examples of these views are:

1. A full FBM model in some FBM visualization (like cogNIAM, ORM, FCO-IM)
2. An overview diagram, pointing out the main concepts of the FBM model
3. A derivation rule hierarchy (what derivation rule is input for which other derivation rule)
4. A list of concepts (in different sorting algoritms)
5. A set of test cases for validation
6. A set of derivation rules and constraints

Due to size, it is not possible to display all of these views here and we limit it to a representation of the fact types (Fig. 3).

Domestic tax duty owner has Financial advantages from own home in Tax year

Domestic tax duty owner with own home	Tax year	Amount (VT)
ID	Year number	Financial advantages from own home
444	2018	1430
555	2018	2960

1:   Domestic tax duty owner with own home <ID> has as financial advantages
from <Financial advantages from own home> euros in tax year <Year number>.

Domestic tax duty owner has Taxable revenues from own home in Tax year

Domestic tax duty owner with own home	Tax year	Amount (VT)
ID	Year number	Taxable revenues from own home
444	2018	1130
555	2018	2260

1:   Domestic tax duty owner with own home <ID> has as taxable revenues from own
home <Taxable revenues from own home> euros in tax year <Year number>.

Domestic tax duty owner has Deductible costs charged from own home in Tax year

Domestic tax duty owner with own home	Tax year	Amount (VT)
ID	Year number	Deductible costs charged from own home
444	2018	300
555	2018	700

1:   Domestic tax duty owner with own home <ID> has as Deductible costs charged from
own home <Deductible costs charged own home > euros in tax year <Year number>.

Fig. 3. Fact types of example case

4   Overview of the Best Practice

Application of the Best Practice approach has important benefits for the process of
translating legislation into IT specifications. We summarize them here:

1. Legislation and associated policies become traceable to specifications and vice
   versa. This facilitates determining the impact of legislative change.
2. The translation is explicitly done with recording intermediate steps. The results are
   re-usable and validable.
3. Interpretations and intermediate steps in the translation are recorded in a structured
   manner, with the result that knowledge transfer is possible. Therefore duplication of
   work and different interpretations can be limited.
4. It becomes possible that government agencies can provide insight into their logic of
   law execution and the link to the underlying legislation.
5. The analysis of legislation is carried out multidisciplinary. Knowledge and specific
   skills are combined resulting in better specifications.

To achieve these benefits, the following steps are defined, combined with a multidisciplinary approach and supported by tooling:

1. Determine the purpose of the analysis
2. Gather the relevant original (legal) texts

3. In an iterative way:
   a. Determine the decision which is the result of this iteration
   b. Determine the text part that will be analysed
   c. Analyse that text with the use of Fact Based Modeling techniques, combined with legal knowledge (classifications, annotations, relationships, Law Validation Integration Diagram)
   d. Validate the results of the text analysis by means of concrete examples
   e. Construct all aspects of the conceptual model related to that text
   f. Construct all requested views of the conceptual model related to that text

The result is a Law model, a FBM model and rules model. Per fact type all variables and roles, concrete facts (data records and example sentences), fact communication patterns, definition of concepts, uniqueness constraints, derivation rules and other conceptual constraints (data quality rules) are recorded. These models make it possible to have multiple views:

1. Overview diagram of the collection of fact types (stratification)
2. Hierarchy of derivation rules (decision structure)
3. Glossary (both alphabetical and knowledge sequence)
4. Collection of validation cases (test cases, facts, scenarios)
5. Collection of rules (derivation rules, restriction rules.

5 Future Development

The Best Practice is used as a starting point for Business Rules Management. In another project of the Dutch Tax and Customs Administration, the Best Practice is also used as a part of the vertical data architecture approach [6]. Architects of both projects underline the value of combining Data and Rules modelling, as pointed out in [5]. Furthermore, future development will focus on education in this Best Practice and further developing the underlying Cognitatie-software [7] in a way that besided the text analysis, also the conceptual data modeling and rules modeling is fully supported.

Also the used classification types will be reviewed very strictly. In the current Best Practice a set of classifications is defined, but this will probably change a little bit in the near future, as with new projects, sometimes a need for a new classification arises. But this will only concern little changes in the classification scheme as the current is already used in multiple projects.

Finally, in the introduction is stated that an integration between data, rules, semantics and processes is needed. To accomplish this, the Best Practice needs to be extended for integration of process modelling.

6 Summary

In this paper a Best Practice for analysis of documents, with main focus on legal texts, is described. The need for the Best Practice arised from business side and mainly focusses on how to get in control of the translation from text to specifications.

The Best Practice consists of several steps, performed in a multidisciplinary team, where the capabilities of a (legal) domain expert and a knowledge modeler are optimally combined. The end result is the captured knowledge of the domain expert (like interpretation, relations between the textual elements, etc.) in a structured way, which makes it possible to use this knowledge in many ways. Also a conceptual data and rules model is created, also containing all semantics of the used concepts, which can be the starting point for implementation in an (automated) system.

Cognitatie [7] supports all traceability and impact analysis by default.

References

1. Lokin, M., van Kempen, M.: Transparantie 2.0, Nieuwe transparantie-eisen en hun betekenis voor de regelbeheersing, BRM Conferentie, 7 December 2018 (2018)
2. Lokin, M.: Wendbaar wetgeven De wetgever als systeembeheerder, Proefschrift, VU, October 2018 (2018)
3. Lokin, M., Nijssen, S., Lemmens, I.: CogniLex. In: Ciuciu, I., et al. (eds.) OTM 2015. LNCS, vol. 9416, pp. 235–244. Springer, Cham (2015). https://doi.org/10.1007/978-3-319-26138-6_27
4. Leo, S.: ICT-deskundigen worden pas veel te laat betrokken bij de totstandkoming van nieuwe belastingwetten, Financieel Dagblad (2019). Accessed 28 May 2019
5. Veldhuijzen van Zanten, G.: Gegevens, feiten en regels, ppt van presentatie bij eBRM Conferentie, 7 December 2018 (2018)
6. Bulles, J., Arntz, R., Evers, M.: Fully traceable vertical data architecture. In: On the Move to Meaningful Internet Systems 2019 Workshops, Rhodes, October 2019 (2019)
7. PNA Group Cognitatie (2019). http://www.cognitatie.nl. Accessed 21 July 2019

A Conceptual Model of the Blockchain

Peter Bollen[✉]

School of Business and Economics,
Maastricht University, Maastricht, The Netherlands
p.bollen@maastrichtuniversity.nl

Abstract. Hyperledger Fabric is a very large project under the umbrella of the Linux Foundation, with hundreds of developers involved. In this paper we will illustrate how the application of fact-based modeling will help us in understanding some basic features of the blockchain concept as is used in Hyperledger Fabric (HLF) and that it can serve as a conceptual blueprint of HLF for all involved to use.

Keywords: Hyperledger Fabric · Ledger · World state · Blockchain · Fact-based modeling

1 Introduction

Hyperledger Fabric is a permissioned blockchain application development environment. Hyperledger Fabric is a very large project under the umbrella of the Linux Foundation, with hundreds of developers. Currently no validated conceptual model is accessible by the developers community.

In this paper we will clarify the essential blockchain concepts as they are implemented in Hyperledger Fabric (HLF). In Nijssen and Bollen [1, 2] an introduction into the transaction logic for the Hyperledger Fabric implementation for permissioned blockchain applications was provided. In this paper we will focus on the conceptual building blocks of Hyperledger Fabric [3]: *blocks, blockchain, world state* and *ledger*. We will illustrate how we can build up a conceptual model of Hyperledger Fabric by introducing examples and by applying CogNIAM's fact-based modeling protocol [4–8] on these examples.

2 Modeling Basic the Blockchain Concept

In Fig. 1 we have shown a significant example of blocks in a blockchain. The legend provides those relevant elements that we are interested in for now. We note that for the initial conceptual modeling process that is presented in this paper we restrict ourselves to a universe of discourse that consists of a single blockchain.

© Springer Nature Switzerland AG 2020
C. Debruyne et al. (Eds.): OTM 2019 Workshops, LNCS 11878, pp. 117–126, 2020.
https://doi.org/10.1007/978-3-030-40907-4_12

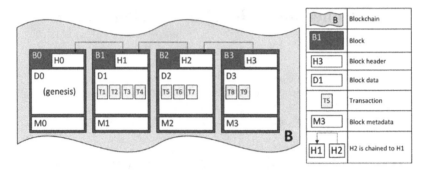

Fig. 1. Example of blocks in a blockchain

Applying step 1 of CogNIAMS's modeling protocol (verbalise) [8] will lead to the verbalization of (a significant part of) the example as follows.

Block B0 is a genesis block
Block B0 has Block header H0
Block B1 has Block header H1
Block B0 has Block data D0
Block B1 has Block data D1
Block data D1 contains Transaction T1
Block data D1 contains Transaction T2
Block data D1 contains Transaction T3
Block data D1 contains Transaction T4
Block data D2 contains Transaction T5
Block B0 has Block meta data M0
Block B1 has Block meta data M1
Block header H3 is chained to Block header H2
Block header H2 is chained to Block header H1

Grouping these sentences and determining which parts are variable and fixed together with the addition of explicit entity types and name classes yield the result of steps 2 and 3 of the CogNIAM modeling protocol: fully qualified sentences.

Block with *block code* |B0| is a genesis block

Block with *block code* |B0| has **Block header** with *block header code* |H0|
Block with *block code* |B1| has **Block header** with *block header code* |H1|

Block with *block code* |B0| has **Block data** with *block data code* |D0|
Block with *block code* |B1| has **Block data** with *block data code* |D1|

Block data with *block data code* |D1| contains Transaction with *transaction code* |T1|
Block data with *block data code* |D2| contains Transaction with *transaction code* |T5|

Block with *block code* |B0| has **Block meta data** with *block meta data code* |M0|
Block with *block code* |B1| has **Block meta data** *with block meta data code* |M1|

Block header with *block header code* |H3| is chained to **Block header** with *block header code* |H2|
Block header with *block header code* |H2| is chained to **Block header** *with block header code* |H1|

At this stage an initial list of concept definitions can be created that at least contains entries for all entity/concept types (depicted in **bold**) and the name classes (depicted in *italic*). We emphasize that the concept definition for name classes includes the semantics of the naming conventions as well. An excerpt of such a list of concept definitions at this stage is given in Table 1.

Table 1. Initial list of concept definitions

Concept	Definition
Block	A [Block] is a data container that contains an ordered set of <transaction>s
Block code	A specific [Block code] is used to identify a specific <Block> within the union of all <Block>s in a given blockchain
Transaction	A [Transaction] captures a change in the world state
Transaction code	A specific [Transaction code] is used to identify a specific <Transaction>. Within the union of all <Transaction>s in a blockchain
Block header	A [Block header] contains the non-transaction data that are contained in a <Block>
Block header code	A specific [Block header code] is used to identify a specific <Block header> within the union of all <Block header>s in a given blockchain
Block data	[Block data] of a <Block> contain an ordered set of <Transactions>
Block data code	A specific [Block data code] is used to identify a specific <Block meta data> within the union of all <Block meta data>s in a given blockchain
Block meta data	[Block meta data] in a <Block> contain block-specific data on the creation of the <Block>
Block meta data code	A specific [Block meta data code] is used to identify a specific <Block data> within the union of all <Block data>s in a given blockchain
H2 is chained to H1	The new <block> with <block header> H2 is added to the blockchain via a chain to the existing <block> with <block header > H1
Genesis block	The first Block in a blockchain that does not contain data

If we inspect the excerpt of the list of concept definitions in Table 1 we notice that the context in which the naming conventions hold, is the context of a single blockchain. We remark here that in general in a permissioned blockchain network multiple channels and corresponding ledgers (that each contain a different blockchain) tailored to these channels might exist. After we have modeled the initial level of blockchain complexity as is illustrated in Fig. 1 we might decide to model the next level of complexity connected to the block header.

3   Modeling the First Level of Complexity in the Blockchain

One of the advantages of the fact-based conceptual modeling approach is that we can extend our universe of discourse with new examples of communication that exist within the domain. In this task we will zoom in on the content of a given (non-genesis) block in the blockchain as given in Fig. 2.

In the following a description of the block-header is provided. A **Block Header** comprises three fields written when a block is created: a *Block number*: An integer starting at 0 (the genesis block) and that is increased by 1 for every new block appended to the blockchain, the *Current block bash* which is the hash of all the transactions contained in the current block and the *previous block hash*: A copy of the hash from the previous block in the blockchain.

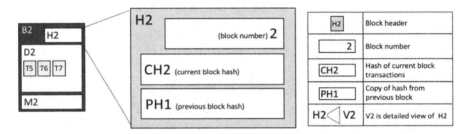

Fig. 2. Example of non-genesis block in a blockchain

The hash fields are internally derived by cryptographically hashing the block data. They ensure that each and every block is inextricably linked to its neighbour, leading to an immutable ledger.

When we apply CogNIAM's modeling protocol on the example in Fig. 2 we get the following result of step 3 (classification and qualification of variables). For sake of comprehension we only list the additional qualified sentences here.

The block that contains **Block header** with *block header code* |H2| has **Block number |2|**
The block that contains **Block header** with *block header code* |H2| has current **Block hash |CH2|**
The block that contains **Block header** with *block header code* |H2| has previous **Block hash |PH1|**

Adding these fact types to the fact types from our first example and deriving the uniqueness, mandatory role and totality integrity rules for this fact model schema leads to the conceptual schema in Fig. 3.

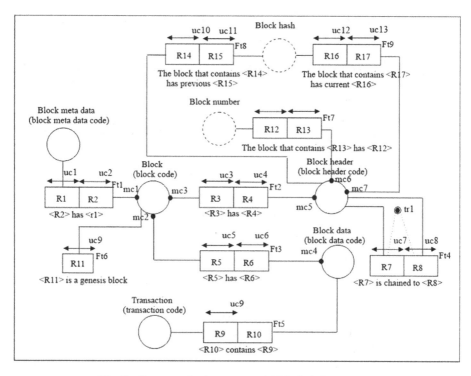

Fig. 3. Conceptual schema essential blockchain concepts

4   Modeling the Second Level of Complexity in the Blockchain

If we analyse the basic logic within a distributed ledger system consensus is very important. It basically means that in a distributed ledger system all peers need to have identical world states and blockchains for the ledger in the channel.

After the consensus protocol has established that the current world-state and blockchain are consistent among the endorsing and committing peers [1, 2] a block can be appended to the blockchain. Thereby the current hash of the 'last' block is used in the consensus determining process. Once this consensus process has established a uniform commitment for adding the new block to the chain, the current hash of this last block becomes the previous hash of the newly added block. In our conceptual model this can be modeled as a derivation rule that inspects the instances of fact type Ft4 and thereby can determine the 'identity' of the last block (in terms of *block header code* or *block code*) by looking up that instance of fact type Ft4 for which instance exists that has no successor block. Then for this block the current block hash can be determined by inspecting the population of fact type Ft9. After the commitment of adding the new block to the blockchain is given an instance of Ft4 is created after the 'baptist fact instances' for the new block have been created, normally by some preset derivation rules, i.e. instances of Ft1, Ft2, Ft3 will be determined, normally the 'next' value in a series of *block header* or *block codes*. Finally new instances of Ft9 will be created by performing a derivation rule on the content of the transactions (Ft5) in the form of a hash function leading to the current hash of the new block. Finally the current hash of the last block will be copied into the previous has of the new block (Ft8). In Table 2 we have summarized the derivation rules in terms of the derived fact types, the input fact types and a natural language description of the insert and query processes and the derivation logic.

Table 2. Processes and derivation rules for the conceptual schema from Fig. 3

Process/ derivation rule	Derived fact type	Input fact type(s)	Derivation rule description
P0	Query	Ft4	Find that block for which the block header code is not chained to a successor
P1	Insert	Ft1	Add new block meta-data
P2	Insert	Ft2	Add new block code
P3	Insert	Ft3/Ft5	Add new block data/transactions in block
Dr1	Ft9	Ft2, Ft3, Ft5	Create current block hash of newly added block
Dr2	Ft8	Ft9	Copy the current block-hash for the block that was a result of process P0 as the previous hash of the newly added block

5   Modeling Transaction Validation in the Blockchain

In this section we will now add another level of complexity in the commitment or validation phase of the Hyperledger Fabric distributed ledger environment [2] in which for every transaction in the proposed block the committers will check the associated endorsement policy and hence for every transaction determine the validation status as either *valid* or *invalid*. We will now add this fact type to our conceptual schema (see Fig. 4).

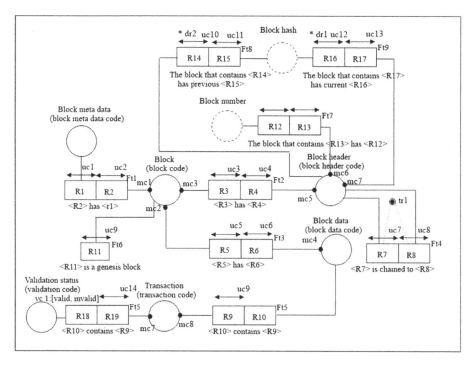

Fig. 4. Conceptual schema blockchain concepts

6   Linking the Blockchain to the World State

In Fig. 5 an example is given of a ledger L. This ledger comprises a world state W and a blockchain, B. W contains four states with keys: CAR1, CAR2, CAR3 and CAR4. B contains two blocks 0 and 1. Block 1 contains four transactions: T1, T2, T3, T4.

Block 0 is the genesis block, though it does not contain any transactions that relate to cars. Block 1 however, contains transactions T1, T2, T3, T4 and these correspond to transactions that created the initial states for CAR0 to CAR3 in the world state. Furthermore, We can see that block 1 is linked to block 0. We can see that the ledger world state contains states that correspond to CAR0, CAR1, CAR2 and CAR3. CAR0 has a value which indicates that it is a blue Toyota Prius, currently owned by Tomoko, and we can see similar states and values for the other cars. Moreover, we can see that all car states are at version number 0, indicating that this is their starting version number – they have not been updated since they were created. So the ledger in HLF contains asserted facts (transactions) and derived facts (states), in which the new world state facts are derived from the old world state facts together with the facts in the validated transaction(s) from the new block that is (gonna be) appended to the blockchain.

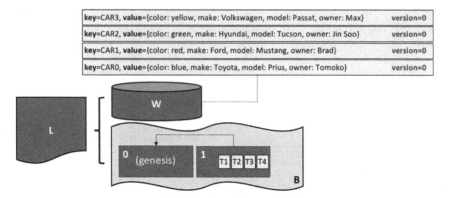

key=CAR3, value={color: yellow, make: Volkswagen, model: Passat, owner: Max}	version=0
key=CAR2, value={color: green, make: Hyundai, model: Tucson, owner: Jin Soo}	version=0
key=CAR1, value={color: red, make: Ford, model: Mustang, owner: Brad}	version=0
key=CAR0, value={color: blue, make: Toyota, model: Prius, owner: Tomoko}	version=0

Fig. 5. Ledger (L), world state (W) and blockchain (B)

When time passes new valid transactions will update the world state(s). In tandem with this update of the world state caused by the outcome of these validated transactions the version numbers for these world state(s) will be increased by 1. When we refer to the Ledger in Fig. 5, the world state is the result of the valid transactions *T1*, *T2*, *T3* and *T4*. Because this is the first state of the key-value pairs the version for all car states is equal to 0.

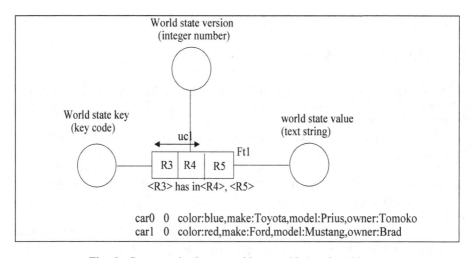

Fig. 6. Conceptual schema world state with (version) history

In Fig. 6 we have shown the conceptual schema of the world state in which conceptually all future world states can be captured. This is possible in spite of the fact that current world state is a snaphot model (see Fig. 7) because in the future all past key-value versions can be derived by executing a derivation rule on the valid transaction updates on the world state and in that sense the version is derived based on the validation statuses of the proposed transactions for these world states.

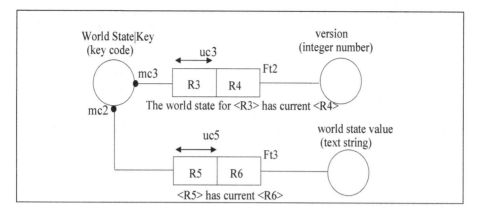

Fig. 7. Conceptual schema: world state as a snapshot

7 Conclusion

In this paper we have introduced the concepts of *block*, *blockchain*, *world state* and *ledger* based on the defining literature on Hyperledger Fabric. We have given a list of concept definitions and we have created a conceptual schema using CogNIAM's modeling protocol. After we have established the basic logic underlying the appending of new blocks to the blockchain it was made clear how the derivation mechanism works for the basic blockchain configuration and what conceptual processes are executed in the validation stage of the blockchain transactions. We are currently in the process of creating conceptual models for additional functionality as it is implemented in HLF, i.e. the blockchain network, organization membership, consortia, identity and private data functionality.

References

1. Nijssen, S., Bollen, P.: The lifecycle of a user transaction in a hyperledger fabric blockchain network part 1: propose and endorse. In: Debruyne, C., Panetto, H., Guédria, W., Bollen, P., Ciuciu, I., Meersman, R. (eds.) OTM 2018. LNCS, vol. 11231, pp. 107–116. Springer, Cham (2019). https://doi.org/10.1007/978-3-030-11683-5_11
2. Nijssen, S., Bollen, P.: The lifecycle of a user transaction in a hyperledger fabric blockchain network part 2: order and validate. In: Debruyne, C., Panetto, H., Guédria, W., Bollen, P., Ciuciu, I., Meersman, R. (eds.) OTM 2018. LNCS, vol. 11231, pp. 150–158. Springer, Cham (2019). https://doi.org/10.1007/978-3-030-11683-5_16
3. Hyperledger-Fabricdocs Documentation. Release master, January 2019
4. Lemmens, I., van de Laar, B., Saton, J., Bulles, J.: How to fulfil regulatory requirements consistently: a semantic-based approach. In: Debruyne, C., et al. (eds.) OTM 2017. LNCS, vol. 10697, pp. 202–211. Springer, Cham (2018). https://doi.org/10.1007/978-3-319-73805-5_21

5. Nijssen, M., Lemmens, I.: Verbalization for business rules and two flavors of verbalization for fact examples. In: Meersman, R., Tari, Z., Herrero, P. (eds.) OTM 2008. LNCS, vol. 5333, pp. 760–769. Springer, Heidelberg (2008). https://doi.org/10.1007/978-3-540-88875-8_100

6. Moberts, R., Nieuwland, R., Janse, Y., Peters, M., Bouwmeester, H., Dieteren, S.: Business object model: a semantic-conceptual basis for transition and optimal business management. In: Ciuciu, I., et al. (eds.) OTM 2015. LNCS, vol. 9416, pp. 245–253. Springer, Cham (2015). https://doi.org/10.1007/978-3-319-26138-6_28

7. Nijssen, S., Piprani, B.: 1975-2015: Lessons Learned with Applying FBM in Professional Practice. In: Ciuciu, I., et al. (eds.) OTM 2015. LNCS, vol. 9416, pp. 266–275. Springer, Cham (2015). https://doi.org/10.1007/978-3-319-26138-6_30

8. Bollen, P.: Enterprise resource planning requirements process: the need for semantic verification. In: Piazolo, F., Felderer, M. (eds.) Innovation and Future of Enterprise Information Systems. LNISO, vol. 4, pp. 53–67. Springer, Heidelberg (2013). https://doi.org/10.1007/978-3-642-37021-2_6

Creating a Space System Ontology Using "Fact Based Modeling" and "Model Driven Development" Principles

Kaiton Buitendijk$^{(\boxtimes)}$ and Carla Arauco Flores

GorillaIT, Arnhem, The Netherlands
kaiton.buitendijk@gorillait.nl
http://www.gorillait.nl

Abstract. In this practical paper we describe our ongoing project of building a candidate skeleton for the new Space System Ontology that is to be used by the space system community; starting from the vision: being able to achieve semantic interoperability instead of focusing on technical interoperability), through our approach: Fact Based Modeling (FBM) and Model Driven Development (MDD) and finally ending with the results: an Object Role Model containing the semantic model of the Space System Ontology. This project is based on the already existing meta-model of Arcadia, a field proven method for model based system engineering. By reverse engineering the UML-based meta-model of a tool supporting the method, we were able to remove the technical HOW's and restore the true conceptual meaning of the meta-model. We will describe the algorithms we used for automatically reverse engineering UML-based meta-models to ORM-models, we will talk about the value of connecting the conceptual model to real-life examples by visualizing, and introduce the process of automatically generating editors in order to verify completeness and correctness by populating the model. We will conclude with general findings while reverse engineering UML-based models and some tips on how to solve typical modeling problems that arises when transforming object oriented artifacts to their semantic equivalents.

Keywords: Ontology · Semantic interoperability · Fact-oriented modeling · ORM · ESA · ECSS · Global conceptual model · Model Driven Development · Model driven architecure · Code generation · Reverse engineering · ECORE · Eclipse

1 Introduction

Developing space systems implies complex activities involving many parties. It requires efficient and effective information exchange during the overall space development and operations life-cycle. According to the European Space Agency (ESA), this can only be achieved by realizing semantic interoperability between all involved parties [1]. ESA stands not alone on this; the space system community is moving towards the definition of a Space System Ontology (SSO) that

© Springer Nature Switzerland AG 2020
C. Debruyne et al. (Eds.): OTM 2019 Workshops, LNCS 11878, pp. 127–138, 2020.
https://doi.org/10.1007/978-3-030-40907-4_13

has the potential to embrace the complete life-cycle of a space system, supporting this interoperability [2]. ESA is currently assessing the possibility to reverse engineer the widely used system engineering methodology Arcadia[1], supported by the tool Capella[2], to provide a conceptual skeleton for the SSO.

2   The Project - A Conceptual Skeleton for the SSO

GorillaIT has been asked by ESA to provide a conceptual skeleton for the Space System Ontology. In this paper we describe our project of building this conceptual skeleton. Both ESA and GorillaIT are big proponents of the Object Role Modeling method for semantic modeling. After years of applying many of the theoretical ideas presented by the Fact Based Modeling community in our daily work, we want to share how we applied those ideas during this project.

3   The Three Fundamental Pillars of This Project

3.1   The Need for Semantic Interoperability

ESA formulated a few fundamental starting points for this project. Firstly, the skeleton for the Space System Ontology should be a semantic conceptual model, focusing on the WHAT (instead of technical HOW). This vision to establish a formalization of the European Cooperation for Space Standardization (ECSS) vision focusing on semantics and semantic interoperability is described in ECSS-E-TM-10-23A [4] and graphically summarized in Fig. 1 on page 2.).

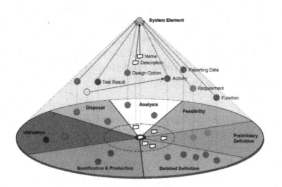

Fig. 1. ECSS-E-ST-10-23 looks at standardizing the information model ensuring the overall consistency of the model through all phases

---

[1] Arcadia. The method. https://www.polarsys.org/capella/arcadia.html.
[2] Capella. The tool. https://www.polarsys.org/capella/.

3.2   The Use of Object Role Modeling

Secondly, Object Role Modeling (ORM) [3], is chosen as the required method to develop a global conceptual data model. ORM is primarily a method for modeling an information system at the conceptual level. The focus of ORM is on data modeling, since the data perspective is the most stable and it provides a formal foundation on which operations can be defined. For correctness, clarity and adaptability, information systems are best specified first at the conceptual level, using concepts and language that people can readily understand. ESA requires that the tool NORMA is used for this project.

3.3   The Reuse of Knowledge, by Reverse Engineering Arcadia

Thirdly, instead of starting from scratch, the work should be based on a reverse engineered conceptual model from the already existing meta-model of Arcadia, a method for model based system engineering that has already been used by the space community for years. This way this project can solely concentrate on solving the semantics and ontology aspects, instead of also having to solve system based engineering difficulties and problems that already have been solved by the Arcadia-team in the past.

4   Introducing: Arcadia, Capella, Ecore and the Meta-model

4.1   Arcadia

Arcadia is a method devoted to systems & architecture engineering. It describes the detailed reasoning to understand the real customer need, define and share the product architecture among all engineering stakeholders and early validate its design and justify it. Five major steps structure the engineering activities, each one dealing with specific engineering issues, grouped by the needs and the solution. The steps describing the understanding part are "Operational analysis" and "System Need analysis". The steps describing the solution are "Logical analysis", "Physical analysis" and "End-Product Breakdown Structure".

4.2   Capella

Capella is the tool supporting the method Arcadia. It provides methodological guidance, intuitive model editing and viewing capabilities for Systems, Software and Hardware Architects. The tool itself is built using the Eclipse Modeling Framework (EMF). From a model specification, EMF provides tools and run-time support to produce a set of Java classes for the model, along with a set of adapter classes that enable viewing and command-based editing of the model, and basic editors[3]. The meta model of Capella is what ESA expects to be a robust foundation for the new Space System Ontology.

---

[3] Eclipse Modeling Framework https://www.eclipse.org/modeling/emf/.

4.3   Ecore and the Capella Meta-model

The meta model of the tool Capella is stored physically in an EMF-file. This core EMF includes a meta model (Ecore) for describing models and run-time support for the models including change notification, persistence support with default serialization and a very efficient reflective API for manipulating EMF Objects generically.

5   The General Approach

The approach for this project is to reuse the knowledge of the Arcadia method by fully and adequately reverse engineering the meta-model of Capella. In general, the steps of the approach are:

– Reuse the existing knowledge by studying the Arcadia method and using the physical meta-model from Capella to automatically convert Ecore to ORM
– Analyze the knowledge by mapping concepts of the meta-model to the theory and by analyzing the tool Capella and consult with Arcadia and Capella-experts
– Model the analyzed knowledge by remodelling non-semantic structures, adding semantics and adding missing constraints.

The project followed this approach and the resulting milestones will be discussed in the following paragraphs.

6   The Results so Far

6.1   Milestone Product 1: A ORM-model Automatically Converted from Ecore

To get a starting model there were two options:

1. start with an empty ORM-model and model fact by fact, object by object what we understood from the Capella-metamodel and manually copying sentences and information, thus filtering information before entering in the ORM-model.
2. or start with blindly automatically copying everything from Ecore to ORM, and cleaning the ORM-Model afterwards.

It was decided to go for the latter option, for the reason that: 1. a tool capable of importing Ecore already existed, 2. the project team was very proficient with ORM and NORMA, 3. the project team had very deep technical knowledge on how to read ORM-files and about the inner working of NORMA, 4. we had an idea how to automatically report progress using ORM and 5. ESA had a strong preference for that option.

The first milestone was an ORM-model that holds all the structure and information of the Arcadia meta-model, without worrying if the imported makes sense for including in a semantic model. This information is stored in multiple Ecore-files and these are used to generate Capella (using EMF). Since Arcadia is an open-source tool, these files are easily found and can be downloaded from the internet[4].

Matt Curland, one of the main developers of NORMA, created a specialized plugin for NORMA that can import Ecore-files into an ORM-file. This tool has the following functionality:

- It converts Ecore-classes to ORM-objects.
- It converts Ecore-attributes to ORM-facts with correct mandatoriness and correct uniqueness constraints.
- It converts Ecore-relationships to ORM-facts with correct mandatoriness and correct uniqueness constraints.
- It converts all Ecore-properties to ORM-custom-attributes, so that all knowledge will be converted in the ORM-model.
- It converts Ecore typing hierarchies (supertype/subtype) into ORM equivalents.

Using this tool, the structure of Capella was imported into an ORM-model. After dragging elements to diagrams to visualize what was imported, it could immediately be recognized that it looked very different compared to manually made ORM models. Examples are cryptic sentences and object names, only binary fact-types, no objectified fact-types, no uniqueness constraints spanning multiple roles and enormous super-type/sub-type structures.

6.2   Milestone Product 2: Identifying Main Challenges of What Was Imported

The result of using the Ecore-importer was an ORM model with approximately 1200 facts. The first task was to identify the main challenges.

Challenge 1: Cryptic Imported Fact Names. While importing, the Ecore-importer uses an algorithm to name all facts and provide basic fact-sentences. Most of the time it concatenates class names together with attribute names, or in case of a reference, it concatenates a class name together with the reference name and with the referenced class name. The quality of the output is highly dependent of the naming by the original designers of the Ecore-metamodel. Names were not self-explanatory and because of this understanding the intended meaning of the meta-model was difficult.

Challenge 2: Huge Inheritance Structures. One challenge was the huge super-type/sub-typing structure. As an example, the class "Operational analysis" had an inheritance structure of 28 classes. This inheritance structure is common to most (close to 90%) classes we imported from Ecore. Many of the class names were not self-explanatory. Many sub classes also had common super types for unknown reasons, which made understanding the model very difficult.

---

[4] https://git.polarsys.org/c/capella/capella.git/.

Challenge 3: Understanding the General Structure. Normally, when looking at a ORM-diagram, it is easy to guess the general structure of the model by recognizing main concepts and from there follow the structure to the more detailed facts. Looking at the imported model, no easy starting points could be found and therefore understanding the structure was difficult.

6.3   Milestone Product 3: Mapping the Meta-model to Capella-Theory

The Information Sources. Having identified the major challenges to tackle, the next task was to understand the model. The Arcadia method and the tool Capella are very detailed described in books and websites [5] [6] [7] [8]. Next to that a Capella expert was consulted.

Our Modeling Approach in NORMA. Our starting point for our ORM skeleton was an ORM-model with lots of elements imported, but without any diagrams. The following modeling approach was used in NORMA;

- understand the meaning of the elements before dragging ORM-elements into the diagram.
- create a ORM-diagram for the big overview. With only the main concepts and facts connecting those main entities.
- create an ORM-diagram per Arcadia-perspective.
- add semantics by improving sentences of the dragged facts.
- add or improve constraints, such as uniqueness and mandatory.

Finding the Starting Points. Starting from the theory, Arcadia is grouped in 5 different perspectives, each concerning a different phase of the life-cycle with system based engineering. These are: Operational Analysis, System Analysis, Logical Architecture, Physical Architecture and End-Product Breakdown Structure Architecture. Objects corresponding to these perspectives could be found in the ORM-model. Using these five different root entities as starting points, it was easier to untangle the meaning of the meta-model.

Grouping All Entities by the Corresponding Arcadia Perspectives. The next step was to group all the imported ORM-entities to their containing perspectives. The theory of Arcadia described the main concepts. Figure 2 on page 7 shows, as an example, the entities of the Operational Analysis-perspective. Those tables are also available for the other perspectives and can be freely found on the internet[9].

---

[5] https://www.elsevier.com/books/model-based-system-and-architecture-engineering-with-the-arcadia-method/voirin/978-1-78548-169-7.

[6] https://www.elsevier.com/books/systems-architecture-modeling-with-the-arcadia-method/roques/978-1-78548-168-0.

[7] https://www.polarsys.org/capella/arcadia.html.

[8] https://www.polarsys.org/capella/index.html.

[9] https://www.polarsys.org/capella/resources/Datasheet_Arcadia.pdf.

With this information the main entities and structure of the meta-model of Arcadia could be recognized, resulting in a ORM-diagram with a first version of the skeleton of our project.

Connecting the First Version of the Skeleton Visually to the Theory. We realized that to make an ontology successful, it has to be used and understood by the users. We already experienced the difficulties in connecting the Arcadia-theory

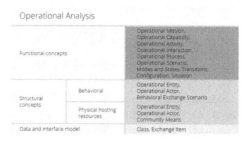

Fig. 2. The main concepts of the perspective Operational Analysis as described in the theory of Arcadia.

to the meta-model, and even after getting familiar with the theory and meta-model, it was difficult to explain and share our knowledge with the stakeholders. For that reason a big-picture was created, visually connecting the Arcadia-theory with the ORM-model.

This picture consisted of five horizontal lanes, one per Arcadia perspective, starting at the top with "Operational Analysis" and ending at the bottom with "EPBS". These lanes were divided vertically in columns. The first column consisted of the graphical figure used on the Arcadia website to describe the five different perspectives[10]. The second and third column described the main Arcadia-concepts per perspective, again using graphical material found on the website of Arcadia. The last column contained the ORM-model.

By horizontally dividing all the columns people could easily recognize which Arcadia entities belong to which perspective and how they are called and relate to each other and how the were modelled in the ORM-model.

Using Posters to Improve Communication and Understanding. The big picture was printed out as a big poster. Hanging it on the wall it really invited all stakeholders to start discussing about it. The visual connection from the ORM-elements to the theory improved communication and understanding compared to just having the ORM-model on a computer-screen together with the Arcadia-books alongside. For that reason it was decided to create one poster per perspective. Each poster showed the meta-model of the perspective in ORM. Next to that, modeling examples in Capella were included, next to the corresponding facts in ORM. That way, it made understanding the meaning and use of every ORM-element easier.

In Fig. 3, a small part of the poster of the perspective Operational Analysis is shown. It shows a small part of the meta-model; an "Operational Activity" can be a parent of an other "Operational Activity". Just reading the ORM-model, it may be difficult to understand what the fact is trying to express,

---

[10] https://www.polarsys.org/capella/arcadia.html.

Fig. 3. An ORM-fact type expressing that an "Operational Activity" can be a parent of an other "Operational Activity"

but with a corresponding example of an Arcadia-model we see it is easier to understand. At the end we created all five posters, with all of the main fact-types in the ORM-model included, accompanied with a corresponding example of an Arcadia-model.

6.4   Milestone Product 3: A Clean ORM-Model

Having the big skeleton in place, we started with cleaning the ORM-model.

First sentences were added to the facts that were understood by mapping it to the Arcadia-theory. In case the imported names or the theory did not help us, the Capella-expert was consulted for the meaning of the facts and for suggestions for naming.

Secondly, the huge inheritance structures had to be solved. All the elements in the imported ORM-model inherit from a concept called Element. Sometimes a class inherited from numerous other classes, for which no reason could be found in the Arcadia theory. After consulting the Arcadia-expert it was concluded that many of those classes were introduced solely for technical reasons; without those classes, the Capella-tool could not be programmed (it uses those classes to draw, to facilitate programming or to group functionality) and therefore those technical classes were removed from the model.

Thirdly, there were imported structures that could be remodeled more elegantly in ORM. As an example, the Arcadia-theory indicates the fact that an "Operational Entity" involves an "Entity", what sounds as a simple fact that can easily expressed in ORM. The imported structure for that fact looked very different as shown in Fig. 4 on page 9.

After consulting with the Capella-experts, who suggested that the structure did not have any semantic meaning, it was decided to model it like Fig. 5 on page 9.

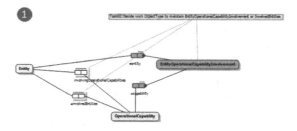

Fig. 4. Simple according to the theory, but complicated in Ecore meta-model

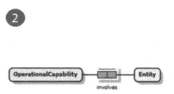

Fig. 5. After consulting the experts, it was modeled in a much simpler way

Establishing Modeling Rules. While reverse engineering and remodeling it occurred often that certain structures found in the reverse engineered structure (in this case Ecore) could not be understood. The big pitfall was to spend hours on finding out and discussing about why the original designers structured it like that. To prevent that we used the following steps to make modeling decisions:

1. Use the reverse engineered structure as a base. In this case: Ecore reversed engineered with the Ecore-importer.
2. If we cannot understand the reason why it is structured like it is reversed engineered, we try to find this reason by understanding the theory (by reading books & literature, consulting experts).
3. If we cannot find the reason of the structure in theory we focus on understanding the reason by investigating the tool Capella.
4. If we cannot find the reason of the structure by investigating Tool or Theory, we just look at what is expressed semantically/functionally and we model the most simple way to express this in ORM.

6.5   Milestone Product 4: An Automatic Way to Report Progress Reverse Engineering Ecore to ORM

Having imported almost 1200 facts from Ecore to ORM, we had to come up with a way to report progress. The people that created the Ecore meta-model obviously thought a lot about the structure and therefore we wanted to be able to report what happened with every imported fact; keep it (with reference to ORM-element), remodel it (with reference to ORM-element) or delete it (with a reason why). To do that manually is prone to errors (and takes lots of time) and therefore a way to automate this process had to be created.

For that purpose, a program, based on Acceleo[11], was created that could generate Excel-reports, reporting all the entities, attributes and references. Essential for the approach was that every row, for tracking reasons, was automatically given a unique identifier. Next, an extended attribute was added, called "ExcelUniqueId" to our Norma-model. Extended attributes is a functionally provided by Norma. It gives the modeler the functionality of adding extra properties on ORM-elements (such as facts, objects and constraints). Every time the modeler modeled an element of the Ecore-model in ORM, this extended attribute was filled in, referring back to the original row in the Excel-report. Lastly, a program was created that could read our ORM-file, read the excel-report and for every row in excel find the corresponding ORM-element (by looking for the value of the extended attribute "ExcelUniqueId". In case the program could not find a corresponding ORM-element OR a reason for deletion (typed by the modeler in the excel-sheet) it reported for that element that it was still "to do". That way, it is possible to fully trace back what happened with all the information in the original Ecore-file and report the progress of the project (Fig. 6).

Big Reduction of Facts Reported. After modeling and being able to report we found an interesting outcome. As described earlier, a big part of the structure was modeled for technical reasons and did not have any semantic value or could be remodeled more elegantly. After deleting and remodeling, the number of facts reduced drastically. A reduction of almost 50%.

A	B	C	D	E
1		No. of facts		
2 Ecore-model	Modeled	Delete	Total	% Done
3 Capability	34	3	37	100
4 Deployment	7	0	7	100
5 Trace	18	0	18	100
6 Project management	25	1	26	100
7 requirement	17	5	22	100

Fig. 6. An example automatically-generated Excel-report by combining ORM-models with Excel-sheet.

6.6   Milestone Product 5: An ORM Model with Constraints Added

Ecore supports various ways to check models and prevent errors. Nevertheless, many rules on a typical meta model can not be enforced just by using Ecore-functionality. EMF therefore provides an architecture for attaching rules written Java-code to the Ecore-model. The programmers of the tool Capella used this functionality to write hundreds of constraints. We found out that a lot of the constraints that were programmed in Java could be expressed elegantly using normal ORM-constructs. As an example, the Capella programmers had to enforce a rule that a "Functional Chain Involvement" should either involve a Function or a Functional Exchange. The constraint is not possible to enforce using Ecore and therefore they created a Java-function consisting of tens of lines of code. In Fig. 7 on page 11 is shown how we added this constraint in the ORM-model.

---

[11] https://www.eclipse.org/acceleo/.

7   Conclusions

At the time of writing, this is still an ongoing project.

Summarizing our achievements until now:

- A first skeleton of the Space System Ontology, including all the perspectives of Arcadia.
- Using automatic converting, we are sure we included all information from the Capella meta-model Ecore-models.
- Using automatic reporting, we know that every element in the original meta-model has been covered by our modeling process.
- We found a way to visually connect the theory of the meta-model with the ORM-model by making posters.
- We found that with reversing Ecore, at least for this project, the amount of facts reduced with almost 50% without losing semantic value.
- We found out that many constraints that conventionally have to be programmed, can be elegantly modeled in ORM.

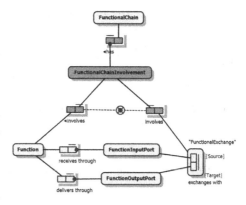

For each FunctionalChainInvolvement, **exactly one of the following holds:**
that FunctionalChainInvolvement involves **some** FunctionalExchange;
that FunctionalChainInvolvement involves **some** Function.

Fig. 7. A constraint that had to be programmed in tens of lines of Java code originally, but could be easily modeled using ORM.

8   The Road Ahead

8.1   Validation by Examples

Right now we are in the phase of validating the meta-model for correctness and completeness. It is already foreseen that it is difficult to be sure if the model is correct and complete without actually populating it with concrete examples. The next concrete steps are therefore:

- Find real world examples for populating the first version of the Space System ontology. Take typical off-the-shelve-components that are relevant to the space system industry and try to populate the meta model.
- Validate if the model is correct (the structure of the meta-model can hold semantically the needed information).
- Validate if the model is complete (all information needed to describe the component can be semantically described using the provided semantics of the ORM-model).

8.2   Generate Application with Editor-Functionality for the Space System Ontology

GorillaIT has years of experience in automatically generating working software by using Model Driven Development methods. We do that by transforming ORM models into working applications. Our vision on application generation corresponds with that of the ESA. Currently, we are in the process of automatically converting the ORM model of the skeleton in a working application supplying basis editor-functionality to populate the model. Next to that, We will create a list of examples and iteratively we will populate the generated application with all the data of the examples. In case the model is not correct or not complete, we re-analyze the example, adapt the model, regenerate the application and try to populate the application again. We will repeat this process until the model is correct and complete.

Acknowledgements. We thank ESA (Serge Valera and Quirien Wijnands) for asking us for this project. Thanks to Gerald Garcia for helping us with the Capella, Ecore and Arcadia.

References

1. Lemmens, I., Sgaramella, F., Valera, S.: Development of tooling to support fact-oriented modeling at ESA. In: Meersman, R., Herrero, P., Dillon, T. (eds.) OTM 2009. LNCS, vol. 5872, pp. 714–722. Springer, Heidelberg (2009). https://doi.org/10.1007/978-3-642-05290-3_87
2. Garcia, G.: Foreword Book. ESA-GorillaIT, Arnhem (2019)
3. Halpin, T., Microsoft Corporation: Object role modeling. In: Bernus, P., Mertins, K., Schmidt, G. (eds.) Handbook on Architectures of Information Systems, ch. 4. Springer, Berlin (1998)
4. Valera, S.: ECSS, ECSS-E-TM-10-23A: Space Engineering – Space system data Repository, Noordwijk, The Netherlands (2011)

Industry Case Studies Program 2019 – Industry Day (ICSP 2019)

Industry Case Studies Program PC Chairs Message

Cloud computing, service-oriented architecture, business process modelling, enterprise architecture, enterprise integration, semantic interoperability—what is an enterprise systems administrator to do with the constant stream of industry hype surrounding him, constantly bathing him with (apparently) new ideas and new "technologies"? It is nearly impossible, and the academic literature does not help solving the problem, with hyped "technologies" catching on in the academic world just as easily as the industrial world. The most unfortunate thing is that these technologies are actually useful, and the press hype only hides that value. What the enterprise information manager really cares about is integrated, interoperable infrastructures, industrial IoT, that support interoperable information systems, so he can deliver valuable information to management in time to make correct decisions about the use and delivery of enterprise resources, whether those are raw materials for manufacturing, people to carry out key business processes, or the management of shipping choices for correct delivery to customers.

The OTM conference series have established itself as a major international forum for exchanging ideas and results on scientific research for practitioners in fields such as computer supported cooperative work, middleware, Internet/Web data management, electronic commerce, workflow management, knowledge flow, agent technologies and software architectures, Cyber Physical Systems and IoT, to name a few. The recent popularity and interest in service-oriented architectures & domains require capabilities for on-demand composition of services. These emerging technologies represent a significant need for highly interoperable systems.

As a part of OnTheMove 2019, the Industry Case Studies Program on "Industry Applications and Standard initiatives for Cooperative Information Systems - The evolving role of Cyber Physical Systems in Industry 4.0 implementation", supported by OMG, IIC (Industrial Internet Consortium), IFAC TC 5.3 "Enterprise Integration and Networking" and the SIG INTEROP Grande-Région, emphasized Research/Industry cooperation on these future trends. The focus of the program is on a discussion of ideas where research areas address interoperable information systems and infrastructure. Three short papers have been presented, focusing on industry leaders, standardization initiatives, European and international projects consortiums and discussing how projects within their organizations addressed software, systems and architecture interoperability. Each paper has been reviewed by an international Programme Committee composed of representatives of Academia, Industry and Standardisation initiatives. We thank them for their dedication and interest.

We hope that you find this industry-focused part of the program valuable as feedback from industry practitioners, and we thank the authors for the time and effort taken to contribute to the program.

Wided Guédria
Hervé Panetto
Gash Bhullar
The OTM Industry Case Studies Program Chairs

Translating a Legacy Stack to Microservices Using a Modernization Facade with Performance Optimization for Container Deployments

Prabal Mahanta and Suchin Chouta[✉]

SAP Labs Pvt. Ltd., Bangalore, India
{p.mahanta, suchin.chouta}@sap.com

Abstract. We often find it challenging to translate a legacy system when the software business is critical. Adding to the misery of technical debt is the "Broken Window" concept which adds more complexity in exercising dynamic context resolutions for independent services alongside governance and data management. This often leads to a maze of disoriented services with high interdependency. To seriously adopt "Operate what you Build" phenomena, we need a granular facade approach to understand the business requirement and translate it to the architectural operators. The paper tries to provide an approach to establish platform independent interfaces, bounded domain contexts, eliminating non-critical legacy components and incremental quality aware methods to translate a legacy system to microservices. Along with the architectural objects, the paper will also present granular level of performance management of the translated application to consider factors like - system, container, network and application service itself.

Keywords: Microservice · Performance · Facade · Modernization · Containers

1 Introduction

The only constant in Software engineering is "evolution". As we evolve our business process, the software systems become more and more complex calling for intelligent implementations and to scale the scenarios we need to define software components as independent units which offers services via a defined set of interfaces [1].

When we design an architecture, we need to adhere to commonly used design guidelines. All of which will have its own advantages and disadvantages so we would need to assess them during the development cycle to overcome challenges while scaling our solutions.

We also see that automating the design phase will require an effort from the perspective of incorporating the design patterns for setting up the structure of an architecture and structural patterns for the overall application, but this requires a strong framework for processing and analysing the performance benefits from identified implementations.

© Springer Nature Switzerland AG 2020
C. Debruyne et al. (Eds.): OTM 2019 Workshops, LNCS 11878, pp. 143–154, 2020.
https://doi.org/10.1007/978-3-030-40907-4_14

Challenge in product development currently is the delivery strategy and based on which we need to design the architecture with the perspective of scale and extension. In case of products being designed ground up, it is comparatively easier than monoliths being translated using modernization facades. In designing such systems or creating a migration strategy with refactoring, it is critical that we take into consideration the business requirements along with the operational costs.

Redefining or transformation of technology paradigm requires people, business and technology reliability be considered also dwell upon the future aspects. For e.g. – there are instances where we may need to design microservices but need not necessarily use container technology for deployment. Similarly, we may design a business system, but it is not important to push machine learning cases for each of the business processes (Fig. 1).

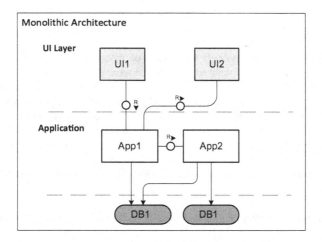

Fig. 1. Monolithic architecture based application

With the translations, we need to consider the fact that software would have technical debt and design issues with lots of dead code (Fig. 2).

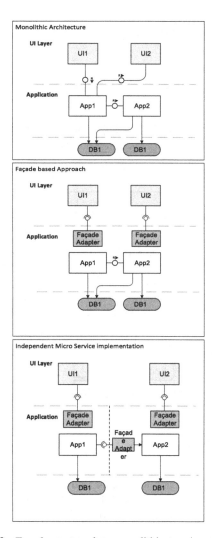

Fig. 2. Facades to translate monolithic to microservice

Refactoring monolithic systems are difficult, but we need to start small with small sections where we would need to disintegrate the overall architecture into self-autonomous microservices which can run independently [2] (Fig. 3).

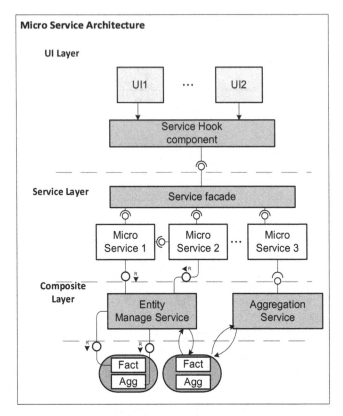

Fig. 3. Translations for monolithic applications into microservices are identified and implemented

We try to provide an approach to observe and translate a legacy to a modernized architecture. The section will cover the drawbacks of doing such translations also how we need to constantly optimize our architectures.

2 Architecture Analysis Framework

With the ongoing demand of having customized features for meeting business needs, we need to deep dive into implementation details. It is seen that if we ignore few of the corner cases, it becomes impossible to implement the optimizations later in the life-cycle of product development. The perception in general is that if we ignore the technical details, the project details are left ignored throughout the product lifecycle leading to a broken window effect.

Aligning to programming practices, this ignorance of not dwelling deep into details of the architecture will also add to poor design and will reflect it on organization when the product is released. There is a constant need to monitor and improve our architecture based on key parameters like performance and scalability.

Such monitoring and analysis activity will provide a good notion of where the broken windows are in the product artefact and the landscape [3]. This will help in determining and drilling down to the core requirements and coming up with strategies to perform preventive but scalable maintenance.

Now to address any transformation of monolith, we need to define methods and tools for migrating legacy applications to cloud development. The main reason for the requirement of transformation is because legacy systems are not agile enough to incorporate new features fast enough to meet the market needs. In some cases, it is difficult to directly migrate the architectures to microservices so there we need to focus predominantly on the aspect of business requirement. Business scenarios which would demand the integration between the newly designed service. In such architecture pattern implementation, we often have the issue of technical debt that hinders such integration scenarios.

Scenarios vary from business to technical, which may require either a migration from on premise to cloud only to have an integration scenario enabled or consistency of outcomes from orchestration point of view between cloud solutions and on premise. Modularity, Elasticity and Portability becomes critical in arriving at a solution.

Let us summarize the requirements from point of view of a developer and an architect which are –

a. Methodology to analyze based on scenario requirement
b. Approach to modernize based on evaluation

Based on the scenario requirement, we may also need to design Composite Microservices where services are independent which also contains business logic, inter service communication, build the integration to legacy, external services and shared DB etc. If we consider IOT based business scenarios, we need to develop and deploy special services which offers routing, versioning security layer, API management capabilities such as monetization, spike arrest etc.

Framework for such evaluation would also require analysis in cases where Microservices allow building product suite instead of projects. The same service can be reused in more than one process or over different business groups.

The ability of scale up and down is a key characteristic of microservices which helps in abstracting the underlying infrastructure and dependencies from a develop alongside enabling easy integration and smooth deployments.

Next comes the important task of assessments which includes analysis and impact of business processes on systems, architectures and dependencies. Structural and Flow analysis and mapping of abstracted business data on control flow of the graph edges [4].

Overall standardization of reliable and adaptable systems is useful for rationalizing, alignment and modularizing the application in focus. Based on the evaluation there are extractions which can then be migrated to a specific transformation scenario [5].

After the transformation scenario is processed, we would have a decomposed system with artefacts representing either of the following:

a. Function Modules
b. Inter Function Calls
c. Data relationships

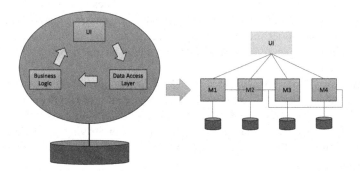

Fig. 4. Translation of core monolith into autonomous services

The framework that we worked on requires requirements and business scenarios be designed in terms of three key factors such as – Producer (SP), Broker (SB) and Consumer (SC). Once your scenarios are identified then individual costs such as Use case (UC), Design (DC), Implementation (IC), Process (PC) and Development (DV) are determined (Fig. 4).

Before we move into the cost discussion let us visualize the steps that required for modernization (Fig. 5).

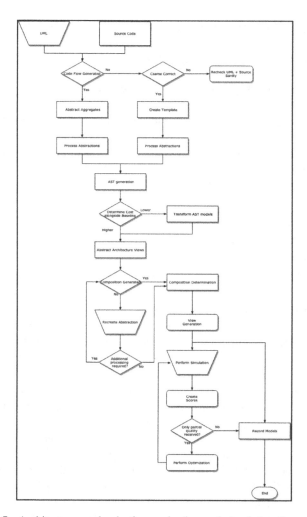

Fig. 5. Architecture modernization evaluation and simulation framework

The total costs are then calculated using the following matrix (Fig. 6):

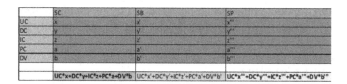

	SC	SB	SP
UC	x	x'	x'''
DC	y	y'	y'''
IC	z	z'	z'''
PC	a	a'	a'''
DV	b	b'	b'''
	UC*x+DC*y+IC*z+PC*a+DV*b	UC*x'+DC*y'+IC*z'+PC*a'+DV*b'	UC*x'''+DC*y'''+IC*z'''+PC*a'''+DV*b'''

Fig. 6. Calculation matrix for identification of service requirement actor

As intuitive it is, we can determine the cost of the producer, broker, consumer but the most of cost would determine the use case requirements and the key actor the service would play in the overall product. For e.g. – If SC > SB > SP, then the service re-engineering is required to develop consumers.

Following up on the simulations, there are determination requirement for functional and data dependencies. These simulations require benchmarks and for achieving benchmarks we use the traditional c packages for evaluating performance of code flows and instrument the flows to achieve near 0 performance within the function modules. The components are determined by producing and simulating errors to determine whether we have function modules. Functional dependencies where the component uses other parts of the system in order to carry out its functionality or other parts of the system use the components or parts of them. As per the traditional code flow analysis, the following aspects are covered as part of abstractions. This is also simulated across the business scenarios based on the following parameters [6] -

a. Data dictionary
b. Metrics at class, and function level
c. Invocation tree
d. Cross reference objects
e. Unused functions and objects

While we handle legacy systems, we also need to optimize sql queries and for database optimizations we would like to create predefined assumption to value add using the in-memory techniques. Algorithms like Adjacency list, Path enumeration, Nested sets, Transitive closure are the generic methods to exploit the problem of hierarchical data traversal. When we explore the sql domain, then we can find that direct algorithms like Warshall's Algorithm [7] and Warren's algorithm [8] are explored where we have to choose the optimal processing order but with the study by Agarwal et al. [9] this mode of execution can be excluded and there are also multiple studies on optimization of set based recursive queries by Ordonez [10].

The room for improvement exists using SQL recursion in columnar database where there is limited work done including Tinnefeld et al., where they propose that the data representation is with pre order and post order encoding [11] which proposes a data model different from parent child data representation.

For each service, which we would analyze for simulation and transformation from an existing legacy system, we cover interface analysis and vulnerability with open-source open-standards. Hence for an overall product design or a legacy architecture we analyze the dependency between the user interface classes or objects with predefined translations of services, interlinked services and dead code dependency. Based on which we apply UI module refactoring, but we don't try to simulate UI interfaces with actions which is still part of the continued work that we are currently pursuing.

3   Results and Conclusion

We took various complex architectures for evaluation with the intention to reconstruct legacy built-in system to translate into functional artefacts with methods to conjugate the performance of the translation with that of the previous system (Fig. 7).

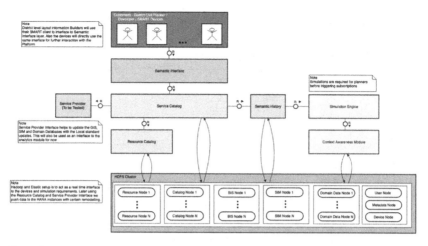

Fig. 7. Refactored TAM representation of legacy system based in SmartCity (demo) application

For a specific scenario, we were able to modernize the depth of implementation from the point of view of discovery of devices from edge systems.

In this case we took a specific simulated scenario and maintained cost for developing performance points within the code flows to optimize the efficiency of handling data and managing quality (Fig. 8).

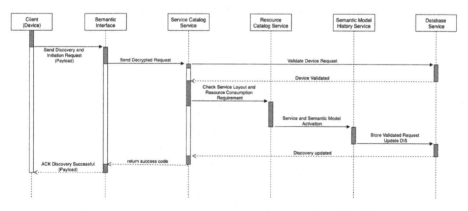

Fig. 8. Sequence diagram of specific service post modernization which achieved 70% performance boost

The specific challenge that we faced was when we had to simulate data. The fundamental problem in uncontrolled generation of data is to manage them (Fig. 9).

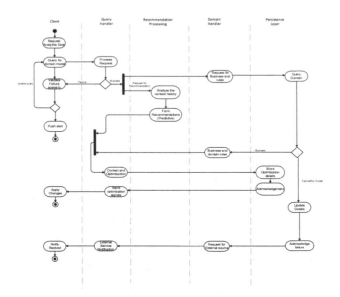

Fig. 9. Activity diagram of modernized legacy system.

The process involved in the generation of data is required to be parameterized or logged to prevent any loss of information during the analysis phase. The next in the cycle comes to unification of the data for both input and output and ease the process of managing them in a more compressed format as well as design more robust tools around the data structure (Fig. 10).

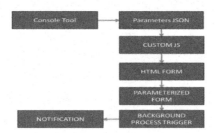

Fig. 10. Incorporating in the overall flow with data generation optimizations

Using the above logical flow, the user experience becomes simplified and researchers can perform activity runs for getting their readings for any experiment and are not required to monitor as the system provides the mechanism of notification for confirmation of the experiment runs.

The user data for runs in terms of logs and the output results are stored in a column store and single structure data structure holds the output files in in-memory so that once the next tool runs the execution can progress faster and using the shared memory the runs are made efficient. The in-memory data structure for logs also makes it possible to query to the point of failure faster and the management of data is thus made easier as compression on columnar store tables are more effective. If we try to aggregate the usability aspects that will be helpful for a new user in a domain with complex and cluster of tools, then we can serve the experience better in a manner that saves a researcher's time and effort. For critical simulation of data flow optimizations, we used a hardware configuration of 1 TB RAM and 40-core processor on a top Sensor company data where there were 6 levels with input sizes varying from 250k to 1 million records and output size varying from 1000 to 10000 for each input size.

The set based hierarchy traversal involves queries of the form where R and T can be considered as tables with j and i rows respectively [12]:

$$R = R \ U \ (R \bowtie T)$$

The result of $R \bowtie T$ gets added to R itself. Since R is joined once with T recursion is linear. Table R is joined with T based on some comparison between R:j and T:i. [10]. In this paper equi-join (R: j = T:i) predicate is considered. The number of iteration passes would be same as the navigation level (λ). Hence the execution time T can be represented as:

$$T \alpha \lambda$$

Translations are critical but we also need to assess if the activities are cost effective too. Micro service architecture is described as elastic, resilient, composable, minimal, and complete, modernization help to build performant solution services are small, fine granular to perform a single functionality. Leverage different programming languages based on the operations performed by services, which is key point for performance improvement with modernization Taking our research forward to identify ML techniques which can assist in determination of translation points in an architecture along with performance optimizations. The workflow will also be evaluated in dynamic environment where Machine Learning and Artificial Intelligence based Applications will also be considered for performance translations in terms of algorithm recommendations.

References

1. Kiviluoma, K., Koskinen, J., Mikkonen, T.: Run-time monitoring of behavioral profiles with aspects. In: Koskimies, K., Kuzniarz, L., Nummenmaa, J., Zhang, Z. (eds.) Proceedings of the NWUML 2005: The 3rd Nordic Workshop on UML and Software Modeling, Tampere, Finland, 29–31 August 2005 (2005)
2. Carrasco, A., van Bladel, B., Demeyer, S.: Migrating towards microservices: migration and architecture smells. In: Proceedings of the 2nd International Workshop on Refactoring. ACM (2018)
3. Welsh, B.C., Braga, A.A., Bruinsma, G.J.N.: Reimagining broken windows: from theory to policy. J. Res. Crime Delinq. **52**(4), 447–463 (2015)

4. O'Brien, L., Smith, D., Lewis, G.: Supporting migration to services using software architecture reconstruction. In: 13th IEEE International Workshop on Software Technology and Engineering Practice (STEP 2005). IEEE (2005)
5. Arcelli, F., Tosi, C., Zanoni, M.: Can design pattern detection be useful for legacy system migration towards SOA? In: Proceedings of the 2nd International Workshop on Systems Development in SOA Environments. ACM (2008)
6. Ulrich, W.: A status on OMG architecture-driven modernization task force. In: Proceedings EDOC Workshop on Model-Driven Evolution of Legacy Systems (MELS). IEEE Computer Society Digital Library (2004)
7. Papadimitriou, C., Sideri, M.: On the Floyd-Warshall algorithm for logic programs. J. Logic Program. **41**(1), 129–137 (1999)
8. Drozdek's, A.: Data Structures and Algorithms in C++, p. 173. PWS Publishing, Boston (1996)
9. Agrawal, R., Jagadish, H.V.: Multiprocessor transitive closure algorithms. In: Proceedings of the International Symposium on Databases in Parallel and Distributed Systems, pp. 56–66. December 1988. ACM SIGMOD Record, December 1991
10. Ordonez, C.: Optimization of linear recursive queries in SQL. IEEE Transactions on knowledge and Data Engineering **22**(2), 264–277 (2009)
11. Tinnefeld, C., Wagner, B., Plattner, H.: Operating on Hierarchical Enterprise Data in an In-Memory Column Store (2012)
12. Saad, Y., Suchomel, B.: ARMS: An algebraic recursive multilevel solver for general sparse linear systems. Numer. Linear Algebra Appl. **9**(5), 359–378 (2002)

A Hybrid Approach to Insightful Business Impacts

Prabal Mahanta and Abdul-Gafoor Mohamed[(✉)]

SAP Labs Pvt. Ltd., Bangalore, India
{p.mahanta, abdul-gafoor.mohamed}@sap.com

Abstract. Organizations often end up with wasted space when handling datasets generated as code-application logs. Every dataset be it semi-structured, unstructured is monitored and insights are driven be it predictive, prescriptive or descriptive.

Now we often replicate data to an application space for analysis and these datasets are often cause a critical problem which is not cost effective. Using this paper we try to evaluate cost effective ways of doing decentralised in-situ and in-transit data analysis with the objective of providing business impact insights.

We also discuss techniques for queue management, scenario based hypothesis for various business requirements and the approach to achieve cost effective analysis mechanisms. Based on the scenarios, we also try to bring in the importance of the in-situ techniques as data movement and storage is itself energy hungry problem when it comes to simulation and analytics.

Keywords: Data analytics · Data movement · In-situ · In-transit · Insights · Intelligence

1 Introduction

1.1 Journey of Data in Business Domains

For any business domain, the journey of data starts with the connected sources, disparate sources, creating the variety of data. With the business transactions, grows the depth of the data creating the volume of data. As the business starts to grow, additional hands lead to inconsistencies contributing to variations in the data. By the time data reaches the business users for analyses the complexity would have increased multi-fold, creating data cleansing needs and raising questions about the data quality. In summary, the data created or arrived at via multiple channels needs to be transformed into providing real business values efficiently to nurture insights [1].

From digitization of data at an earlier state to connected device data to semantic web linked data, evolution of data has been impressive but in effect, the methods used to provide the end to end process overview has been overwhelming and as stated above about effectiveness and efficiency, there has been a drift [2]. This drift is due to poor understanding of the data culture leading to creation of multiple data lakes and hence redundancy of business transactional data as well as master data [3].

© Springer Nature Switzerland AG 2020
C. Debruyne et al. (Eds.): OTM 2019 Workshops, LNCS 11878, pp. 155–160, 2020.
https://doi.org/10.1007/978-3-030-40907-4_15

With the expansion of domains in business space, the requirement of handling data, managing data, curation of insights from the data for a productive business impact becomes critical. When we discuss about areas like supply chain, inter-net of things, semantic web applications, genomics, we see that variety and depth of data becomes a grey area for investigations based on a centralized manner of analysis [4].

1.2   In-situ and In-transit Processing

The late nineties saw many corporations in the industry adopt software methodologies. In the context of Agile methodologies, I/O (input-output) calls were seldom a constraint for data scientists. However, I/O is crucial to warrant optimizations when it comes to data analysis. Data sources should be extremely accessible for discovering, exploring and transforming data using the discovered data relationships. Data analysis and Data curation are prime focus areas from the data scientist's perspective that lead to successful business strategies [5]. Such pivotal factors help the analysts simulate the semantic interaction of data and record not only outcomes but also the reasoning and factors influencing those outcomes. It then becomes a simpler task to build or manipulate visualizations automatically using machine learning methods [6].

A key innovation that fits into the grand scheme of things is this – To visualize a complete end-to-end process that involves complex data processing and analytics, with a potential to use Machine Learning in arriving at an outcome of an Intelligence Based Visualization [7]. This is the need of the hour due to data proliferation at many organizations worldwide.

After the plateauing of the data warehouses in the modern data world, we observe that diversity [8] of the data presents a challenge in operationalizing a data model without performance bottlenecks, for both structured and unstructured [9]. For data scientists to tackle performance out of the box, a hybrid approach towards schema and table management should be adopted while also pursuing the best of both worlds for data processing – 'in-situ' and 'in-transit' [10].

The overall analysis process should include conceptualization, operationalization and measurement with semantic propagation studies, facilitating the introduction of Artificial Intelligence in augmenting data pipelines. The expected outcome of this analysis will be in the form of recommendations and also to find optimal solutions for specific business problems.

Our evaluation of the performance optimizations using the hybrid approach for in-situ and in-transit have surfaced issues with large scale adoption of data lakes [11]. Many organizations jumped on the bandwagon of data lakes over the last decade in trying to address data challenges within their enterprises, but they have mushroomed given rise to different challenges such as:

- Unorganized data spanning across several repositories (data chaos) [3]
- Lacking a pro-active approach and an ability to seek predictive outcomes [12]
- Very little value in mining the data lakes for analysis [13]

Adopting hybrid analytics not only addresses the above drawbacks but also provides a scalable model to the overall solution in a cloud platform. The hybrid approach allows asynchronous calls back and forth between data sources, encouraging node sharing for computation and analytics [14]. This approach also facilitates real-time decision making, which on-the-fly contributes to positive business outcomes (Fig. 1).

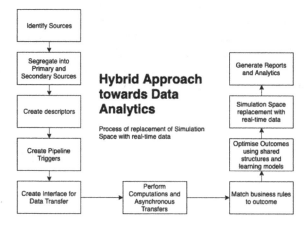

Fig. 1. A hybrid approach to replace simulated space to allow in-situ and in-transit data analysis

2 Managing the Right Data Scenarios

Big Data is not only characterized by certain data attributes – volume, variety, velocity, veracity, but also extends to certain dimensions – legal, economic, organizational, and technological. While tackling any *big data* scenario, the reliance on certain business rules defined by product experts and subject matter experts help immensely in streamlining the data economics for both the producers and consumers [15].

With the ever-changing business requirements, we need evolving approaches to handle infrastructure and data issues. Here we need to address the proposition of creating and managing traceable scientific data over the process lifecycle. This enables better infrastructure mapping, provisioning and component designs thereby addressing the quality of the overall process, resulting in outcomes that are better perceived.

In each scenario, it is imperative to automate *master data management* based on the transaction semantics, processed by the relevant business/research activity. Once we address the automation aspect, we can use the user semantics to handle data in a variety of formats to add real value to data outcomes with corresponding visualizations.

For an analyst, it is key to pick the right algorithm for the sake of efficiency. It is also important to keep in mind space paradigm while addressing the problem of manifesting a business process. Not only is the algorithm important to generate specific outcomes, but we also need to ensure that we operationalize the product environments.

Next, we need to address scalability. In a typical tractable problem, the running time in linear scale can take up to 4×10^6 computations for a problem size of 1500/s and also this can ramp up to 10x optimizations. The numbers for computation handling ability and optimizations decrease for any algorithm as the complexity of data and problem increases [16].

If we consider a business scenario where the problem size increases to 1million, assuming we have not taken care of addressing fault tolerance and the scale-out problem, then we can expect the cost space for bug fixes increases to n-times of optimizations of linear for a non-linear bug fix. This emphasizes the need to consider keys aspects like fault tolerance, scale-out and hybrid data management as part of the design [17].

Quality and Governance are also key elements while handling multitude of business and making information more valuable. The idea of building an end-to-end process framework for big data is driven by the need to have a balance between the risk and value factors, so that it fosters evolutionary growth of the data and optimizes management [15] (Fig. 2).

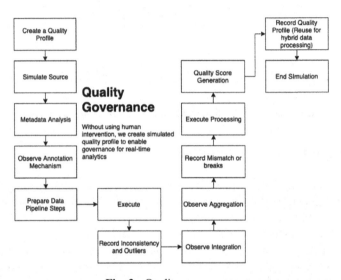

Fig. 2. Quality governance

With the widespread adoption cloud platforms, we need to use an intelligent mapping of policies with well-designed models. The focus of the governance and quality modules should be to create a value proposition for the business, and not create any constraints that limit access to such data.

3   A Discrete Approach Towards Intelligent Data Valuations

Orchestration of data starts with ingestion of data – raw or otherwise – which is then classified into structured, unstructured, semi-structured. This helps with the exploration of data channeling it into domain-specific processing – supervised or unsupervised – eventually leveraging the power of Artificial Intelligence for better analysis and insights. Data scientists would like to reduce manual involvement in these cases and adopting machine-based recommendations facilitates the evolutionary design for a big data framework. This evolution should be characteristic and not enforced as a deliverable feature.

We would also like to introduce Dimension Clustering for readers interested in additional techniques. Dimension Clustering is critical in many data management scenarios to derive value, contributing to enhanced accuracy, completeness, accessibility, consistency and integrity of the data. Many of the features, say in a large framework can be translated to data processes by using the framework itself [18].

It is also important to focus on the *structural characteristic awareness* of the data – a number of qualities are fine-tuned and adapted to the requirements of specific business domains. It helps with the flexibility and consistency of outcomes catering to business scenarios. User experience is another crucial aspect in almost every domain. With the evolving business mindset and behavior, influenced by the modern consumer devices, platforms are expected to adopt seamless patterns with smooth transitions. This approach to provide consistency in user experience surfaces as a critical factor for the future of any platform in terms of survivability.

A data framework shouldn't impose Artificial Intelligence in every scenario but accelerate data discovery and processing in specific business scenarios. Defining Structural Economics [20] for a business is also critical – better achieved with experience semantics gained from business users. Relaxations and Heuristics tend to follow the process; hence it is critical to understand whether some of the business objectives really require artificial intelligence intervention. To achieve this, we recommend business users work closely with the developers to understand key semantics of data discovery in specific business scenarios [19].

4 Conclusion

The stark reality is that enterprises are craving for a platform that not only caters to business scenarios but also enhances the overall experience of the business users and research engineers in the enterprise. User experience that caters to be context specific greatly contributes to the productivity and usability of any data analytics platform.

By focusing on this approach while designing a framework, we can also achieve both data and user experience consistencies in business domains. The key aspect we can achieve with this practice is how the synthesized data can align better with the business scenarios. That way process simulations meet the expectations of production standards. The business case for evolutionary platforms is still a work in progress, as scaling for different business scenarios requires potentially a few more years of understanding the semantics.

References

1. Bitton, D., et al.: One platform for mining structured and unstructured data: dream or reality? In: Proceedings of the 32nd International Conference on Very Large Data Bases. VLDB Endowment (2006)
2. Faerber, F., et al.: Towards a web-scale data management ecosystem demonstrated by SAP HANA. In: 2015 IEEE 31st International Conference on Data Engineering. IEEE (2015)

3. Fang, H.: Managing data lakes in big data era: what's a data lake and why has it became popular in data management ecosystem. In: 2015 IEEE International Conference on Cyber Technology in Automation, Control, and Intelligent Systems (CYBER). IEEE (2015)

4. Tsai, C.-W., et al.: Big data analytics: a survey. J. Big Data 2(1), 21 (2015)

5. Shin, D.-H.: Demystifying big data: anatomy of big data developmental process. Telecommun. Policy 40(9), 837–854 (2016)

6. Bennett, J.C., et al.: Combining in-situ and in-transit processing to enable extreme-scale scientific analysis. In: Proceedings of the International Conference on High Performance Computing, Networking, Storage and Analysis. IEEE Computer Society Press (2012)

7. Samek, W., Wiegand, T., Müller, K.-R.: Explainable artificial intelligence: understanding, visualizing and interpreting deep learning models. arXiv preprint arXiv:1708.08296 (2017)

8. Laney, D.: 3D data management: controlling data volume, velocity and variety. META Group Res. Note 6(70), 1 (2001)

9. Gandomi, A., Haider, M.: Beyond the hype: big data concepts, methods, and analytics. Int. J. Inf. Manag. 35(2), 137–144 (2015)

10. Zafar, R., et al.: Big data: the NoSQL and RDBMS review. In: 2016 International Conference on Information and Communication Technology (ICICTM). IEEE (2016)

11. Dixon, J.: Union of the State – A Data Lake Use Case. James Dixon's Blog, 22 January 2015. jamesdixon.wordpress.com/2015/01/22/union-of-the-state-a-data-lake-use-case/

12. Hai, R., Geisler, S., Quix, C.: Constance: an intelligent data lake system. In: Proceedings of the 2016 International Conference on Management of Data. ACM (2016)

13. Gao, Y., Huang, S., Parameswaran, A.: Navigating the data lake with datamaran: automatically extracting structure from log datasets. In: Proceedings of the 2018 International Conference on Management of Data. ACM (2018)

14. Brown, N., et al.: In situ data analytics for highly scalable cloud modelling on Cray machines. Concurrency Comput.: Pract. Exp. 30(1), e4331 (2018)

15. Hashem, I.A.T., et al.: The rise of "big data" on cloud computing: review and open research issues. Inf. Syst. 47, 98–115 (2015)

16. Danziger, P.: Big o notation. Source internet. http://www.scs.ryerson.ca/∼mth110/Handouts/PD/bigO.pdf. Accessed Apr 2010

17. Batini, C., et al.: From data quality to big data quality. In: Big Data: Concepts, Methodologies, Tools, and Applications, pp. 1934–1956. IGI Global (2016)

18. Feldman, D., Schmidt, M., Sohler, C.: Turning big data into tiny data: constant-size coresets for k-means, PCA and projective clustering. In: Proceedings of the Twenty-Fourth Annual ACM-SIAM Symposium on Discrete Algorithms. Society for Industrial and Applied Mathematics (2013)

19. Madnick, S., Zhu, H.: Improving data quality through effective use of data semantics. Data Knowl. Eng. 59(2), 460–475 (2006)

20. Chen, H., Chiang, R.H.L., Storey, V.C.: Business intelligence and analytics: From big data to big impact. MIS Q. 36(4), 1165–1188 (2012)

Digital Transformation – A Call for Business User Experience Driven Development

Prabal Mahanta$^{(\boxtimes)}$ and Abdul-Gafoor Mohamed

SAP Labs Pvt. Ltd., Bangalore, India
{p.mahanta, abdul-gafoor.mohamed}@sap.com

Abstract. In order to transform organizations digitally, it is critical to understand and analyse the disruption effects from the point of view of the business model or a target consumer group. While organizations layout their roadmap to achieve transformations, they often invest in techniques and methodologies without a vision on business analytics, intelligence and end up creating a non-manageable platform and data graveyard. The illusion of achieving the silver lining in analytics and data insights for business is creating a critical roadblock in the path of optimized and scalable mechanisms of developing a well-oiled data management system.

With the growing practices in designing business data management and analytics systems, it is a complex problem to design a scalable and a mature system. Here, we try to discuss on how to, with the changing dimension of platform offerings, use portability as one of the key parameters to scale efficiently and effectively. Also, artificial intelligence (AI) becomes a key component in many optimizations in specific scenario of software applications but when it comes to business data management, we only use it for insights, predictions and seldom map the power of AI to manage the data effectively. We discuss various approaches to address the criticality of the business scenarios and how we can implement the focus on data at its core.

Keywords: Business intelligence · Business strategy · Portability · Metadata management

1 Introduction

1.1 Surviving the Digital Disruption

The ability of any organisation to sustain success in dynamic environments is a critical measure of its strategy. Dynamic environments are a result of economic evolution and the change in supply-demand cycle due to trends in the market. Hence, to be successful in both the explorations and exploitation phases, organizations are required to have effective and efficient business management, control and certainty in workflows ensuring business success. In order to implement successful strategies, we need to create explorations and research a core part of product lifecycle which will support innovation of application supporting the business strategy, leadership alignment and structural integrity.

© Springer Nature Switzerland AG 2020
C. Debruyne et al. (Eds.): OTM 2019 Workshops, LNCS 11878, pp. 161–166, 2020.
https://doi.org/10.1007/978-3-030-40907-4_16

Variations in consumer behavior, diverse business scenarios and implementation landscapes, we are deep into digital disruption where the processes as well as the states of implementations are required to be agile. This also leads to another factor to be taken into consideration which is the cost of time and space when it comes to lifecycle of an application. With the influx of multiple personalized business implementations, it becomes critical for organizations to have an effective strategy to deflect the competition and scale it for coming decades [1]. From business ranging from small to enterprise level, it is seen that the differentiating factor is not only the economic relevance but also the cultural outlook which lays the foundation of success in a business domain [2]. An implementation strategy to be successful for any business domain, it is critical to nurture and provide a scope for verified alternatives to traditional solution with the scope for dynamicity and functional supremacy [3].

To achieve scalable solutions, most organizations drifted towards market approach which is no longer an assured method for organizational success be it first to market or creating a niche market [4]. This is also due to the fact that functionally complete and correct product has more consumption than a product which meets the business user's requirements partially. The nature of current business demands from an ROI perspective must be evaluated with economics taken into consideration. The key to achieve sustainability in the rapid technology drift is to have a "secure, functionally correct and business enabled feature" product. This requires organizations to evaluate business product requirement analysis with design thinking and business user experience. This helps developers to churn productive code which enables the business users and none of the important aspects of the user experience are lost [5].

Technology advancements like blockchain, artificial intelligence which have created tremors in the traditional approach for business processes are also responsible for creating a drift from the traditional approaches for diverse aspects of business. Translated processes into an assisted model to enable business users with power to perform the operations for business excellence can be on e of the many techniques that can be implemented [6]. Making businesses go digital now need not only alignment with the IT but also the research initiatives for competitive edge in present consumer-based ecosystem. This strategy takes time to nurture and we need to focus on this approach with a research mindset as we see that optimized outcomes are critical out of this phase.

1.2   Transforming Business Using Intelligence

Intelligence assists in realizing the differential value of business need of an organization and as an end user it will focus on leveraging the best of methods to perform operations with minimal cost and a reliable technology [7].

Assuming the present chaos around the intelligence requirements, it is necessary that the intelligence requirements in business scenarios are well evaluated and applied after requirements are verified by business users. It is critical to evaluate customer centric requirements with the aid of past usage of the product and a contextual data to come up with the best approach to be implemented for the current business requirement. This implementation can be the place where we imply intelligence be it artificial or supervised based on the business needs [8].

One of the key elements that require the inception of intelligence is the visualization area. The need for intelligent visualization is very critical to address since it is the same aspect of the software product that enables usage to its maximum intend. Learning from user experiences into curating a model to facilitate user based analytical experience is key to achieve consistency from a usage point of view of an application. There are several factors that we need to take into consideration for a well perceived application which is not limited to user dynamic based output, etc.

Trying to automate all scenarios at once is always going to lead to failure but incrementally if we want to select the right scenarios for intelligence based implementation then it is the correct approach to achieve end to end automation since it will clearly isolate the scenarios and events where human behavior cannot be replicated and simulated. The key is not to see human as cost based key indicator but the importance of an experienced business user and the eye for the detail cannot be simulated or replaced. This understanding is critical to create a respectful balance between the artificial intelligence and human intelligence [9].

Let us take up a scenario here in case of a software product, in each phase of development we foresee a need to automate continuous delivery and continuous integration perspective and in doing so we perform an automated end to end scenario testing. Despite this certain feature may not be perceived well in terms of accessibility so this we will not be able to achieve without the experience of an accessibility tester or a user. The experience that experts bring into the lifecycle helps increase the end user experience after the product is released into the market making it a quality driven product hence creating an edge in the competitive market since the business end users may desire such scenarios [10].

2 Workflow for Strategic Success

For achieving any strategic value addition for any product, it is required that we fully understand and model the business environment and outcomes of a similar strategy in an organization. Creating of a workflow for strategic success is critical but making it transparent for the internal community is even more important since it creates the notion of trust and positive mindset in the development community in case of a software product and likewise in any other product industry [11].

The workflow may have all the elements that we have mentioned in the figure below or additional components based on the organizational requirements. We all will start with the business scenarios and explore the digital opportunities that can suit the business scenario more from an adoption point of view. Why exploring digital and business scenarios together is important? It will leverage the power of providing a strong business model with the context of relevance and sustainability for the idea or the product.

To nurture the idea or the feature it is also critical to portray the business scenario with the techniques of design thinking, discovery models and brainstorming at all levels of implementation need and ownership. This will provide an outlook for exploring the business requirements in terms of return on investment model.

Now when we have this core outline then we can map it back to the organizational environment and start creating decision models which later can be simulated for refinement and focus for market value addition. This practice will create a blueprint for feature/product which can again be again refined using the current organizational strategies.

When we follow this approach, we also touch upon an important aspect of the strategy requirement and that is to provide a holistic outcome in terms of product/feature relevance. To achieve business relevance, we constantly need to change the organizational conditions and refine our product blueprint for a better sustenance and also a competitive edge in the market.

To discuss more on sustainability of a software product, it is key that we use it as a measure of quality. This particular parameter will take care of the dimension in socio-economics, environment, technology, functionality and perception. Critical for any software product is to align with relevance since sustainability will help realize the key model to evaluate concern weights over evaluation for market leadership [12] (Fig. 1).

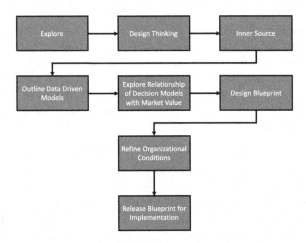

Fig. 1. Workflow for strategic evaluation

The second half of the strategic dominance will only be featured if it is successfully achieved using an implementation process. This implementation process will be critical for providing a market edge for a product against its competitors. In order to perform analytics optimally, we need portable data analysis models to enable analyst across all domains to directly do the analysis on the source of the data and avoid data lakes. For doing so, we need strategically align the architecture to support such practices. Key features like materialized data, schema and presentation are critical for any data pipeline adoption and performance for workloads in a scale is also crucial for any platform success.

3   Conclusion

For realizing the true potential of business transformation, there are technology and culture aspects that go together and hence it is ideal for an organization to evaluate various techniques to pursue excellence in the field of data transformation and analytics using data pipelines and nurture future use cases using artificial intelligence.

Customer experience alongside developer experience [13] is critical to analyze the business scenarios and not only provide an artificial intelligence flavor to it. It is important to understand the end user experience hence empathy for the end user will be an additional parameter to focus during digital transformation.

Using this experience to nurture features can mature the strategy and also provide a uniqueness for any product tackling any business scenario. Portability of user experiences and analysis model should also be looked upon for strategy alignment in any organization. We are currently working on translating the strategy work into a working model for business excellence and is an ongoing activity of our research work.

References

1. da Costa, L.S., Pereira, L., Akkari, A.: A proposed framework to identify digital transformation maturity in small industries. In: 4th Workshop on Innovative Engineering for Fluid Power (WIEFP 2018), 28–30 November, Sao Paulo, Brazil, no. 156. Linköping University Electronic Press (2018)
2. Kahre, C., Hoffmann, D., Ahlemann, F.: Beyond business-IT alignment-digital business strategies as a paradigmatic shift: a review and research agenda (2017)
3. Lainema, T., Nurmi, S.: Applying an authentic, dynamic learning environment in real world business. Comput. Educ. **47**(1), 94–115 (2006)
4. Kontić, L., Vidicki, Đ.: Strategy for digital organization: testing a measurement tool for digital transformation. Strateg. Manag. **23**(1), 29–35 (2018)
5. Crouch, S., et al.: The Software Sustainability Institute: changing research software attitudes and practices. Comput. Sci. Eng. **15**(6), 74 (2014)
6. Baldassarre, B., et al.: Bridging sustainable business model innovation and user-driven innovation: a process for sustainable value proposition design. J. Clean. Prod. **147**, 175–186 (2017)
7. Larson, D., Chang, V.: A review and future direction of agile, business intelligence, analytics and data science. Int. J. Inf. Manage. **36**(5), 700–710 (2016)
8. Rădescu, R., Muraru, V.: Study platform for complex data analysis of telecommunications and social network applications using business intelligence. In: The International Scientific Conference eLearning and Software for Education, vol. 1. "Carol I" National Defence University (2019)
9. Jarrahi, M.H.: Artificial intelligence and the future of work: human-AI symbiosis in organizational decision making. Bus. Horiz. **61**(4), 577–586 (2018)
10. Scandaroli, A., et al.: Behavior-driven development as an approach to improve software quality and communication across remote business stakeholders, developers and QA: two case studies. In: Proceedings of the 14th International Conference on Global Software Engineering. IEEE Press (2019)

11. Tavanti, M., Davis, E.B.: Integrating sustainability mindset and impact competencies in management education: directions, models, and strategies. In: Contemporary Perspectives in Corporate Social Performance and Policy. Management Education for Corporate Social Performance, pp. 223–241 (2017)
12. Bačić, D., Fadlalla, A.: Business information visualization intellectual contributions: an integrative framework of visualization capabilities and dimensions of visual intelligence. Decis. Support Syst. **89**, 77–86 (2016)
13. Mahanta, P., Kaur, B.: User experience and agile software practices – an industry perspective. In: Debruyne, C., et al. (eds.) OTM 2017. LNCS, vol. 10697, pp. 232–235. Springer, Cham (2018). https://doi.org/10.1007/978-3-319-73805-5_24

8th International Workshop on Methods, Evaluation, Tools and Applications Towards a Data-Driven e-Society (Meta4eS 2019)

Meta4eS 2019 PC Co-chairs' Message

The future eSociety, addressed with our workshop, is a data-driven and e-inclusive society based on the availability of large amounts of data and the extensive use of digital technologies at all levels of interaction between its members. It is a society that evolves based on knowledge and that empowers individuals by creating virtual communities that benefit from social inclusion, access to information, enhanced interaction, participation and freedom of expression, among other.

In this context, the role of the ICT in the way people and organizations exchange information and interact in the social cyberspace is crucial. Large amounts of data, known as Big Data, are being generated from these interactions, and a growing number of services and applications emerge from it. The Meta4eS initiative takes into account methods for the creation, acquisition, storage, processing and consumption of increasing amounts of data and tools that make possible their application to real-life situations for the benefit of the society, as well as their evaluation. The final aim is to enable the society at large to benefit from data-driven technologies, based on better, accountable decision-making. These include data storage management and processing, data analysis, information extraction, information visualization, privacy and trust, etc.

To discuss, demonstrate and share best practices, ideas and results, the 8th International Workshop on Methods, Evaluation, Tools and Applications towards a Data-driven eSociety (Meta4eS 2019), with a special focus on cross-disciplinary communities and applications associated with Big Data in any possible domain and their impact on the eSociety, brings together researchers, professionals and experts interested to present original research results in this area.

We are happy to announce that, for its eigth edition, the workshop raised interest and good participation in the research community. After a thorough review process, with each submission refereed by at least three members of the workshop Program Committee, we accepted 2 full papers and 4 short papers covering topics such as data management, data catalogs, open data understandability, data quality, natural language processing, data-driven services, decision modeling, artificial intelligence, data analysis and applied to the fields of e-Health, human activity monitoring, ambient assisted living, user profiling, chatbots and human resources.

We thank the Program Committee members for their time and effort in ensuring the quality during the review process, as well as all the authors and the workshop attendees for the original ideas and the inspiring discussions. We also thank the OTM 2019 Organizing Committee members for their continuous support. We are confident that Meta4eS will bring an important contribution towards the future eSociety.

October 2019
Ioana Ciuciu
Anna Fensel

Defining a Master Data Management Approach for Increasing Open Data Understandability

Susana Cadena-Vela[1]([⊠]) (ID), Jose-Norberto Mazón[2]([⊠]) (ID), and Andrés Fuster-Guilló[2]([⊠]) (ID)

[1] Central University of Ecuador, Quito, Ecuador
scadena@uce.edu.ec
[2] University of Alicante, Alicante, Spain
{jnmazon,fuster}@ua.es

Abstract. Reusing open data is an opportunity for eSociety to create value through the development of novel data-intensive IT services and products. However, reusing open data is hampered by lack of data understandability. Actually, accessing open data requires additional information (i.e., metadata) that describes its content in order to make it understandable: if open data is misinterpreted ambiguities and misunderstandings will discourage eSociety for reusing it. In addition, services and products created by using incomprehensible open data may not generate enough confidence in potential users, thus becoming unsuccessful. Unfortunately, in order to improve the comprehensibility of the data, current proposals focus on creating metadata when open data is being published, thus overlooking metadata coming from data sources. In order to overcome this gap, our research proposes a framework to consider data sources metadata within a Master Data Management approach in order to improve understandability of the corresponding (shortly published) open data.

Keywords: Open data · Understandability · Data quality · Master data management

1 Introduction

Open data portals are nowadays the most used interface for potential reusers (companies and persons from the eSociety) to access the information that an organization publishes in the Web. Undertaking an open data project to create such a portal can be complex for organizations as they face up to several problems such as dispersed (low-quality) data sources and lack of governance to publish data, among others [1]. Consequently, organizations that are involving in an open data project generally decide to publish data sets without considering strategies to support decisions on how to do it [11]. It is worth noting that the most-widely strategy for opening data is based on how easy releasing data is according to legal issues (such as transparency laws) thus ignoring other technical issues (such as management of metadata) [9]. Interestingly, metadata is a key enabler for open data interpretation [2], since effectively accessing open data requires metadata that

© Springer Nature Switzerland AG 2020
C. Debruyne et al. (Eds.): OTM 2019 Workshops, LNCS 11878, pp. 169–178, 2020.
https://doi.org/10.1007/978-3-030-40907-4_17

describes its content, as well its reusing conditions and other features, in order to make it understandable. Actually, if open data is misinterpreted ambiguities and misunderstandings will discourage eSociety for reusing it. In addition, services and products created by using incomprehensible open data may not generate enough confidence in potential users, thus becoming unsuccessful. This scenario increases the risk of having a limited number of datasets being reused because they are not understandable, causing open data portals to be abandoned shortly after launch [3].

Although there are standards, such as ISO/IEC 25024, that define understandability as the ability of data to be read and interpreted by users considering appropriate languages, symbols and units [4], to the best of our knowledge, no mechanism has been considered up to now to address understandability of open data from the data sources.

In order to overcome this gap, this paper introduces a framework that extends several good practices and standards such as ISO 25000[1] and ISO 8000[2], in order to consider data sources metadata within a Master Data Management (MDM) approach, thus improving understandability of the corresponding (shortly published) open data. According to ISO 8000, MDM aims at managing data of an organization to provide a unique point of view (known as master file). Figure 1 shows an overview of the structure of our framework. Data sources are at the core of our framework, since organizations must consider integration of a disparate of data sources within an open data project. Therefore, one of the elements to develop when publishing data is a master file, as a strategy for integrating heterogeneous metadata from different data sources. Our framework adapts the concept of master data file to define an open master data file. This novel artifact (together with an open data dictionary) contains all the required information from the data sources for publishing understandable data. Moreover, governance should be improved within the organization to develop an open data project. For this purpose, we propose to identify stakeholders (i.e., Chief Data Officer or CDO, open data manager and potential reusers) and define their roles and tasks within our framework.

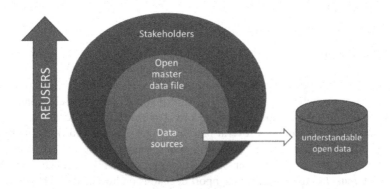

Fig. 1. Overview of the framework.

---

[1] https://www.iso.org/standard/64764.html.

[2] https://www.iso.org/standard/51653.html.

In order to evaluate our framework, several interviews and focus groups have been conducted by considering indicators extended from the ISO 25000.

This paper is organized as follows: next section reviews some important related work, Sect. 3 describes our framework to publish understandable open data, while Sect. 4 states the evaluation of our framework. Finally, conclusions and future work are explained in the last section.

2 Related Work

Many studies (as the one presented in [5]) states that there is a quality problem with open data, which has a negative impact on open government initiatives. One of the elements that affects quality is the data sources heterogeneity [6], since the implementation of open portals involves the integration of data from disparate (data) sources, whether these sources are formal or informal.

Considering the results presented in [7], we can conclude that open data have a constant growth of information, but the great heterogeneity in the portals has caused a low quality of metadata, which prevents them from being understood and used. Recommendations derived from this study are as follows:

– Providing a schema/ethics/model for their metadata that adapts to standards.
– Automatically deriving metadata values directly from data (e.g., size, format, etc.).
– Restricting certain metadata values to a predefined list of options (e.g., for license descriptions, field formats, etc.) and checking/validating the compliance of certain metadata values (e.g., URLs, emails).

Specifically, among data quality criteria, according to [8], the failure to address open data understandability becomes a significant risk that hampers the effective reuse of open data for developing novel data-intensive IT products and services. Therefore, it is necessary to conduct research on publish more understandable open data in order to improve how data is exploited to generate both social and economic impact.

The study conducted in [9] shows that existing organizations are not paying enough attention to management of the datasets, resources, and associated metadata that they are currently publishing on an open data portal. Also, according to the aforementioned ISO standards, one of the elements of quality is understandability that involves several characteristics such as: the degree of use of comprehensible symbols, metadata and the data dictionary that uses a common vocabulary, the data model and the linked master data. Therefore, understandability, is one of the barriers to the growth of open data and it is conditioned by the metadata. In order to improve open data understandability, in this paper we propose to create an open master data file, which brings together the various data sources, adding features required in opening processes such as license, level of anonymization among others. In order to fully support the understandability of the published open data, our open master data file is included in a framework for opening data containing several levels that consider understandability of open data from early stages of an open data project.

3 Framework for Opening Understandable Data

In this section, a framework is proposed to improve the comprehensibility of data sets to be published. Our framework is based on information systems best practices (such as Master Data Management) and standards (such as ISO 8000 and 25000), thus being structured in several tasks, grouped into three levels: strategic, tactical and operational. Categories, illustrated in Fig. 2, are explained next.

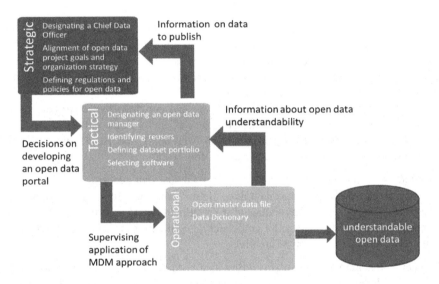

Fig. 2. Overview our framework for publishing understandable open data.

3.1 Strategic Level

This level contains those tasks that facilitate the alignment of open data projects with the corporate strategy of the organization that is willing to publish data. Tasks within this level aim to encourage a proper maintenance of open data project as an organizational asset. The following tasks are proposed:

– Designating a CDO (Chief Data Officer) [10], aiming at developing a data management strategy to achieve a company's goals considering (i) internal structure and external context of the company, (ii) useful dataspaces for the company, and (iii) generated value impact from data. Specifically, a CDO is in charge of developing strategies for implementing, managing and supervising an open data project [11].

– Aligning open data project goals with organization strategy by (i) defining the purpose of the open data project (e.g., complying with laws and regulations or promoting an entrepreneurship scenario); as well as (ii) identifying data to be published by considering goals of the organization.

- Defining organization regulations and policies for open data project, considering current laws related to open data and transparency, as well as data privacy laws.

3.2 Tactical Level

This level contains tasks required for executing the decisions made according to the strategy level. These tasks are related to the exploitation of the open data to obtain value. The suggested tasks within this level are as follows:

- Designating an open data manager (i.e., person in charge of defining and manipulating the open data). Open data manager generates the data set according to the requirements stated by the CDO, thus creating an open data portal. The open data manager must have knowledge of databases and Semantic Web technologies. Suggested activities are: describing data sources and their status (e.g., automatized or manual), defining publication policies, data standards to be used, as well as privacy regulations and laws. In addition, open data manager will be in charge of defining the levels of aggregation of existing data and the level of aggregation required for publication. Data manager will support the creation of metadata of the published open data (by means of an open master data file, as explained in the next section).
- Identifying potential reusers in order to know which data sets are most required for publication. The reusers can be both internal to the organization or external. While internal reusers are easy to detect, potential external reusers are infomediaries who generate value from published data and their support is important to identify how open data would be used.
- Creating a portfolio of data sets for opening, i.e., determining the data that should be published and when. A trade-off analysis between reusers requirements and available data sets should be used to prioritize data to open. Also, portfolio includes the right licenses for open data as well as data privacy concerns.
- Selecting software tools for implementing open data portal. Technical characteristics and the budget of the organization should be considered for selecting this tool from among those available [12], e.g. CKAN[3] or Socrata[4].

3.3 Operational Level

This level focuses on defining an open master data file in order to add all the metadata that allow publication of understandable open data, including a data dictionary describing the data.

---

[3] https://ckan.org/.

[4] https://dev.socrata.com/.

3.4 Defining the Open Master Data File

As data to open comes from a disparate of data sources in an organization, a centralized repository of metadata is required for opening that data in an understandable manner. To do so, we propose to use an MDM approach to create an open data master file by considering the following activities:

– Data inquiry: aiming at identifying that data in the information system of the organization that potential reusers may require. A unique document is created containing the following information: identification of the data source, data privacy concerns, required license for reusing and anonymization of dataset.
– Data integration: to evaluate the data quality of data sources as well as the integration process required for linking data sources before publishing them as open data.
– Data definition: establishing data publication formats and license for reusers.

Therefore, once data to be published is detected in the data inquiry stage the open master data file support linking heterogeneous data sources to define a unified data. The open master data file therefore contains all the metadata from the data sources that would be required for publishing them as understandable open data. In order to define metadata of the open data master file within our approach, we define a metadata structure (described in Table 1) based on DCAT (Data Catalog Vocabulary) [13] and OAI-PMH (Open Archive Initiative Protocol for Metadata Handling) [14].

Table 1. Metadata structure.

Metadata	Description	Property
Identifier	Unique identifier of a dataset from the organization data sources. It should not be modified in time	dct:identifier
Name	Title of the dataset	dct:title
Description	Comprehensive textual description of the data set	dct:description
Creation date	Date of creation of the dataset	dct:issued
Update_frequency	Approximate frequency in which data updates of the dataset	dct: accrualPeriodicity
Opendatamaster	The update is through an open master data file	fw: openmasterdata
Owner_dataset	Contact for the person responsible for the dataset	fw: responsibledata
Anonymization	State of anonymization of the dataset.	fw_anonymization
Data_manager	Contact of the open data manager of the organization	fw_managerportal
License	License applicable to the dataset (i.e., reusing conditions)	dct:license
Language	Language of publication	dct_language
Organization	Web site of the organization	dct_organization
Keywords	Search keywords for the dataset	dct_keywords

3.4.1 Building the Open Data Dictionary

The data dictionary contains information of datasets and their descriptions (called attributes). For the sake of understandability, the meaning of the data to open must be explicitly described as well as its structure. Therefore, the following information of each data set is considered: name, description, domain and data type.

4 Evaluation of Our Framework

Our framework has been defined by using Action Research: a participatory method where research is done incremental and iteratively [15]. Action Research acquires knowledge and validates it with stakeholders by means of cycles that would result in the final proposal of our framework. The stages performed are as follows:

- Identifying the issues that guide the research, in this case an open data set to be understandable for reuser.
- Reviewing of the barriers for open data, standards and good practices [4].
- Analysis of the collected information in order to structure it, thus proposing a framework for published understandable open data.
- Sharing the results through semi-structured interviews with 17 managers of open data portals and creating focus groups with persons coming from three sectors: government, civil society and academia. Each discussion group is composed of six persons aiming at validating and improving the proposed framework.

Our framework for publishing understandable open data was presented to stakeholders within the validation meetings by means of some samples coming from the metadata structure (see Table 1). A sample is shown in Table 2.

Table 2. Sample metadata.

Metadata	Description
Identifier	30339983
Name	Travel information of public authorities and functionaries of an organization
Description	Information on travel allowances or national allocations of authorities and public officials of the organization in January 2018
Creation date	June 8, 2018
Update_frequency	Monthly
Opendatamaster	Yes
Owner_dataset	managerportal@organization.gov.ec
Anonymization	Yes
Organization_manager_portal	datamanager@organization.gov.ec
License	Attribution 4.0 International (CC BY 4.0)
Language	Spanish
Organization	Organization.gov.ec
Keywords	allowances, salaries

Table 3 shows indicators for evaluation of understandability of open data, from the viewpoint of reuse potential. Indicators are defined based on ISO 25000 standard.

Table 3. Proposed indicators.

Indicator	Description
Percentage between the number of data values presented by unknown symbols and the number of data that the revision of the symbols is requested	Understanding of symbols. Percentage of use of understandable symbols
Percentage of the data set that the description is understood as opposed to the ones that are not understood	Semantic comprehension. Relationship between the recognized common vocabulary and the terms or definitions used in the data dictionary
The percentage between the number of data values defined in the data dictionary using a common vocabulary in relation to the number of data values defined in the data dictionary	Data dictionary comprehension. Relationship of understanding of terms used in a common vocabulary
Percentage between the number of metadata understood as opposed to the metadata of interest for the potential re-users in a specific context of use	Understanding metadata. Relationship between understanding the meaning of data elements
The percentage of data sets that are understood by the license, its application vs. those that are not understood	Comprehensibility of the license to use. Relationship between knowing the use that can be given to a license and the spectrum of application
Percentage of anonymization criteria understood as opposed to those that were not understood	Comprehensibility of anonymization standards and their application

The results of the research were evaluated from the conducted interviews with the managers of the open data portals:

- Out of the 17 interviews carried out, 9 interviewees are responsible for already implemented open data portals with published data (specifically, a total of 512 published open data sets), 6 interviewees have already implemented open data portals (with no published data) and 2 interviewees have only approved the open data portal project.
- Regarding the open data projects, 61% did not consider reusers in their initial process for opening data due to several reasons: (i) person in charge of the open data project ignores importance of considering them, (ii) it was required to publish open data in a short period of time, and (iii) developing an open data portal was considered a pilot project. Furthermore, 80% of interviewees consider that reusers must participate in early stages of an open data project.
- 40% of the interviewees did not consider quality of the data sources before publication of open data. They argued (i) lack of knowledge, (ii) performing costly

manual cleaning processes, (iii) lack of documentation, as well as (iii) pressing needs of publishing open data.

– 70% of the interviewees did not apply any mechanisms for considering metadata in a formal manner, and even more, 35% of them were unaware of MDM concept.

Also, the focus groups were carried out (three iterations) and the following results were obtained:

– First iteration of the focus group states the need to include anonymization standards for open data and metadata in order to guide the publisher.
– Second iteration of the focus group concludes that the proposed framework is useful but it is requested to add data protection regulations.
– Third interaction concludes that framework must be applied with support of appropriate staff.

5   Conclusions and Future Work

In this paper, we have described a framework for opening more understandable data by defining two novel artifacts that are applied to the data sources: an open master data file and an open data dictionary. These artifacts are located at the operational level of our framework, while we propose two extra levels: strategic and tactical.

Our approach is useful for supporting open data managers in publishing more understandable open data for the eSociety by considering, in the data sources, those metadata useful for opening data. We have performed an evaluation with open data managers to show the feasibility of our framework. We found that using our proposed open master data file and the open data dictionary is useful for the open data managers. As an avenue for future work we propose to explicitly consider potential reusers and infomediaries in our framework. Furthermore, we will explore how automate the application of our framework. Finally, we will extend the evaluation of our framework apart from the focus groups and interviews already performed, by conducting a usability study of the proposed framework.

Acknowledgements. This work has been partially supported by the Publi@City project (TIN2016-78103-C2-2-R) from Spanish Ministry of Economy and Competitiveness.

References

1. Reis, J.R., Viterbo, J., Bernardini, F.: A rationale for data governance as an approach to tackle recurrent drawbacks in open data portals. In: Proceedings of the 19th Annual International Conference on Digital Government Research: Governance in the Data Age, pp. 73:1–73:9 (2018)
2. Zuiderwijk, A., Helbig, N., Gil-García, J.R., Janssen, M.: Special issue on innovation through open data: a review of the state-of-the-art and an emerging research agenda: guest editors' introduction. J. Theor. Appl. Electron. Commer. Res. **9**(2), 1–8 (2014)

3. Benitez, F., Comber, A., Huerta, J.: Improve the reusability of open How much data is generated every minute? (2018)
4. ISO: International Standard Iso ISO/IEC 25024, 2015, vol. 2015 (2013)
5. Kubler, S., Robert, J., Le Traon, Y., Umbrich, J., Neumaier, S.: Open data portal quality comparison using AHP. In: Proceedings of the 17th International Digital Government Research Conference on Digital Government Research, pp. 397–407 (2016)
6. Heinrich, B., Klier, M., Schiller, A., Wagner, G.: Assessing data quality – a probability-based metric for semantic consistency. Decis. Support Syst. **110**, 95–106 (2018)
7. Umbrich, J., Neumaier, S., Polleres, A.: Quality assessment and evolution of open data portals. In: Proceedings of 2015 International Conference Future Internet Things Cloud, FiCloud 2015, 2015 International Conference Open Big Data, OBD 2015, pp. 404–411 (2015)
8. Sadiq, S., Indulska, M.: Open data: quality over quantity. Int. J. Inf. Manag. **37**(3), 150–154 (2017)
9. Kubler, S., Robert, J., Neumaier, S., Umbrich, J., Le Traon, Y.: Comparison of metadata quality in open data portals using the analytic hierarchy process. Gov. Inf. Q. **35**(1), 13–29 (2018)
10. Prieto, A.E., Mazon, J.-N., Lozano-Tello, A.: Framework for prioritization of open data publication: an application to smart cities. IEEE Trans. Emerg. Top. Comput. **6750**(c), 1 (2019)
11. Kassen, M.: A promising phenomenon of open data: a case study of the Chicago open data project. Gov. Inf. Q. **30**(4), 508–513 (2013)
12. Attard, J., Orlandi, F., Scerri, S., Auer, S.: A systematic review of open government data initiatives. Gov. Inf. Q. **32**(4), 399–418 (2015)
13. Missier, P., Belhajjame, K., Cheney, J.: The W3C PROV family of specifications for modelling provenance metadata. In: Proceedings of the 16th International Conference on Extending Database Technology, pp. 773–776 (2013)
14. Devarakonda, R., Palanisamy, G., Green, J.M., Wilson, B.E.: Data sharing and retrieval using OAI-PMH. Earth Sci. Informatics **4**(1), 1–5 (2011)
15. Avison, D.E., Davison, R.M., Malaurent, J.: Information systems action research: debunking myths and overcoming barriers. Inf. Manag. **55**(2), 177–187 (2018)

Human-Activity Recognition
with Smartphone Sensors

Dănuţ Ilisei and Dan Mircea Suciu[(✉)]

Babeş-Bolyai University, Cluj-Napoca, Romania
idie2141@scs.ubbcluj.ro, tzutzu@cs.ubbcluj.ro

Abstract. The aim of the Human-Activity Recognition (HAR) is to identify the actions carried out by an individual given a data set of parameters recorded by sensors. Successful HAR research has focused on the recognition of relatively simple activities, as sitting or walking and its applications are mainly useful in the fields of healthcare, tele-immersion or fitness tracking. One of the most affordable ways to recognize human activities is to make use of smartphones. This paper draws a comparison line between several ways of processing and training the data provided by smartphone sensors, in order to achieve an accurate score when recognizing the user's activity.

Keywords: Human-Activity Recognition · Recurrence plots · Neural networks

1 Introduction

Lower sensor prices, extensive scale adoption of portable computing gadgets and a developing level of interconnection between electronic devices cause a massive increase in produced information. Their high computational power, small size, and ease of use enable individuals to communicate with the gadgets as a feature of their day by day living. The type of data and its processing can vary depending on the problem we want to solve in our society.

Without any doubt, the potential of these sensors is considerable large. Particularly, the recognition of human activities is a task of high interest that can be solved by these means. The aim of the Human-Activity Recognition (HAR) is to identify the actions carried out by an individual given a data set of parameters recorded by sensors. The applications of HAR are useful especially in the fields of health care, tele-immersion or fitness tracking [12].

HAR capability could be implemented in two ways: using external or wearable sensors. On one hand, the external sensors are fixed in predetermined focal points because the recognition of the activities will be dependent entirely on the interaction between them and the users (an example of such sensor could be a camera recognizing activities from video sequences).

On the other hand, the wearable sensors are attached to the user's body. The measured attributes are related to the user's movement using accelerometer and gyroscope sensors. They can output various measurements such as attitude, gravity, user's acceleration or rotation rate. In order to be feasible and easy to integrate with

© Springer Nature Switzerland AG 2020
C. Debruyne et al. (Eds.): OTM 2019 Workshops, LNCS 11878, pp. 179–188, 2020.
https://doi.org/10.1007/978-3-030-40907-4_18

real-world applications, this kind of wearable sensors has to be small, powerful and used in small numbers. By minimizing their number and lessening the interaction with the user, the complexity will be reduced, and more comfort will be provided for the user. Nevertheless, more sensors mean more accuracy: one cannot tell if the user is moving his arm by having a sensor placed at his waist. The number of sensors and their positions must be carefully chosen depending on which kind of activity it is required to be recognized. There will always be a tradeoff between the comfort of the user and the accuracy, therefore, a well-balanced relationship between them is required.

Considering the arguments brought previously, one of the best and most affordable ways to recognize human activities is to make use of smartphones. These indispensable gadgets bring up new research opportunities for this kind of applications where the user can produce a big amount of data just by doing his daily activities. A big advantage of smartphones is the minimal users' effort because every individual nowadays carries at least one. The latest devices come with embedded built-in sensors such as accelerometers, gyroscopes, microphones, cameras, etc. These devices are present in our daily living and provide an alternative solution for the HAR problem.

The objective of this paper is to analyze the feasibility of a human activity recognition system. The next section presents a theoretical background of the subject alongside with previous results obtained in the field of human activity recognition. The third and fourth sections present the results obtained during the research and the last section contains some conclusions and future prospects.

2   Human Activity Recognition with Smartphone Sensors

Smartphones are becoming a ubiquitous part of our life. Their evolution along with the development of other branches such as the increasing sensing and computing power has made possible to have a lot of health, game or sports tracking on our mobile devices. These applications are made possible in most of the cases by analyzing accelerometer data. Nevertheless, unlike wearable devices, smartphones are more versatile, meaning that they could be carried in various and uncertain positions. For instance, sometimes one could grab the phone in the hand and walk then put it in the pocket and after that in the jacket. This is one of the biggest impediments so far when it comes to human activity recognition with smartphone sensors. If one wants to be able to recognize activities with this approach, a standard must be established. If the model is trained using phones located in the pocket, then the user has to place the phone in the same place when he wants to use the recognition framework [5].

Different classification techniques have been used by researchers when solving the HAR problem. Usually, the patterns of input data are associated with the activities under consideration. The classification techniques used by researchers are supervised as well as unsupervised allowing the automatically inference of classes from data. The most used and accurate algorithms are k-Nearest Neighbors (k-NN) [8], Support Vector Machines (SVMs) [7], Random Forests (RF) [3], Gaussian Mixture Models (GMM) [2], Markov Chains [10] and Hidden Markov Models (HMM) [4].

K-Nearest Neighbors is a supervised classification technique which is also called a direct classification method because it does not need a learning process to classify the data. However, the whole storage of the data is required. The similarity between the training data and the new observation is used when it comes to classifying new data. The test or observation data is assigned to the most common class using a majority vote of its k nearest neighbors. The difference between neighbors of observation is computed using a distance measurement called the similarity function. For example, the Euclidean distance can be used as a similarity function. The complexity of the function increases when new samples are assigned to the class. Forster et al. used this technique in his paper for solving the HAR problem and achieved an accuracy of 95.8% for 9 activities. The misclassifications occurred because of insufficient discrimination between walking and walking downstairs [6].

Support Vector Machines is a classification technique which is inspired by statistical learning theory. This method consists of minimizing the empirical risk (which is represented by a cost function) and at the same time, maximizes the distance between the separating hyperplane and the data. The SVM method is a standard linear classification but using "kernel tricks" a non-linear classification method can be obtained. SVM is a binary decision technique which draws a decision boundary between the classes. In order to ensure a multi-classification technique pairwise classification can be used which makes this method ineffective when it comes to large amounts of data. The authors applied this method to classify falls and other activities. The recognition percentage was between 84% and 96% [7].

Random Forest is an algorithm based on combinations of decision-trees. They are used for various machine learning tasks. The single-tree classifier is improved by combining the bootstrap aggregation method and randomization when selecting partitions of data nodes in the construction of the decision tree. The trees that make up the forest constitute a majority vote that is decisive for the assignment of new observation vectors. Random decision forests also correct for decision trees' habit of overfitting to their training set. In [3], the authors classified different activities such as driving a car, being on a train or walking by comparing different machine learning methods. They have proved that the Random Forest algorithm is better than SVMs or Naïve Bayes for this kind of motion activities.

A Gaussian Mixture Model is a probabilistic approach, usually used in an unsupervised fashion. This method stands out from other standard probabilistic models by estimating the data by a single Gaussian component density. The proportions and mean vectors of a GMM and other parameters used by this method are approximated using the expectation-maximization algorithm. This method could be adapted for the HAR problem by constructed features for human activities. By this means, different GMMs could be learned for different activities. After this step, by selecting the GMM with the highest probability, the classification can be performed. The setback of this algorithm is that it is not guaranteed that the global minimum converges when initializing the expectation-maximization algorithm [1].

The Markov chain is represented by a discrete-time stochastic process covering a limited number of states where the current state is dependent on the previous one. When it comes to human activity recognition, each state represents an activity. The difference between the Hidden Markov Model and a Markov chain is made by the fact that the second one is well adapted to model sequential while the first is more general. The HMM assumes that the current model is owned by a hidden state (activity in the case of HAR). After the HMM is trained, using the Viterbi algorithm [9], the most likely sequence of activities is determined. This method has the same setback as the GMM, it is not guaranteed the convergence to the global minimum and the initialization of the expectation-maximization has to be carefully chosen. The HMM algorithm has been used by the authors in different HAR problems such as classification of daily living activities using a two-level classification schema or in an unsupervised fashion [13].

Dinh Le and Van Nguyen describe in [6] a system based on 3 modules: the *feature extraction*, the *dimensionality reduction* and *the classification*.

The *feature extraction* part of this system responsibility is to preprocess the raw sensor data received as inputs from sensors. Once the preprocessing is done, the feature extraction can be started. This process consists of two parts: Data Collection and Feature Extraction. The first one is responsible for collecting data from accelerometers and gyroscopes. The received raw data could contain noise which has to be eliminated by applying noise filters and low-pass filter techniques. After the noise is eliminated, the data is passed to the feature extraction model in order to extract the features. They are the most important part of this model because the classification is done by learning the features. The *dimensionality reduction* component is used for reducing the computational complexity. This is very important when it comes to the user experience because a fast response time for the recognition process is mandatory. The process is done in 2 steps: Features Selection and Instance Selection. The feature selection part will reduce the number of features that will be learned by the algorithm by identifying the redundant ones. The redundant features are those that do not contribute to any information during the learning process. After the most effective features are selected, the instance selection improves the efficiency of the current classifiers with respect to classification time. It reduces the size of the training data by selecting the best instances and uses them only during the classification time. After these steps are completed, the *classification* part recognizes the activity. For this method, the authors chose to use the Naïve Bayes and Decision Tree algorithms. The accuracy obtained for with the Naïve Bayes algorithm was 91% and for the Decision Tree was 96%. Also, the experiment showed that the performance of the reduced dataset was significant better achieving 15% better accuracy [4].

3   Analysis of Motion Sensor Data

The data used for our research include time series data generated by accelerometer and gyroscope sensors. The main attributes of those sensors were the attitude, the gravity, the user acceleration, and the rotation rate. It was produced with an iPhone 6s using the SensingKit application. The phone was placed in the participant's front pocket. A number of 24 participants with different age, gender, height, and weight performed 6 activities in 15 trials. They did these activities under the same circumstances and environment. There were short and long trials; the long ones last around 2 to 3 min and the short ones last from 30 s to 1 min. The activities they performed were walking downstairs, walking upstairs, walking, jogging, sitting and standing. All participants were asked to wear flat shoes. The accelerometer measures the sum of two acceleration vectors: gravity and user acceleration. Thus, a time series with 12 features resulted: attitude.roll, attitude.pitch, attitude.yaw, gravity.x, gravity.y, gravity.z, rotationRate.x, rotationRate.y, rotationRate.z, userAcceleration.x, userAcceleration.y, userAcceleration.z. The data was collected by Malekzadeh et al. on organizing the workshop on privacy by design in distributed systems and contains 1.412.864 time stamps distributed between the participants and activities [14].

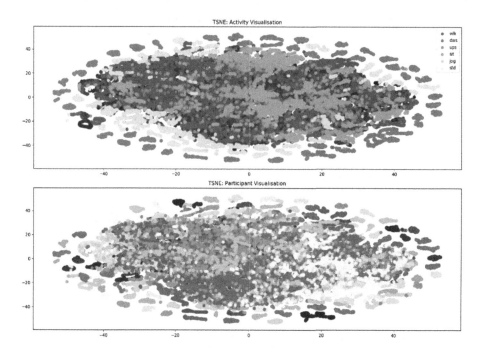

Fig. 1. Activity and participant visualization using t-SNE

We used t-Distributed Stochastic Neighbor Embedding technique, a machine learning algorithm for dimensionality reduction [15], in order to investigate the separability of the activities. Figure 1 shows the results of this algorithm applied to our dataset. The activity visualization plot is promising, showing that most of the activities are separable. However, there are some interlaid activities, such as walking upstairs and walking downstairs activities. This is not concerning, because those activities are similar and other specific algorithms could be better for separating these activities. The participant visualization plot shows personal information about the participant (each color represents a participant). We can see that everyone has a unique style of performing these activities. Therefore, the sensors inside the smartphone have the potential of recognizing who is using the smartphone.

In order to have a more thorough study of the high degree of accuracy achieved when recognizing the walking activity, we also investigate the walking signature of each participant from the 24-total set of participants.

It can be seen in Fig. 2 that some participant's plots contain outliers which could be interpreted as different activities such as start or stop walking or even unbalanced steps of the participants. Even though the plots are explicit, showing that each participant has a unique style. Taking into consideration the accuracy obtained during the classification and the plot it can be concluded that each person has a unique style. Because in our example we have the data of only 24 participants, that makes it easy to recognize the person. If there are over one billion participants providing data for their walking style, it would be almost impossible for every participant to have a unique style. If that would be the case, more groups could be established, and participants could be classified regarding their similarities. They could be grouped based on their height, weight, age, and even gender.

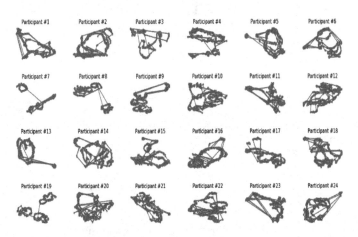

Fig. 2. The walking style for 24 persons

4 Recurrence Plots

Based on the results presented in [11], we used Deep Convolutional Neural Network to represent recurrence plots for all captured activities. The solution presented in this paper is that the time series data is transformed into a recurrence plot. By this means, each time series sequence becomes an image. A recurrence plot is a plot showing, for each moment i in time, the times at which a phase space trajectory visits roughly the same area in the phase space as at the time i. This method has been chosen mainly because time series are characterized by a distinct recurrent behavior such as periodicities and irregular cyclicities. To put it simply, the purpose of this conversion is to reveal in which points some trajectories return to a previous state.

Figure 3 illustrates step-by-step how time series data is converted into a recurrence plot. The left figure is a simple example of a time series signal (x) with 12 data points. In the middle is described the 2D phase space trajectory which is constructed from x by the time delay embedding ($\tau = 1$). States in the phase space are shown with bold dots: s_1: (x_1, x_2), s_2: (x_2, x_3), ..., s_{11}: (x_{11}, x_{12}). In the right figure is described the recurrence plot R, which is an 11×11 square matrix with $R_{i,j} = dist(s_i, s_j)$.

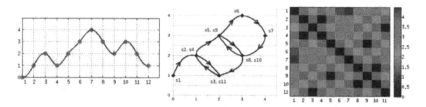

Fig. 3. From time series signal to recurrence plot [11].

In order to have an organized working pipeline, we divided our method into three steps. During the first step, the data is pre-processed, in the second step we construct and compile the Convolutional Neural Network and the third step consist of training and evaluating the model.

The pre-processing part of this method intends to bring the initial data to a state which is compatible with the compiled Convolutional Neural Network. In order to do that, the given time series data was converted to a recurrence plot using the sklearn framework. After this, the obtained recurrence plots have been resized to 32×32 pixels. This has been done because the obtained recurrence plots did not have the same size, since that the time series data did not have the same length (the time series length was between 30 s and 3 min). The 32×32 pixels scale has been chosen because of the computational limits, otherwise, a larger scale may perform better, because fewer data would have been lost. Then, the data is labeled and normalized in order to be properly fed into the algorithm. Also, the data have been split into 15% test data and 85% train data.

A sample of the recurrence plots obtained is presented in Fig. 4. Here it can be observed that all the activities have some degree of periodicities. This is a good sign considering that we need our activities to have repetitive sequences in order to be good practice for the recurrence plot method. Also, it can be seen in the figure that the recurrence plots for the pairs: walking & jogging, sitting & standing, downstairs & upstairs are similar. This is because those activities rely on the same type of motion, and this means that they will have similar periodicities. Therefore, the experiments were divided into two categories: trying to recognize each activity and trying to recognize the grouped activities, more precisely, the following types of activities: walking & jogging, sitting & standing and downstairs & upstairs.

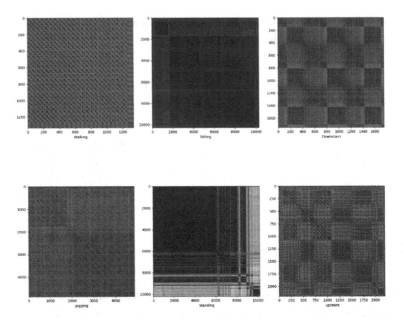

Fig. 4. Recurrence plots for each activity: walking, sitting, downstairs, jogging, standing and upstairs

The Convolutional Neural Network was built using the Sequential Keras model. The first layer is a convolutional one and has a number of 32 filters with a size of 3 × 3. The activation function used is relu. The input shape of this layer is (1, 32, 32), which means that has only one input channel (because the pixels are on a grey scale, from 0 to 1), and 32, 32 is the size of the input image which was already scaled at this size. It has a max pooling 2d layer which down-samples the image in order to reduce the over-fitting. After this, the results are passed to a drop out layer, where 40% of neurons are dropped out, so it reduces complexity. This is done because the results without this layer had signed of overfitting. After those three layers, the results are passed into other three layers which will have the same order and configuration: convolutional, max pooling and drop out layer. In order to be able to classify those results, we needed to transfer all the data from a Convolutional Neural Network to an Artificial Neural Network. This step is done using a flatten layer. It is followed by a dense layer which is fully connected with 64 outputs. The results are passed to a dropout layer with 50% of neurons dropped and then to a dense layer with 6 layers. Therefore, we have the Convolutional Neural Network which extracts the feature and an Artificial Neural Network which put them together and gives a probabilistic distribution of the results with the SoftMax activation function.

After the pre-processing and the setup process were done, the model was trained with the data and then evaluated. The model has been trained in 150 batches. The results for the first trial, with 6 different types of activities lied around 70% percent. The wrong recognition of the activities during the evaluation process has been done because of the similarities between activities with the same type of motion, like walking upstairs or walking downstairs. They have very similar recurrence plots. In terms of the results obtained grouping the activities in two by two, they were considerably better. The results of this method were 89%.

5 Conclusions

The main goal of our research was to investigate how feasible is to recognize some activities performed by humans based on the information captured from their smartphone sensors. It has been studied the ability to recognize only 6 activities, but there are more activities that people do daily and could be recognized.

The paper has been proven that within a time interval between 30 s and 3 min the mobile device that someone is carrying is able to determine with accuracies from 75% to 90% if that person is doing one of the studied activities. This time is very short considering the amount of time an average person is carrying his/her phone. At the same time, the conducted experiment showed that each person has a different walking signature. The system knows who the person is just by walking, with a precision of 95%. The data gathered for this research has been done with only one smartphone by accessing two sensors: accelerometer and gyroscope.

References

1. Attal, F., Mohammed, S., Dedabrishvili, M., Chamroukhi, F., Oukhellou, L., Amirat, Y.: Physical human activity recognition using wearable sensors. Sensors **15**(12), 31314–31338 (2015)
2. Baum, L.E., Petrie, T.: Statistical inference for probabilistic functions of finite state Markov chains. Ann. Math. Stat. **37**(6), 1554–1563 (1966)
3. Bedogni, L., Di Felice, M., Bononi, L.: By train or by car? Detecting the user's motion type through smartphone sensors data. In: Proceedings of the 2012 IFIP Wireless Days (WD), Dublin, Ireland, pp. 1–6 (2012)
4. Bishop, C.M.: Pattern Recognition and Machine Learning. Springer, Heidelberg (2006)
5. Chen, Y., Shen, C.: Performance analysis of smartphone-sensor behavior for human activity recognition. IEEE Access **5**, 3095–3110 (2017)
6. Dinh Le, T., Van Nguyen, C.: Human activity recognition by smartphone. In: 2nd National Foundation for Science and Technology Development Conference on Information and Computer Science (NICS), 16–18 September (2015)
7. Doukas, C., Maglogiannis, I.: Advanced patient or elder fall detection based on movement and sound data. In: Proceedings of the 2008 Second International Conference on Pervasive Computing Technologies for Healthcare, Pervasive Health, Tampere, Finland, pp. 103–107 (2008)
8. Foerster, F., Smeja, M., Fahrenberg, J.: Detection of posture and motion by accelerometry: a validation study in ambulatory monitoring. Comput. Hum. Behav. **15**(5), 571–583 (1999)
9. Forney Jr., G.D.: The Viterbi algorithm. Proc. IEEE **61**(3), 268–278 (1973)
10. Gagniuc, P.A.: Markov Chains: From Theory to Implementation and Experimentation. Wiley, Hoboken (2017)

11. Hatami, N., Gavet, Y., Debayle, J.: Classification of time series images using deep convolutional neural networks. In: Ecole Nationale Superieure des Mines de Saint-Etienne, SPIN/LGF CNRS UMR 5307, 158 cours Fauriel, 42023 Saint-Etienne, France (2017)
12. Kim, E., Helal, S., Cook, D.: Human activity recognition and pattern discovery. IEEE Pervasive Comput. **9**(1), 48 (2010)
13. Lester, J., Choudhury, T., Kern, N., Borriello, G., Hannaford, B.: A hybrid discriminative/generative approach for modeling human activities. In: Proceedings of the IJCAI 2005 19th International Joint Conference on Artificial Intelligence, Edinburgh, UK, 30 July–5 August, pp. 766–772 (2005)
14. Malekzadeh, M., Clegg, R.G., Cavallaro, A., Haddadi, H.: Protecting sensory data against sensitive inferences. In: 1st Workshop on Privacy by Design in Distributed Systems, W-P2DS 2018, Porto, Portugal, 23–26 April. ACM (2018)
15. Van der Maaten, L., Hinton, G.E.: Visualizing data using tSNE. J. Mach. Learn. Res. **9**, 2579–2605 (2008)

Chatbots as a Job Candidate Evaluation Tool

Short Paper

Andrei-Ionuț Carțiș and Dan Mircea Suciu$^{(\boxtimes)}$

Babeș Bolyai University, 400084 Cluj-Napoca, Romania
cais1345@scs.ubbcluj.ro, tzutzu@cs.ubbcluj.ro

Abstract. Nowadays there is a constant interest in solving the problem of recruiting new personal in a constantly changing environment, while reducing the time invested into the process. We propose a solution that uses an intelligent chatbot which drives the screening interview. The users (job candidates) will feel like they talk to a real person and not just filling a simple webform for another job interview. At the same time, the chatbot can evaluate the data provided by users and score them through a sentiment analysis algorithm based on IBM Watson Personality Insights service. Our solution is meant to replace the first step in the interviewing process and to automatically elaborate a job candidate profile.

Keywords: Chatbots · Natural language processing · Data analysis

1 Introduction

The aim of the paper is to describe a software solution which automatizes the process of profiling job candidates and analyses their soft skills for the recruitment team of a company, in order to find a proper match for an open position.

Chatbots are computer programs that simulate a human conversation by using artificial intelligence or various other techniques [6]. They have expanded their area of applications and can be seen performing many repetitive tasks, in order to help humans in their work. This approach allows us to take advantage of the "ELIZA effect", which might have contributed to the speed they have spread across various domains of activity. The phenomenon refers to the people's tendency to assume, without being aware, that computer behaviour is analogous to human ones. This is known in literature as anthropomorphism [12].

The domain of Human Resources is in a constant development. Once with the technological advance, recruiting has moved more and more in the online ecosystem, with companies lowering their expectations in some hard skills, but increasing their requirements for soft skills [11]. Our proposed solution offers an interactive form of addressing soft skills of future possible employees, without having them take a test just for this matter.

The rest of this paper is as follows: Sect. 2 gives an overview of related work, while Sect. 3 presents an overview of our approach. The paper is concluded in Sect. 4 with a discussion of further work.

© Springer Nature Switzerland AG 2020
C. Debruyne et al. (Eds.): OTM 2019 Workshops, LNCS 11878, pp. 189–193, 2020.
https://doi.org/10.1007/978-3-030-40907-4_19

2 Related Work

As the place for hiring new work force has slowly shifted to the online environment, recruitment must keep it up with the change. However, this is still dependent to the human factor and it is highly time consuming, since it is more difficult to properly multi-task while discussing with different candidates.

One of the solutions for helping the HR departments during the recruitment process is the (HR)^2 agent [3]. The main advantage of this solution is that it can take away some of the tasks involved in the process. This is a solution proposed for the professional platform, LinkedIn. It should interact with the candidates and let the company know when there is a match.

The steps they have proposed involve mapping the candidate's skills with a master contract, which will be filled with the skills of the potential future employee. This is an iterative process that offers feedback throughout the entire process. One of the biggest disadvantages of this solution is that by relying on *LinkedIn* data, it can wrongly identify some skills in a person that might not have it.

Another relevant software solution is *Paradox-Olivia* (source paradox.ai), which discusses with candidates over the phone. It analyses the answers in order to decide what questions to ask further on. The system is capable of scheduling meetings with the candidates and even sends them reminders.

Nevertheless, for the moment we can say that there is no such software system capable of aiding the recruitment staff in the process in terms of soft skills. Soft skills are personality traits and features that affect the way we interact with each other and which cover various characteristics like leadership, communication, dutifulness and many others. [10] The task of identifying them is complex for a human but follows certain patters for specific roles.

One of the best solutions on the market with respect to the matter of identifying feelings comes from IBM [4, 9]. They offer a set of cognitive services that can enhance chatbots with new capabilities, like sentiment, tone or chat analysis. Its mechanism allows for a deeper understanding of emotions, by putting things into context, rather than simply matching phrases or keywords.

3 Our Approach

We propose a chatbot for collecting information from a job candidate. A psychological analysis is performed on the candidate's answers and a report is generated. The main goal is to perform this in a conversational way, offering to the users a friendly experience.

We are researching in this paper the possibility to develop a generic chatbot that can create objective feedback in the interview process performed by recruiters. Our goal is to offer employers a way of identifying personality traits in candidates in an objective and much faster way. Instead of a manager sitting in a room and following the conversation, our solution is to let the chatbot take the seat of the highly skilled professional and perform a deeper analysis of the candidate's words in order to obtain its personality traits. In order to have a better interaction, we would use natural language processing to communicate with the user.

Developing a chatbot might not be as straight forward as a web interface implementation, but it has a better long-run return of investment [5]. For the implementation of the chatbot, we have decided to go with the solution offered by Microsoft: Bot Framework. This is a multiplatform solution offered to build chatbots that can be enchanted with various cognitive services from the same provider. This allows developers to quickly create a solution that can be integrated in various channels, the most relevant being *Skype, Slack, Email, Facebook* and *SMS* [7].

One of the main advantages of the Microsoft Bot Framework is that it allows automatic translations to different languages. It also manages the client-side state of the application. The main component is the Bot Connector, which is a REST API that allows our chatbot to exchange messages with different channels via HTTPS, using a JSON format [2].

The code is written using the development platform of choice, which interacts with the bot through a specialized controller. In order to create a relationship between the two sides, messages are posted to the endpoint from or to the channel of interest.

The advantage of this modularization is that we can connect multiple services out of the box or with only a few steps required to implement them. Next phase in creating the overall infrastructure is to add the natural language capability to our system for which we used Language Understanding Intelligent Service (LUIS) [13].

Figure 1 presents the interaction of a system with LUIS. Sentences, here labelled as utterances, are fed to a pre-trained model in order to learn from the context where it specializes itself.

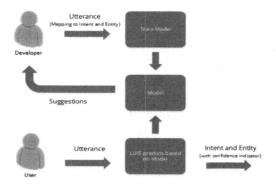

Fig. 1. Luis.ai flow diagram

In addition, we used the IBM Watson personality insights cognitive service in order to analyse the user profile. The report consists of a list of traits and percentages representing the intensity in the analysed text.

At the same time, we get to know what things the candidate values most. We also have a special field containing the needs of that person, like challenges, curiosity and others. This is important for the recruitment staff, in order to know what drives and what motivates a person. Based on the values, we can see the traits which he expresses through speech and that characterize the person.

Relying on studies that prove the old personality type model is worse than focusing on traits, we agreed to follow this approach for more accurate results [1]. The cognitive service offered by IBM analyses the input and applies the results on the five-factors personality model [8]. In this way, instead of finding the personality of a person, we focus on their traits and what value they could bring to fill a role.

The entire system is asynchronous, so there will be no waiting time for the user. It will not block the interface while performing computations.

Our solution offers a report based on the five-factors personality model, which is different from classic personality tests currently available. In this way, the system can offer a novel approach for how soft skills are addressed. The system then builds a report based on how strong a sentiment is present in the text. Here is a fragment of it:

> *Personal: After analysing the answers, here are the results. Smith seems to need to work on his attitude a bit more. Modesty is not one of his strengths and is rather low. The way he speaks classifies him as a rather quite intelligent and calculated person. As an individual, his task orientation is normal, does not seem to have a special orientation towards fulfilling tasks in any special manner. The candidate seems like a person oriented to achieving more than it is expected. It makes efforts to achieve what is needed.*
>
> *Motivational: We analyse what are the most important factors that motivates a person and their needs, like stability, need for challenges, liberty or diversity. For personal and professional development, the candidate seems to like pursuing achievements and strives for excellence. Challenges would be a good motivation and would have a great return of investment if this is met. Here is how important some aspects are for Smith: stability 61.4%, challenges 93.24%, liberty 55.7%*

When a candidate takes an interview for a company, we analyse only his answers. The questions are constructed in such a manner that it will try to drag out some of the skills, like modesty and see how the person expresses themselves. This can be done through simple questions like *"Describe a situation when you worked without any guidance in an unusual situation"*.

The report is constructed on top of the five-factors personality model, as well as using the candidate's needs and values. The service can identify those by using a mix between new learning models that rely on statistical models based on scores obtained from focus groups and other traditional approaches. While needs address what is important for that person, values cover factors that can influence someone into taking a decision.

4 Conclusions and Future Work

The current solution can be extended in several directions. Since we use a chatbot in order to aid the recruiters from various fields and countries, we can use localization. This comes as an out of the box for our system, as it takes into consideration in what language the user is writing, based on the locale settings.

Another improvement is to make the weights of the result configurable. When applying for a job, there are some generic requirements. However, some soft skills might be considered hard skills, like for a managing job, where it is a must to have communication skill. This would allow companies to tailor their needs and to obtain those results that are most important to them. Depending on the position, one might require more advanced skills or higher score than others and having it configurable can bring more value.

References

1. Asendorpf, J.B.: Head-to-head comparison of the predictive validity of personality types and dimensions. Eur. J. Pers. **17**, 327–346 (2003)
2. Fagna, A.: Introduction to Microsoft Azure Bot Service & LUIS. http://medium.com/@ashish_fagna. Accessed 07 Sept 2018
3. Garimella, U., Paruchuri, P.: (HR)^2: An Agent for Helping HR with Recruitment, Agent Technologies and Systems (2015)
4. Gliozzo, A., et al.: Building Cognitive Applications with IBM Watson Services: vol. 1 Getting Started, IBM Redbooks (2017)
5. Gobbi, F.: The Future of Chatbots: ROI, Customer Loyalty, and Revenues, AIExpo (2017)
6. Irwin, P.: What's the Turing Test and Which AI Passes It? The Stanford Encyclopedia of Philosophy (2017)
7. Mayo, J.: Bot Framework – A Multiplatform Approach to Building Chatbots, Pearson Education Inc., (2017)
8. McCrea, R.R., John, O.P.: He introduction to the five-factor model and its applications. J. Pers. **60**(2), 175–215 (1992)
9. Nasukawa, T., Yi, J.: Sentiment analysis: capturing favorability using natural language processing. In: K-CAP 2003 Proceedings of the 2nd International Conference on Knowledge Capture, pp. 70–77 (2003)
10. Schooley, R.: Why Soft Skills Missing in Today's Applicants, Murray State Theses (2017)
11. Schulz, B.: The Importance of Soft Skills: Education beyond academic knowledge. J. Lang. Commun. **2**(1), 146–154 (2008)
12. Wardrip-Fruin, N.: Expressive Processing: Digital Fictions, Computer Games, and Software Studies. The MIT Press, Cambridge (2009)
13. Williams, J., Kamal, E., Ashour, M., Amr, H., Miller, J., Zweig, G.: Fast and easy language understanding for dialog systems with microsoft language understanding intelligent service (LUIS). In: Proceedings of the 16th Annual Meeting of the Special Interest Group on Discourse and Dialogue, pp. 159–161 (2015)

Big Data Management: A Case Study on Medical Data

Vlad Sulea and Ioana Ciuciu[(✉)] [iD]

Computer Science Department, Babes-Bolyai University,
Cluj-Napoca 400084, Romania
svhpl391@scs.ubbcluj.ro, ioana.ciuciu@cs.ubbcluj.ro

Abstract. The paper introduces an approach for scalable data management in the context of Big Data. The main objective of the study is to design and implement a metadata model and a data catalog solution based on emerging Big Data technologies. The solution is scalable and integrates the following components: (1) the data sources; (2) a file scanner; (3) the metadata storage and processing component; and (4) a visualization component. The approach and its underlying metadata model are demonstrated with a toy use case from the medical domain, and can be easily adapted and extended to other use cases and requirements.

Keywords: Data management · Big Data · Data catalog · Metadata

1 Introduction and Motivation

Data represents the foundation for progress today. Extracting, storing, managing, processing and analyzing data are essential steps that help explore vast amounts of information in practically every area. Due to the characteristics of the actual data, every data processing operation raises important challenges, such as: (i) the continuously increasing volumes of available data; (ii) the heterogeneity of the data producers and of their corresponding data sources; and (iii) the speed at which data are being generated.

In particular, data management is of great importance. Almost every business is concerned with the way data is handled within their organization. A correct data management enables valuable data analysis and information extraction. A solution in this direction is represented by the data catalogs, considered to be the "new black in data management and analytics" [1]. Data catalogs support data storage and further data analysis by providing mechanisms for organizing and enriching data with metadata. However, as in every phase of the data pipeline today, the data management is faced with important challenges, due to the particularities of Big Data [2].

The main objective of the present study is to address the Big Data-related challenges with a scalable approach for data catalogs, in view of efficient data management. We propose an integrative solution relying on Big Data technologies and a (meta)data model. We have chosen the medical field for show casing our approach, since it is one of the domains faced with multiple challenges related to Big Data (e.g., data volume, data heterogeneity, speed of the incoming data). The metamodel and the case study can

© Springer Nature Switzerland AG 2020
C. Debruyne et al. (Eds.): OTM 2019 Workshops, LNCS 11878, pp. 194–198, 2020.
https://doi.org/10.1007/978-3-030-40907-4_20

be easily extended and adapted to other business domains. The paper is organized as follows: Sect. 2 is the related work of this study; Sect. 3 illustrates the approach, built around a medical case study; and Sect. 4 concludes the paper.

2 Related Work

The selection of data catalog tools has grown rapidly in the recent years. Data catalog tools exist today in different forms. As described by the Eckerson Group [3] one can distinguish several types of data catalogs: (i) standalone catalogs to support data set search and evaluation; (ii) catalogs integrated with data preparation; (iii) catalogs integrated with data analysis; and (iv) fully integrated solution catalogs. A data catalog reference model and market study is provided in [4], in support for companies and their specific needs. In [5], a data catalog capability model is proposed, addressing five main capabilities required by companies in view of increasing the level of data utilization: discovery, trust, provision, collaboration and data governance. Collibra [6], one of the key leaders in machine learning data catalogs (MLDC), as identified in [7], discusses the main needs of a data catalog: automatic metadata creation, business friendly language, freeform tagging, sync and notify and integration with the company's data governance platform [8]. The importance of Machine Learning to extract valuable insights from data in a data catalog is discussed in [9]. The metadata management in the context of Big Data is addressed by Informatica with a scalable architecture in [10].

Regarding the metadata creation, best practices are available at [11], while in [12] it is argued that any metadata management solution should start with identifying the business subject areas. An inventory of metadata types in a data catalog is proposed in [13].

Well-known Data Catalog solutions include the Google Cloud Data Catalog [14], a fully managed and scalable metadata management service with an easy-to-use search interface for data discovery, Amazon Informatica Enterprise Data Catalog on AWS [15] and BridgeHead's Healthcare Data Management Solution [16] which represents a solution for data management and storage in hospitals.

As compared to the related work, our solution aims at providing a low-cost implementation and operational solution. It is based on Hadoop and NoSQL, providing low-cost high scalability and flexibility of the data model.

3 Approach: Proposed Solution for a Data Catalog

The present approach integrates within a data engineering pipeline introduced in [17], with focus on data management (and data storage). The data catalog solution proposed in this study is depicted in Fig. 1. It contains the following components: (1) Data Sources – are the data files ingested from various departments of a medical center. These files can be structured or unstructured. Structured data is ingested with Apache Sqoop [18]. (2) File Scanner – is a program developed in Java for scanning the Hadoop HDFS [19] file structure and retrieving metadata related to the medical data stored, according to the metamodel proposed next. It uses the Hadoop File System API.

(3) Metadata storing and processing – developed using Apache Hive [20] and with the possibility of implementing MongoDB [21] in case the metadata stored in the catalog needs be accessible from outside the internal network. (4) Visualization component - developed using the Tableau [22] visualization tool.

The technical choices made in this work are motivated by the ease of integration with the Hadoop framework, in order to ensure scalable data storage and processing.

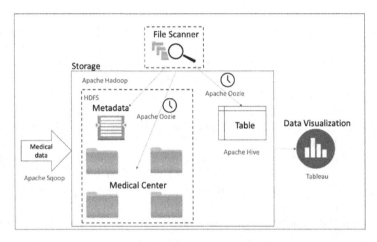

Fig. 1. Proposed scalable solution for a data catalog.

The Metadata Model. It contains all the information needed about a file in the file system. Metadata models are stored and represent the source where the mechanism responsible for querying will look and try to find the information desired by the user, in this case, medical doctors or authorized persons. The proposed model has the following structure: FileID, FileName, FilePath, FileExtension, FileSize, FileCreationTime, LastAccessTime, LastModificationTime. Note that the model is simplified for the proof of concept.

The File Scanner. It is written in Java using the Hadoop File System API to get access to the data stored in HDFS and to write the output (metadata model) back to HDFS. The core of the program is a recursive algorithm which scans the directory hierarchy and processes the documents inside, extracting the corresponding metadata. In order to avoid heap space-related issues, the implementation is using a queue. The algorithm gets the file path from queue, and then checks if that file path refers to a file or a directory. In case that the file path is a file, dedicated methods are called in order to process and extract metadata about that file. The metadata is also saved in JSON format in MongoDB which will be later used if the Data Catalog is used from multiple external users. Finally, the list containing all the metadata models is converted to a CSV file. This file is saved back to HDFS where the next step takes place.

Metadata Storage and Processing. The table in Hive is logically made up of the data being stored. Hive has two types of tables: managed tables (also known as internal tables) and external tables. In case of a managed table, Hive manages the data by default. This means that Hive moves the data into its warehouse directory. On the other hand, external tables tell Hive to refer to the data that is located outside the warehouse directory. In this work, the implementation uses an external table to create a structure that can be queried. In this way, creation and deletion of the data can be easily controlled. The location of the external data is specified at the table creation time. Using the EXTERNAL keyword, Apache Hive is told that it is not in charge of managing the data. This is a useful feature because it means that the data is lazily created after creating the table. Hive will not move the data into its warehouse directory and will not even check whether the external location exists at the time it is defined. One of the most important aspects considered when the external table was chosen is the fact that in case of a "DROP TABLE" statement the data will remain intact; only the metadata for that table will be deleted. Also, the data files are modified by the file scanner program and they are also used by visualization software. This implies that some custom queries will be applied, which could compromise the data in case of a managed table.

Process Automation. Apache Oozie [23] was used in order to automate the whole process. There were two hot spots where the Oozie scheduler was implemented: (1) The file scanner: Oozie has the option to automate a simple Java application. The file scanner program was exported as a JAR file and scheduled using Oozie to run every five minutes. This action ensures that the data catalog is continuously updated with metadata about the newly added files. (2) The updated Hive external table: The external table, which represents the structure queried by the visualization layer, has to be updated with the new information from the CSV file generated by file scanner program. For this task, the scheduler was set to run every five minutes, asynchronous with file scanner job.

Case Study. In the demonstrating scenario of this study, the dataset is represented by all the files from a medical center (e.g., x-ray images, CT scans, blood analysis, urine analysis), grouped by department. Examples of reports on the medical center file structure include: (1) Listing the number of files for every file extension in the directory hierarchy; (2) Searching for a specific file name; (3) Queries containing constraints such as timespan and file extension.

4 Conclusion

This study addressed the problem of Big Data Management in a medical center. One of the main contributions of this work is to propose a low-cost, easy maintainable system for data governance. The main focus was to study and combine existing technologies specific to Big Data, in order to provide a scalable solution for Big Data Management in the form of a data catalog. The proposed solution can be exploited in other scenarios, with specific constraints, thus enlarging the potential of using stored data and discover valuable hidden information. This contribution allows to use the proposed implementation as a foundation to solve problems with higher complexity.

The subject approached in this article has many possible adaptations and scenarios. Future work concerns the evaluation of the solution, as well as the use of other emerging technologies. Other possible extensions include: (1) A decision algorithm for file categorization, to automatically decide where an incoming file should be stored in the file hierarchy; (2) A relevant extension of the metadata model for machine learning algorithms, in view of point (1); and (3) Improvement of the performance of the data processing using realtime frameworks such as Apache Spark.

References

1. Edjlali, R., Duncan, A.D., De Simoni, G., Zaidi, E.: Data Catalogs Are the New Black in Data Management and Analytics. Gartner Research (2017)
2. Bullivant, R.: Data Catalogues Might be the New Black, But Metadata Discovery to Provision Them Can be Tricky. Silwood (2018)
3. Wells, D: The Ultimate Guide to Data Catalogs, Key Things to Consider When Selecting a Data Catalog. Eckerson Group (2018)
4. Corporate Data Quality (CDQ), Data Catalog. https://www.cc-cdq.ch/data-catalogs. Accessed 31 Jul 2019
5. Bieh-Zimmert, O., Engel, M., Kraus, S.: Cataloging Data. A capability maturity model for data catalogs, Deloitte Analytics Institute, Whitepaper (2018)
6. Collibra. https://www.collibra.com/. Accessed 31 Jul 2019
7. Goetz, M., Leganza, G., Hoberman, E., Hartig, K.: The Forrester Wave™: Machine Learning Data Catalogs, Q2 2018 (2018)
8. Collibra, 5 Things Your Data Catalog Needs (But Doesn't Have). https://www.collibra.com/blog/5-things-data-catalog-needs-doesnt/. Accessed 31 Jul 2019
9. Brown, A.: Data Catalogs and the Maturation of the Machine Learning Market (2018)
10. Pathak, G.: A Big Metadata Problem, Metadata Management that Scales: Dealing with Big Metadata (2017)
11. Stanford Libraries, Creating Metadata. https://library.stanford.edu/research/data-management-services/data-best-practices/creating-metadata. Accessed 31 Jul 2019
12. Mosely, M.: Metadata Subject Areas (2010)
13. Knight, M.: To Drive Business Success Implement a Data Catalog and Data Inventory (2018)
14. Data Catalog, Google Cloud. https://cloud.google.com/data-catalog/. Accessed 31 Jul 2019
15. AWS, Informatica Enterprise Data Catalog on AWS. https://aws.amazon.com/quickstart/architecture/informatica-eic/. Accessed 31 Jul 2019
16. BridgeHead. https://www.bridgeheadsoftware.com/healthcare-data-management-hdm/. Accessed 31 Jul 2019
17. Ciuciu, I., Ene, A.B., Lazar, C.: An ICT project case study from education: a technology review for a data engineering pipeline. In: Proceedings of BIS 2019, Seville, Spain (2019)
18. Apache Sqoop. https://sqoop.apache.org/. Accessed 31 Jul 2019
19. Apache Hadoop. https://hadoop.apache.org/. Accessed 31 Jul 2019
20. Apache Hive TM. https://hive.apache.org/. Accessed 31 Jul 2019
21. MongoDB. https://www.mongodb.com/. Accessed 31 Jul 2019
22. Tableau. https://www.tableau.com/. Accessed 31 Jul 2019
23. Apache Oozie. https://oozie.apache.org/. Accessed 31 Jul 2019

Personalizing Smart Services
Based on Data-Driven Personality of User

Izabella Krzeminska[1,2]([envelope]) [iD]

[1] Poznan University of Economics and Business,
al. Niepodlegosci 10, 61-875 Poznan, Poland
[2] Orange Polska, R&D Labs, Obrzezna 7, Warszawa, Poland
Izabella.Krzeminska@orange.com

Abstract. The article presents a research method of creating classification of users needs based on their personality (Big 5) determined on the basis of available digital data. The research is work in progress and is based on a specific use case which is a smart services (home environment) with users interface on a mobile phone. This paper includes the results of preliminary research on the needs of users, formulates research problems and discusses assumptions and the research methods. What distinguishes the proposed solution from others, is that the profile will be available for service just after installing, without the necessity of collecting data about user activity. The idea of data-based users classification, can be used at the early stage, which seems to be important in the adaptation process to any new smart service.

Keywords: User profiling · Service personalizing · Data driven services · Automatic personality recognition · Smart services

1 Introduction and Related Works

Nowadays, when the competitiveness and availability of services is very large, companies focus on adapting services to the user. Traces of digital activity of users are increasingly being used to collect information about the client, as well as profiling or classifying [1]. However, in the case of new and technologically advanced services using artificial intelligence (smart services), the risk of service rejection and discontinuation of using it, seems to be significant in the early beginning of contact with the service. A good illustration of this problem is the Amazon Alexa market research report, published in August 2018 that says "Of the people who did buy something using Alexa voice shopping, about 90% did not try it again" [2]. Moreover in the same report we can read that, despite the high sales success of the Alexa, users seem to limit themselves to using only a few basic functionalities like playing music, checking the weather or checking the news. Customers are not able to learn and use other, more advanced functionalities available in the service. As a result, algorithms based on history of usage are not appropriate, because people hardly get beyond what they know or do not

© Springer Nature Switzerland AG 2020
C. Debruyne et al. (Eds.): OTM 2019 Workshops, LNCS 11878, pp. 199–203, 2020.
https://doi.org/10.1007/978-3-030-40907-4_21

have history of usage. This article presents the idea and methodology of using automatically recognised personality as a classifier of needs. The research is in progress and all preparatory stages are finished. The creation of final statistical models and their validation is in the sphere of plans.

1.1 Personality

Personality is a psychological term, most often understood as a set of relatively constant psychical properties (attributes) for an individual, conditioning the constancy of its behavior and attitudes. There are a number of studies showing a strong relationship between personality and behavior, life satisfaction achievements and preferences e.g. [3].

For this research, the Big Five model is used to describe the personality of an individual. The model has been developed mainly by Costa & McCrae since 1978 and in the 90s it was conrmed in a large number of empirical studies [4,5]. Big 5 model basically claims that there are five dimensional factors of personality.

- **Openness** to experience describes tolerance for new and unknown.
- **Extraversion** describes tolerance for big quantity of stimuli and is also connected with social excintolerancehange.
- **Neuroticism** describes for stress.
- **Agreeableness** is about concentration to others need and willingness for co-operation.
- **Conscientiousness** is about intolerance for chaos and disorder.

1.2 Personality Detected from Digital Footprint

Many researchers have attempted to determine the user's personality based on digital data. Most of the attempts concerned data from social media (Facebook, Twitter) [6–8] or other personal data like call logs [9] or mobile applications [10]. Some of this kind of personality diagnosis were verified and the result was positive [11]. Models of indicating data-driven users' personality are mainly based on analysing of text (e.g. tweets or FB posts) [7,12]). In 2013 [7] researchers prove also that predicting personality based on telephone call logs data is possible. Tracking the digital footprint for detecting the users personality was also broadly investigated by researchers using various kinds of large data sets like text, profile photo, music, film preferences based on the FB likes or relations (SNA) for example: [6,7]. Except the analysing the profile photo in social media, all researches were based on the massive data, collected from the history of social service usage. Therefore, we are looking for methods that allow services for automatic personality recognition based on small amounts of data available at the time of service installation, when history of usage is not existed. Also the assumption refers to determining the personality of each user of the smart service, so the model should be based on the data available in each phone.

2   Research Objectives and Methodology

Taking into account the experience of the related works, as well as the business need, presented above, a research program was created, accompanying the project of creating user-oriented services dedicated to smart home environment. The main goal of the research is to propose **effective and accurate method of recognising the user's personality (Big 5), based on the data available at the moment of installation without having to wait for the data on the user's history to be collected**. An additional goal is to provide evidence that personality can be effectively used in smart services as a classifier. For the fulfilling research objectives, the following research scheme was designed (see Fig. 1):

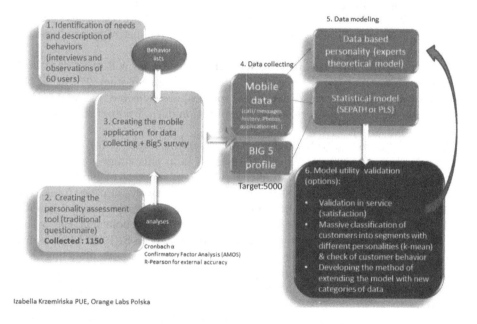

Fig. 1. Research Scheme & Methods

1. Preliminary qualitative research Carried out to identify needs and collect descriptions of discriminating behavior. Survey conducted in 2018 (own research[1]), delivered clear evidence that personality dimensions are good enough for discriminating users needs and expectations. For example, people

---

[1] The research was carried out in 2018, on 60 users of mobile phones, aged 20–29, men and women, (homogeneous group due to emphasize the diversity resulting from personality). The study was a multi-stage: filling of the personality questionnaire (Big 5), monthly observation of behaviors in social profiles and in the use of telephone, in-depth structured interviews aimed at getting as much information as possible about behavior patterns. The results of these studies were behavioral metrics for each of Big 5 dimensions.

who are open to experience (high openness) expect non-standard content, have a high level of cognitive needs, and high need to explore (curiosity). In turn, people with low openness expect only a sense of comfort in a world that is well known to them (they like only what they know, they are afraid of unknown). For high on conscientiousness people important are those functionalities that help in the implementation of the need for control. On the other hand people with a low conscientiousness, who accept life in chaos and disorder, need only very basic control functionalities and will never be interested in the use of advanced calendar or notebook functions. Moreover, respondents confirm that the services based on artificial intelligence are currently not adapted to them and this is the primary reason for their rejection or dissatisfaction with available services.

2. Creation the personality assessment tool which can be used for this specific research (low number of questions (25) and tool tested and created for online or mobile app usage). All standard psychometric procedures are applied.

3. Developing the mobile application dedicated for collecting data from mobile phone and Big 5 assessment (25 questions from stage 2). So far the data from the following user activities (sources) are collected and analyzed on a mobile phone of a user: telco data, application data, Photos, phone settings and statistics.

4. Main research fieldwork is data collecting required for creating the model, planned 5000 participants. Research is in this stage now. The data collected are: mobile phone data, available in the moment of service installation (single drop without additional logging the activity) and Big 5 metrics.

5. Creating the personality model There is an idea to create 2 models. The first will be theoretical model coherent with psychological Big 5 theory. The second will be pure statistical model based on SEPATH (structural equations path modelling) or PLS (partial least squares path modeling).

6. Validation stage e.g in interactive service which allow experimental manipulation based on personality adapted service. Or in laboratory simulation way comparing satisfaction metrics or checking the purchasing behaviour after massive classification of whole data base of mobile customers.The final shape will highly depend on the phase of maturity of the created parallel service as well as on the availability of data on service platform.

The stages 1, 2 and 3 are finished. The research is now on stage 4 (collecting data for statistical models). The future works concern the stages 5 and 6. The validation stage (6) is now rather a list of proposals and is not completely defined. Stage 5 and stage 6 will run cyclically until satisfactory results are achieved. It will also be repeated if the data-set is expanded or the assumptions changed.

3   Conclusion and Future Work

The presented user-oriented research program is conducted simultaneously with service development. It seems that extending the list of variables describing users with features related to, personality and creating universal methods measuring these features is a natural step in the development of intelligent and smart services. It can be new approach for user-oriented services designing. The challenge for researchers will also be an attempt to verify which of created models is more effective in predicting behavior and personalising the smart services. The solution can be also developed towards a faster and automatic diagnosis of a given person (e-health). Also can be easily transfer to other areas of business, such as creating applications and user interfaces which will be automatically adapted to users' personality.

Considering the desired direction of further research, they are mainly related to the measurement of the impact of service personalization on user satisfaction and the creation of a system monitoring the accuracy of the personality model based on data about user activity in the service. The entire system should also be refined in terms of expanding the data set on which the model is created with new categories of data, e.g. smartwatch devices or sensors installed in a smart home that reflect better the more physical spheres of behavior (eg meals, leaving home, home activities, e.t.c.).

References

1. Kosinski, M., Stillwell, D., Graepel, T.: Private traits and attributes are predictable from digital records of human behavior. Proc. Nat. Acad. Sci. (PNAS) **110**(15), 5802–5805 (2013)
2. Anand, P.: The Reality Behind Voice Shopping Hype'. https://www.theinformation.com/articles/the-reality-behind-voice-shopping-hype?. Accessed 30 Aug 2019
3. Judge, T., Higgins, C., Thoresen, C., Barrick, M.: The big five personality traits, general metal ability and career success across the life span. Pers. Psychol. **52**(3), 621–625 (1999)
4. Costa Jr., P.T., Mc Crae, R.R.: Four ways five factors are basic. Pers. Individ. Differ. **12**(13), 653–665 (1992)
5. Goldberg, L.R.: The development of markers for the big-five factor structure. J. Pers. Soc. Psychol. 99–110, (2016)
6. Liu, L., Preotiuc-Pietro, D., et al.: Analyzing personality through social media profile picture choice. In: Association for the Advancement of Artificial Intelligence (2016)
7. Kern, M.L., et al.: The online social self an open vocabulary approach to personality, University of Pennsylvania, University of Cambridge (2013)
8. Quercia, D., Kosinski, M., Stillwell, D., Crowcroft, J.: Our Twitter profiles, our selves: predicting personality with Twitter. In: IEEE SocialCom (2011)
9. de Montjoye, Y.-E., Quoidbach, J., Robic, F., Pentland, A.: Predicting Personality Using Novel Mobile Phone-Based Metrics. MIT/Harvard University (2013). Ecole Normale Suprieure de Lyon
10. Xu, R., Frey, R.M., Fleisch, E., Ilic, A.: Understanding the impact of personality traits on mobile app adoption insights from a large-scale field study, ETH Zurich (2016)
11. Back, M.D., et al.: Facebook profiles reflect actual personality not self-idealization. Psychol. Sci. **21**(3), 372–374 (2010). https://doi.org/10.1177/0956797609360756
12. Goldbeck, J., et al.: Predicting personality from Twitter. In: IEEE International Conference on Privacy, Security, Risk, and Trust (2011)

Temporary User States Method to Support Home Habitants

Ewelina Szczekocka[1,2](✉) (iD)

[1] Faculty of Informatics and Electronic Economy,
Poznan University of Economics, Poznań, Poland
[2] R&D Labs, Orange Polska, Warsaw, Poland
ewelina.szczekocka@orange.com

Abstract. Major goal of the research introduced in the paper is elaboration of a method delivering temporary user states to personalize databased services for this user. The method addressing a paradigm of ambient living will be used for support people broadly in their everyday life activities, like habitants in their home environments, persons needing assistance (in Ambient Assist Living) and others. It can be applied in new data-based services on 5G platforms, using intelligent ambient environments. A system for home experimentally developed in Orange Labs is one of the solutions where the method can be implemented. This system is aligned with an idea of sensitive home, discovering habitant's affective characteristics, like personality and emotions, based on his data and reacting according to this characteristics. The paper aims at presentation of another affective characteristics based on discovering temporary user states. An important aspect considered is privacy, GDPR compliance and moreover it should include a consideration on ethics.

Keywords: Home habitants support · Sensitive home · Ambient
assisted living · NLP · Big data application

1 Introduction

E-society becomes a reality thanks to new information and communication technologies - ICT (like 5G network, AI). We focus on one of e-society's needs, supporting citizens in their everyday lives, e.g. at home, including Ambient Assist Living, people with dysfunctions. In a context of a global economy it is supported by digital transformations [see a study by World Economic Forum [1]]. There are several challenges and risks accompanying these transformations which require involvement of ethics as well as privacy approach. However it gives also opportunities for innovative data-based services as a major company business value. Orange Group bets on building new data-based services, with respect of regulations, as GDPR and telecom law, which means also a respect to a customer privacy. Among its initiatives, there is Horizon 2020 5G Tours project aiming at

Supported by organization Orange Polska SA & Orange SA.

dynamic use of the 5G network, according to specific customer needs shown in individual use cases. Another example is the Home'In architecture and environment for home services provided by Research Labs which aims at integration of services' management at home, tailoring them for each of habitants and supporting everyday life activities. It will be provided via a Virtual Home Assistant or Virtual Personal Assistant (VHA/VPA). According to [2], in 2020 approximately 75% of worldwide households will have one device with VPA functionality, 20% - at least two devices with VPA and 5% three or more devices, which shows significance of works in this area. The recent progress in Machine Learning (like Deep Learning) stimulates a rise of VHA, offering new possibilities to research on natural language processing.

2   Related Works

Speaking on profiling and personalization of home services, it goes far beyond a classical approach. It requires adoption not only to a user's behaviors, customs but moreover to what a user is (in sense of personality, emotions, i.e. being "sensitive"), taking into account a particular external and internal context (situations but also present state of emotions, etc.). Second, it should be not intrusive (supporting not constraining). Finally it should take into account user intent inferred from a dialogue with VHA. However a broad review of literature was provided regarding profiling and personalization approach, it shows lack of relevant research which would enable home (its interface) to be sensitive enough for a user. Exemplary papers from Body of Knowledge [3–9] provide a broad review on profiling and personalization, as well as customer experience. Most works related to profiling and personalization concern recommendations, recommenders (e.g. on-tag profiling, collaborative filtering, content-based filtering), some works relate to Web users profiling (Web mining, Social Network Analysis), marketing (predicting churn), e-commerce/digital services (customer loyalty scoring, purchasing), among which behavioral profiling can be found. However user profiling and service personalization based on knowledge on a user inferred from his data is not widely considered, few interesting works in our research scope were found, like e.g.: toolbox for mobile phone metadata [10], behavioral profiling for authentication (from mobile data) regarding anomalies [14], modelling users social characteristics (communities, relations) based on mobile data [15], predicting psychology attributes for Social Networks users [16], profiling user's personality using colors [17]. They may be inspiring for a development of a method of characterizing temporary user states through digital signals from his data. As it is concerned with NLP approach in profiling: dialogue state tracking [3] is a core part of a spoken dialogue system. It estimates the beliefs of possible user's goals at every dialogue turn. However, for most current approaches, it's difficult to scale to large dialogue domains. Work presented in [3] addresses those constraints. It uses an ontology to support modelling of state tracking. In [4] a method of predicting user mental states is proposed for the development of more efficient and usable spoken dialogue systems adopting dynamically to user needs. The mental state is built on the basis of the emotional state of a user and his intention based on natural language understanding. A method shows that taking into account the user's mental state improves system performance as well as its perceived quality.

3   Temporary User States and Problem Statement

A business goal for Orange is to elaborate a system supporting lives of home habitants by providing relevant reactions ("sensitive home"). A VHA will serve as a basic interface to Home. Discovering knowledge on a user, based on his different data (within a smart home e.g. data from sensors, dialogue data with a Home interface, as well as users' communications data from his devices) which will evolve along with this user, enabling relevant reactions in near real-time, is a key element of this solution. A research briefly presented in this paper introduces an approach of temporary user states. It can be perceived as an affective parameter in user characteristics next to personality and emotions. Discovering personality enriches user's characteristics with his stable view on the external world while identifying emotions brings knowledge on immediate short-lived reactions to different life situations. Both approaches go beyond state-of-the-art works in user's characteristics (described in the literature). Temporary user states is about temporary (vs. stable as by personality) view on a user reflecting his reactions on different signals of external world coming to him (however not such immediate like emotion but accumulative). Author believes that temporary user states can be determined thanks to discovering specific patterns from user data (e.g. from dialogues, communications, physical reactions). It may be significant for personalization of services (like e.g. adjustment reactions of home), as it offers another perspective on a user (between immediate and stable). First experimental architecture has been developed by Orange research, while ensuring personal data protection and securing users' privacy. It is dedicated to serve affective parameters calculated for a user and decide on reactions of VHA as well as adjust home services at a given context of a user (external - customs, social situations, as well as internal – according to a user personality, emotions expressed). One of the components of this architecture called "Affective Services", see Fig. 1, is dedicated to calculate affective parameters for services. Presently it consists of two subcomponents for calculating: personality (based on Big 5 model) and emotions (from texts). Personality signals from the following anonymized data are analyzed (collected from mobiles): telco data (call and sms logs), mobile applications' data and phone parameters, textual data from tweets, photos, based on achievements of [10–13]. The idea of this research is to add next affective parameter in form of temporary user states.

4   Summary and Future Work

Future work will be dedicated to development of a method for discovering temporary user states in scope of doctoral thesis. Data from natural language dialogue

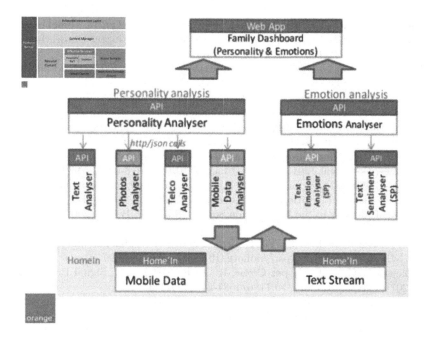

Fig. 1. Architecture of affective services component, consisting on personality and emotions components

(e.g. CRM communication data, data from communication with a VHA, chats for home habitants) will be used as well as data from user communications via mobile devices (in anonymous manner). A method of validation of this solution will be also elaborated. A focus group will be organized as well to check "vitality" of the concept in terms of addressing users' needs. Moreover research activities are planned on how users adopt a fact of discovering such sensitive information like "temporary user states", before experimentation phase with data, which is going to be performed as well. In next steps (out of the scope of this doctoral thesis) work on semantic representation of temporary user states and outcomes from dialogue state tracking can be planned and performed to see how to support decision-making process (use of outcomes from affective services component in order to propose relevant reactions of the system managing home services).

References

1. White Paper: Digital Transformation Initiative. Telecommunication Industry, WEF in Coop. with Accenture (2017). https://www.weforum.org/whitepapers/digital-transformation-initiative
2. Eurpoean Commission Report: The Rise of Virtual Personal Assistants (2018). https://ec.europa.eu/growth/tools-databases/dem/monitor/content/rise-virtual-personal-assistants

3. Hildebrandt, M.: Defining profiling: a new type of knowledge? In: Hildebrandt, M., Gutwirth, S. (eds.) Profiling the European Citizen. Springer, Dordrecht (2008). https://doi.org/10.1007/978-1-4020-6914-7_2
4. Hildebrandt, M.: DuD **30**, 548 (2006). https://doi.org/10.1007/s11623-006-0140-3
5. Kanoje, S., Girase, S., Mukhopadhyay, D.: User profiling trends, techniques and applications. Int. J. Adv. Found. Res. Comput. **1**, 2348–4853 (2014)
6. Bosco, F., Creemers, N., Ferraris, V., Guagnin, D., Koops, B.-J.: Profiling technologies and fundamental rights and values: regulatory challenges and perspectives from European data protection authorities. In: Gutwirth, S., Leenes, R., de Hert, P. (eds.) Reforming European Data Protection Law. LGTS, vol. 20, pp. 3–33. Springer, Dordrecht (2015). https://doi.org/10.1007/978-94-017-9385-8_1
7. Jaquet-Chiffelle, D.O., Benoist, E., Haenni, R., Wenger, F., Zwingelberg, H.: Virtual persons and identities. In: Rannenberg, K., Royer, D., Deuker, A. (eds.) The Future of Identity in the Information Society. Springer, Berlin (2009). https://doi.org/10.1007/978-3-642-01820-6_3
8. Ren, L., Xie, K., Chen, L., Yu, K.: Towards universal dialogue state tracking. In: EMNLP 2018 (2018). https://doi.org/10.18653/v1/d18-1299
9. Callejas, Z., Griol, D., López-Cózar, R.: EURASIP J. Adv. Signal Process. **2011**, 6 (2011). https://doi.org/10.1186/1687-6180-2011-6
10. de Montjoye, Y.-A., Quoidbach, J., Robic, F., Pentland, A.S.: Predicting personality using novel mobile phone-based metrics. In: Greenberg, A.M., Kennedy, W.G., Bos, N.D. (eds.) SBP 2013. LNCS, vol. 7812, pp. 48–55. Springer, Heidelberg (2013). https://doi.org/10.1007/978-3-642-37210-0_6
11. Kern, M., et al.: The online social self an open vocabulary approach to personality. Assessment **21**, 158–169 (2013). https://doi.org/10.1177/1073191113514104
12. Xu, R., Frey, R.M., Fleisch, E., Ilic, A.: Understanding the impact of personality traits on mobile app adoption - insights from a large-scale field study. Comput. Hum. Behav. **62**, 244–256 (2016). https://doi.org/10.1016/j.chb.2016.04.011
13. Liu, L., Preotiuc-Pietro, D., et al.: Analyzing personality through social media profile picture choice. In: ICWSM 2016, Association for the Advancement of Artificial Intelligence (2016)
14. Kałużny, P.: Behavioural profiling authentication based on trajectory based anomaly detection model of user's mobility. In: Abramowicz, W. (ed.) BIS 2017. LNBIP, vol. 303, pp. 242–254. Springer, Cham (2017). https://doi.org/10.1007/978-3-319-69023-0_21
15. Blondel, V., Guillaume, J.-L., Lambiotte, R., Lefebvre, E.: Fast unfolding of communities in large networks. J. Stat. Mech. Theory Exp. **2008**(10), P10008 (2008). https://doi.org/10.1088/1742-5468/2008/10/P10008
16. Khayrullin, R.M., Makarov, I., Zhukov, L.E.: Predicting psychology attributes of a social network user. In: MPRA Paper 82810. University Library of Munich, Germany (2017). https://ideas.repec.org/p/pra/mprapa/82810.html
17. Kabzińska, K., Wieloch, M., Filipiak, D., Filipowska, A.: Profiling user's personality using colours: connecting BFI-44 personality traits and plutchik's wheel of emotions. In: Wilimowska, Z., Borzemski, L., Świątek, J. (eds.) ISAT 2018. AISC, vol. 854, pp. 371–380. Springer, Cham (2019). https://doi.org/10.1007/978-3-319-99993-7_33

1st International Workshop on Security via Information Analytics and Applications (SIAnA 2019)

1st International Workshop on Security via Information Analytics and Applications (SIAnA)

Rhodes, Greece 2019

Message from the Co-chairs

The month of October 2019 marks the inaugural edition of the Workshop on "Security via Information Analytics and Applications" (SIAnA). It has been a part of On The Move Federated Conferences (OTM 2019) and it was held in Rhodes, Greece. The SIAnA Workshop has been established to promote, encourage and facilitate collaboration and exchange of ideas with researchers in the field of cyber-security. Although there are a lot of scientific venues disseminating research results on several aspects of cybersecurity, the SIAnA workshop focuses on technical approaches that concentrate on analytics as an inherent element of the research process.

The goal of the SIAnA workshop is to provide a platform for emerging ideas in solving security problems based on an information point of view. It aims to bring together researchers and practitioners who are interested in addressing security issues using information technology, and work towards possible solutions to such problems. It emphasizes the use, manipulation, and extraction of information for generating solutions to important problems in cybersecurity research.

The first edition of the SIAnA workshop includes four research papers that were presented. These papers addressed cybersecurity problems by analyzing information using machine learning, deep learning, semantic technologies, generative adversary networks, and other relevant techniques.

The SIAnA workshop would not have been made possible without the valuable contributions of the authors, and the assistance of the members of the program committee, the reviewers, supporters, and the colleagues of the OTM organizing team who provided a supporting infrastructure for a successful workshop.

George Karabatis
Aryya Gangopadhyay
The SIAnA 2019 Workshop Co-chairs

SDN-GAN: Generative Adversarial Deep NNs for Synthesizing Cyber Attacks on Software Defined Networks

Ahmed AlEroud[1] and George Karabatis[2(✉)]

[1] Yarmouk University, Irbid, Jordan
ahmed.aleroud@yu.edu.jo
[2] University of Maryland, Baltimore County (UMBC),
Baltimore, MD 21250, USA
georgek@umbc.edu

Abstract. The recent evolution in programmable networks such as SDN opens the possibility to control networks using software controllers. However, such networks are vulnerable to attacks that occur in traditional networks. Several techniques are proposed to handle the security vulnerabilities in SDNs. However, it is challenging to create attack signatures, scenarios, or even intrusion detection rules that are applicable to SDN dynamic environments. Generative Adversarial Deep Neural Networks automates the generation of realistic data in a semi supervised manner. This paper describes an approach that generates synthetic attacks that can target SDNs. It can be used to train SDNs to detect different attack variations. It is based on the most recent OpenFlow models/algorithms and it utilizes similarity with known attack patterns to identify attacks. Such synthesized variations of attack signatures are shown to attack SDNs using adversarial approaches.

Keywords: Cyber-attack detection · Software Defined Networks · Generative Adversarial Networks

1 Introduction

Intrusion Detection Systems (IDS) perform thorough network traffic analysis to make intelligent detection of possible network attacks. Intrusion Protection Systems (IPS) complement IDSs by taking countermeasures or responses to stop detected attacks. Most systems perform both IDS and IPS tasks to protect information assets. In comparison, firewalls use static rules that require continuous monitoring and updating to stay current, and they are written using flow attributes, e.g., port number, IP, MAC address; these are considered the most primitive task that an IDS/IPS performs [9].

The recent evolution in programmable networks such as Software Defined Networks (SDN) opens the possibility to ultimately build network agents that are fully autonomous in the network, handling traffic in a dynamic and programmable manner [1, 21]. SDNs separate the data layer from the control layer. One of the SDN features is the controller global view and knowledge of the network. One or more IDS appliances connected to the controller can receive overall global traffic information. SDNs have

© Springer Nature Switzerland AG 2020
C. Debruyne et al. (Eds.): OTM 2019 Workshops, LNCS 11878, pp. 211–220, 2020.
https://doi.org/10.1007/978-3-030-40907-4_23

the ability to collect network traffic and monitor the network without impacting its performance. A report by [11] discussed implementing an SDN based IDS. The major advantage was related to network load balancing and traffic distribution based on security controls. Rather than including ACLs, an IDS/IPS includes rule engines where those rules study real time traffic and judge whether that traffic can be classified as harmful or not based on rules, signatures, or patterns included in IDS/IPS engines. Firewalls act on L2–L3 level information while IDS/IPS may work at all or most OSI layers information.

Security is one of the major challenges in SDNs. Researchers argue that SDNs are vulnerable and easier to target, and several authors proposed IDSs to protect SDNs. However, it is challenging to identify all attacking techniques that may target SDNs. Adversaries have enough knowledge and motivation to attack and bypass those systems, since most IDSs rely on classification algorithms and it is possible to create examples that evade those classifiers. In this paper we follow an approach that utilizes labeled regular flows to analyze samples of flows generated using SDNs, we then show how it is possible to evade SDN-based IDSs using synthetic samples that are created using Generative Adversarial Networks (GAN). The contributions of this work are as follows:

1. Generation of attack examples on SDNs: it is accomplished through feature perturbation implemented using GAN. The results show that GAN networks are very effective in creating adversarial examples that can fool machine learning detection models for SDN.
2. Synthesis of SDN intrusion detection datasets: to the best of our knowledge, this is the first work to synthesize adversarial examples against GAN, which leaves the door open for new defensive mechanism based on the level of perturbation.
3. Evaluation: The existing GAN cyber security models are tested based on existence or absence of malicious features in attack examples. However, data may also contain suspicious or borderline features, which cannot be classified as benign or attacks. The experimental results proved the success of generating adversarial models for SDN examples using GAN. A significant number of the generated examples evaded different intrusion detection algorithms.

2 Integration of SDNs and IDSs

Several applications can be developed on top of SDNs to control traffic intelligently [4–8, 10, 13]. The SDN controller includes methods to write flow rules in switches' flow tables. We think that the very same task can be extended for SDN-based IDS/IPS. The controller takes two actions based on incoming traffic: first, is the actual decision on what to do with the subject traffic (e.g., drop, forward, flood) and secondly is writing a flow rule in the switch flow table as a response to the subject flow or traffic. SDN-based IDS/IPS should perform similar tasks on a broader context. The single or simple flow in the case of control-flow tables should be extended to include complex flows in the SDN-inference-engine. Below are some design goals for an SDN-based IDS/IPS system:

- Openness and Extensibility: Flexibility of both GAN and SDNs open the possibility to write programs and APIs to interact with the network and generate adversarial examples.
- Flexibility: The developed IDS/IPS system should be flexible to use, configure, and interact with.
- Dynamic behavior: The security system should be able to automatically adjust attack signatures based on network changes. User interaction with the system (e.g. to add rules, datasets, etc.) should be handled with well-defined Deep Learning models enabled by users and applications.

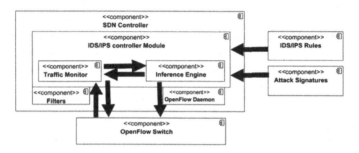

Fig. 1. SDN based IDS/IPS security model

Figure 1 illustrates a high level component diagram of the SDN based IDS/IPS security control. An SDN IDS/IPS module as part of SDN controller should perform the following tasks:

Traffic Monitor: This module communicates with Open Flow switches to submit customized traffic queries and receive traffic information from the network or the switches. This task can be outsourced to applications such as sFlow that can interact with SDN controllers. In this work we utilize our previous technique [17] to create and label flows. There are different ways to pass traffic to the IDS/IPS system. In one approach, the controller can be programmed to pass the traffic to the IDS/IPS in addition to forwarding it to its destination. Another one uses the special ports in Openflow switches [12]. In particular, SDN allows simple and dynamic programming of the packet monitoring system. Switch Port Analyzer (SPAN) is used for monitoring traditional networking components. However, it has several problems and limitations. IDS/IPS SDN-based customized real-time monitoring can be the most significant contribution that SDNs bring to IDS/IPS. This can be categorized in three major aspects: Real time, customized, and beyond L2–L4 information, as described next.

- Real time: SDN controllers can provide monitoring system on-path or real time traffic information without significantly causing overhead in comparison with traditional approaches. Many IDS/IPS systems require to mirror network traffic in order to be investigated.
- Customized traffic monitoring or packet processing: An SDN is largely labeled as "Control programmable networks" where network administrators and programmers

can define monitoring applications to steer and interact with traffic in real time rather than just pulling the whole traffic to the monitoring system.

- Beyond L2–L4 information or intelligence: Current network requirements for security controls, policy management, etc. show a clear need to extend traffic intelligence up to Layer 7. This can help develop smarter control and security services, and allow high level user abstractions to communicate with low level network information. One further advantage of changing the monitoring process from an embedded to a network function, is that the same monitoring function can be used by different management or security services.

Inference Engine: This is the core module of the SDN IDS/IPS system. Rules can vary of complexity between simple flow related ones to more complex pattern recognition algorithms. Sub-modules are dedicated to different ways of detecting security attacks (e.g. signature based, dictionary based, or rule based). For example, a dictionary based module may include a large dataset of known threats in terms of their known ports, IP addresses [3].

Openflow Daemon: It is responsible for inserting and removing the Openflow entries that direct traffic from the outward-facing ports to the necessary module hosts and processing modules and then back out. Communication between detection and mitigation (i.e. traffic monitoring and inference engine modules) is two-way. Algorithms to detect the type of the attack and mitigate it by proposing a solution should try to optimize time and accuracy based on several possible approaches, and deciding which one to use. Machine learning algorithms can be used dynamically for classification and prediction. For experimentation, there are open datasets that can be used to evaluate IDS/IPS systems and algorithms (e.g. DARPA [14–16]). Inputs to the inference engine include IDS/IPS Rules (added and edited by security experts, and they can be written in natural language terms or using a semi-structured format such as SDN policy languages such as, Frenetic and Pyretic) and Attack Signatures.

There are several problems with traditional IDS/IPS inference engines. There is a need for fine grained decisions beyond the (Block/Permit) binary decisions. This is the main reason that false positive and negative alarms are considered the most significant problems related to those decisions. QoS decision can be added to allow further investigation of suspect packets, holding them aside while allowing the next traffic to be investigated. The fact that SDN allows control programmability helps in defining fine grained decisions between *Block* and *Permit.*

IDS/IPS Rules: This is the component that is accessed and updated by network administrators. Network administrators should be able to add or modify certain rules to override built in or dynamic algorithms. In some cases, those added rules can be used as low level or default rules that will be applied if no match of dynamic rules occurs.

The controller or any of its inner modules acts as an Information Flow Processor (IFP) collecting information on behalf of the security controls. IFP is used to process IDS/IPS continuous real time requests. However, implementing IFP based on traditional architectures requires extensive network resources. In one definition IFP is defined as "a tool capable of timely processing large amount of information as it flows from the peripheral to the center of the system" [3]. We follow an approach that utilizes labeled regular flows to analyze different samples of flows generated using SDNs. The objective of this approach is to: (1) examine if we can utilize existing attack signatures to analyze samples of traffic generated by SDNs, and (2) to find out how the traditional IDS behaves when handling a large number of the traffic generated by SDNs.

3   Testing SDN IDS Using Data Generated by GAN

Recently, deep-learning adversarial models have attracted quite an attention in Cyber Security. As opposed to traditional techniques, GANs apply a set of non-linear transformations on an original malicious sample to generate an adversarial example that evades classification models. GANs have shown some promising results in intrusion detection [22]. The GAN structure in this paper consists of a Generator network, a Discriminator network and an intrusion detector that handles both OpenFlow and NonOpenFlow traffic. Feature vectors of attacks against SDNs consist of the regular features of a network traffic that are converted into binary values of 0 and 1. A feature vector is represented using a ternary (i.e., three-valued) features, where -1 describes the malicious features, 1 describes legitimate features, and 0 describes suspicious features. We re-encode ternary features into two-bit binary features using the encoding, 0 to 01, 1 to 00, and 1 to 11. Our approach deals with suspicious features that can be classified as borderline features. The original feature vector contains n-ternary features in the original encoding (i.e., n columns). With the proposed encoding, 2n features are created. Each feature in the original data is encoded using two columns, each containing one binary feature. This encoding scheme is applied to both attacks and benign examples. The Generator creates a perturbed version of attack examples to convert them into adversarial examples. The Discriminator learns to fit the intrusion detector, which is implemented using classification algorithms to identify Denial of Service attacks on SDNs. At each round of the training process, the Discriminator sends a feedback to the Generator to modify its weights during the training process to the point where it guarantees that the Generator creates enough examples to evade the intrusion detector. Intrusion examples consist of a feature vector f with n features. Both the input vector f and a noise vector z are fed to the generator. Using our encoding scheme, f consists of m features where m = 2n. The features in f take the values of 0 and 1 to identify how malicious the feature is where 11 denotes a very malicious feature. The Hyperparameter z is a vector with random entries in the range [0, 1). The proposed structure of the generator consists of three hidden layers, each with 120 neurons. Hidden layers are activated using LeakyReLU. The output layer consists of 2n neurons, two for each feature, which are all activated using sigmoid function in order to return outputs between 0 and 1. The Generator parameters are updated based on the feedback from the Discriminator. The resulting adversarial examples are binarized using a threshold to create a binary vector with two inputs 0 and 1. However, for backpropagation to work non binarized vectors are used. The perturbation done using GAN preserves the semantics of the original data. In attacks against SDN, it is possible to produce new attacks by removing some features and introducing others.

There is a need to update the weights of the generator using the gradient information from the discriminator. The Discriminator and intrusion detector both take the feature vector f as an input. The Discriminator classifies the given flow as a benign or attack using a single output layer with a certain level of uncertainty. Adam optimizer is used as an optimization function. The training data for the discriminator consists of adversarial sample generated by the generator and the benign sample. The ground truth labels for the discriminator are the predictions made by the intrusion detector, not the actual labels of the samples.

Training the generator and discriminator aims at minimizing their loss functions which are measured differently. The predictions of the intrusion detector are used as labels for the discriminators. Therefore, the loss function of the discriminator tries to minimize classification mismatches between the discriminator and the intrusion detector.

4   Experiments and Analysis

4.1   Data Generation

Our approach aggregates flow entries exchanged between controller and the OpenFlow (OF) switches. The analysis of the collected OFs emphasizes on discovering similarity of such flows with non-OFs using appropriate classification techniques. We hypothesized that sampling OFs and testing them using an appropriate intrusion detection mechanism can be used as a mechanism to discover threats on SDNs. The first sample in our experiment is taken from a dataset of one hour of anonymized traffic traces from a Distributed Denial-of-Service (DDoS) attack [19]. This type of attack attempts to block access to the targeted server by consuming computing resources on the server and by consuming all of the network bandwidth connecting the server to the Internet. The second sample contains only IP packets. Each record of the dataset represents a packet of several fields such as, packetSize, sourceIP, destinationIP, sourcePort, destination- Port, TCPFlags, transportProtocol and packetType [20].

4.2   Network Topology

We used Open vSwitch (OVS) as an OpenFlow switch connected to three Linux-based hosts (the attacker, hostl, host2, and host3). The three hosts can only communicate through the OVS switch. We used GENIExperimenter to create this topology [18]. We utilized an Xen VM with a public IP to run an OpenFlow controller, 1 Xen VM to be the OpenFlow switch, and 3 Xen VMs as hosts. In general, the controller just needs to have a public IP address, so that it can exchange messages with the OpenFlow switch.

Table 1. Samples used for training and testing.

Activity type	OF	Non-OF
TCP/SYN flood	6214	3216
UDP flood	–	2512
ICMP flood	6230	3590
Total	12444	9318
TCP/SYN benign traffic	2712	1100
UDP benign traffic	–	–
ICMP benign traffic	5112	4100
Total	7824	5200
Suspicious and benign	20268	14518
% of suspicious flows	0.61	0.64
% of benign flows	0.38	0.35

4.3 Results Without GAN

Table 1 and Fig. 2 show the results of our experiments when changing the percentages of OFs to non-OF flows where the non-OFs are labeled as attacks or benign activities. Figure 2 represents the baseline for the traffic-type (OF or non-OF). The K-NN is used to classify non-OF using similarity with OF attack patterns.

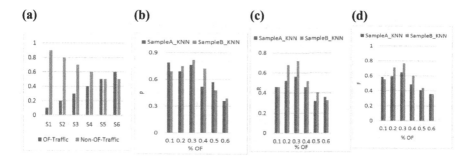

(a)   **(b)**   **(c)**   **(d)**

Fig. 2. (a) OF vs non-OF traffic (b) Precision (c) Recall (d) F-score

The results show that increasing the percentage of OF flows in the testing sample while decreasing the percentage of non-OF flows lowers the attack detection rate in terms of P, R, and F-score.

4.4 Results with GAN

The created instances are used to deceive a machine learning-based detectors that are created using KNN and Random Forest Classification Models. We used the original OF and non-OF data with 0.3 OF from both datasets to generate attacks. The reported values in Table 2 represent the success rate of identifying attacks before and after the data is modified using GAN by varying epoch hyperparameter and changing the machine learning classifier. The noise vector contains 10 dimensions. The intrusion detection rates for adversarial examples is between 0.07–0.53 which clearly shows how GAN can still evade the intrusion detection techniques that work on SDNs. In addition to evasion IDSs, our approach can be used to generate private datasets as proved by the values of conditional privacy reported in Table 2.

Table 2. Results using data generated with GAN

Epoch	Detector type	Conditional privacy	Original attack detection rate	Detection rate after GAN
95	NN	0.44	0.81	0.51
80	NN	0.65	0.81	0.24
29	Random forest	0.39	0.85	0.53
150	SVM	0.95	0.83	0.15
500	NN	1.35	0.81	0.08
140	NN	2.05	0.81	0.04
512	NN	1.40	0.81	0.07

5   Conclusions

Software Defined Networks bring several benefits from the control plan for the data plane. However, decoupling introduces new attacks such as Denial of Service attacks. We proposed techniques to identify attacks on SDNs, we then show how GAN generated data can evade those techniques. The proposed approach synthesizes datasets, taking into consideration the utility- information loss tradeoff. This work can help understand how to use existing attack patterns to discover different attacks that target SDNs. In the future, we plan to create graph-based detectors for different attack types in SDNs and target those models using adversarial examples.

References

1. Alsmadi, I., Xu, D.: Security of software defined networks: a survey. Comput. Secur. **53**, 79–108 (2015)
2. AlEroud, A., Alsmadi, I.: Identifying DoS attacks on software defined networks: a relation context approach. In: NOMS 2016–2016 IEEE/IFIP Network Operations and Management Symposium, pp. 853–857 (2016)

3. Cugola, G., Margara, A.: Processing flows of information: from data stream to complex event processing. ACM Comput. Surv. (CSUR) **44**(3), 15 (2012)
4. Chung, C.J., Khatkar, P., Xing, T., Lee, J., Huang, D.: NICE: network intrusion detection and countermeasure selection in virtual network systems. IEEE Trans. Dependable Secur. Comput. **10**(4), 198–211 (2013)
5. Chung, C.J., Cui, J., Khatkar, P., Huang, D.: Non-intrusive process-based monitoring system to mitigate and prevent VM vulnerability explorations. In: 2013 9th International Conference on Collaborative Computing: Networking, Applications and Worksharing (Collaboratecom), October 2013, pp. 21–30. IEEE (2013)
6. Shirali-Shahreza, S., Ganjali, Y.: Efficient implementation of security applications in openflow controller with flexam. In: 2013 IEEE 21st Annual Symposium on High Performance Interconnects (HOTI), August 2013, pp. 49–54. IEEE (2013)
7. Jeong, C., Ha, T., Narantuya, J., Lim, H., Kim, J.: Scalable network intrusion detection on virtual SDN environment. In: 2014 IEEE 3rd International Conference on Cloud Networking (CloudNet), October 2014, pp. 264–265. IEEE (2014)
8. Lopez, M.E.A., Duarte, O.C.M.B.: Providing elasticity to intrusion detection systems in virtualized software defined networks. In: IEEE ICC (2015)
9. Alsmadi, I.: The integration of access control levels based on SDN. Int. J. High Perform. Comput. Netw. **9**, 281–290 (2016)
10. AlEroud, A., Alsmadi, I.: Identifying DoS attacks on software defined networks: a relation context approach. In: NOMS (2016)
11. Kerner, S.M.: OpenFlow can provide security too. http://www.enterprisenetworkingplanet. com/datacenter/openflowcan-provide-security-too.html. 14 May 2012
12. Hogg, S.: Using SDN to create a packet monitoring system, packet-level monitoring use case with cisco XNC and monitor manager, network world, technical article, December 2013. http://www.networkworld.com/article/2226003/cisco-subnet/using-sdn-to-create-a-packet-monitoring-system.html
13. Skowyra, R., Bahargam, S., Bestavros, A.: Software-defined ids for securing embedded mobile devices. In: High Performance Extreme Computing Conference (HPEC) 2013, pp. 1–7. IEEE (2013)
14. MIT: DARPA intrusion detection evaluation, ed (2012)
15. Stolfo, S.J., Fan, W., Lee, W., Prodromidis, A., Chan, P.K.: Cost-based modeling for fraud and intrusion detection: results from the JAM project. In: Proceedings of the DARPA Information Survivability Conference and Exposition 2000, DISCEX 2000, pp. 130–144 (2000)
16. Tavallaee, M., Bagheri, E., Lu, W., Ghorbani, A.-A.: A detailed analysis of the KDD CUP 99 dataset. In: Proceedings of the Second IEEE Symposium on Computational Intelligence for Security and Defense Applications 2009 (2009)
17. Ding, T., AlEroud, A., Karabatis, G.: Multi-granular aggregation of network flows for security analysis. In: IEEE International Conference on Intelligence and Security Informatics (ISI) 2015, pp. 173–175 (2015)
18. Berman, M., Chase, J.S., Landweber, L., Nakao, A., Ott, M., Raychaudhuri, D., et al.: GENI: a federated testbed for innovative network experiments. Comput. Netw. **61**, 5–23 (2014)
19. The CAIDA "DDoS Attack 2007" dataset. http://www.caida.org

20. Mirza, F., Khayam, S.A.: Network-embedded security using in-network packet marking. http://wisnet.seecs.nust.edu.pk/projects/nes/implementation.html
21. Kreutz, D., Ramos, F., Verissimo, P., Rothenberg, C.E., Azodolmolky, S., Uhlig, S.: Software-defined networking: a comprehensive survey, no. 2014. arXiv preprint arXiv:1406. 0440
22. Zilong, L., Shi, Y., Xue, Z.: IDSGAN: generative adversarial networks for attack gene ration against intrusion detection. arXiv preprint arXiv:1809.02077 (2018)

A Domain Adaptation Technique
for Deep Learning in Cybersecurity

Aryya Gangopadhyay[1]([✉]), Iyanuoluwa Odebode[2], and Yelena Yesha[1]

[1] University of Maryland Baltimore County, Baltimore, MD 21250, USA
gangopad@umbc.edu
[2] Air force Institute of Technology, Dayton, OH, USA

Abstract. In this paper we discuss an algorithm for transfer learning in cybersecurity. In particular, we develop a new image-based representation for the feature set in the source domain and train a convolutional neural network (CNN) using the training data. The CNN model is then augmented with one dense layer in the target domain before applying on the target dataset. The data we have used for our experimental results are taken from the Canadian Institute of Cybersecurity. The results show that transfer learning is feasible in cybersecurity which offers many potential applications including resource-constrained environments such as edge computing.

Keywords: Cybersecurity · Convolutional neural networks · Transfer learning

1 Introduction

While machine learning techniques have been used for intrusion detection systems (IDS) for detecting and classifying cyber attacks, existing techniques are inadequate in detecting the so-called "zero-day" attacks that the deployed models have not been exposed to during training [2]. At the same time cyber attackers continue to create new attack strategies in order to avoid detection. As a result, existing techniques will continue to fail to detect many cyber attacks that are as yet "unseen". Deep learning techniques have the potential to address such shortcomings in current IDS and IPS (intrusion prevention systems). One of the most promising and yet un-explored techniques deals with the possibility of re-using models that have been trained on one attack scenario to be effective in completely different scenarios.

Our goal in this research is to develop deep transfer learning models such that they can be trained in one setting and adapted to another domain. This is the classical definition of transfer learning and domain adaptation of deep learning models. While transfer learning has been successfully deployed in some settings, particularly in image classification, there has been limited research done

Partially supported by NSF grant# 1515358.

in the cybersecurity domain. The benefit of transfer learning is obvious given the enormous resources needed to build deep learning models. Transfer learning also provides the opportunity to deploy deep learning models in resources constrained domains such as in edge computing.

The rest of the paper is organized as follows: in Sect. 2 we discuss the related work in this area. Section 3 describes our methodology. In Sects. 4 and 5 we present the experimental results and our conclusions respectively.

2   Related Work

Traditional machine learning algorithms assume that the feature space of the training data (source domain) is the same as that of the data on which the model is applied (target domain). However, this assumption severely limits the applications of machine learning algorithms, because the amount of data, particularly labeled, available in the target domain may be limited, may have different distributions, or may contain different feature spaces. Hence there is a need to be able to "transfer" machine learning models from source to target domains with the minimum amount of additional effort. However, when the source and target domains are completely unrelated, brute force transfer may result in poor performance, a situation referred to as "negative transfer" [3]. Transfer learning has been applied successfully to various applications such as image processing [5,9], robotics, web mining, and WiFi localization [6–8] . Most of these applications require data in both source and target domains. More recently, [4] proposed a method by which a substantially smaller amount of data in the target domain can be used for domain adaptation. Other recent work on transfer learning and domain adaptation includes cross-domain tagging and cross dataset visual recognition [9–11].

Deep learning has been used in cybersecurity applications such as intrusion detection, malware detection, phishing/spam detection, and website defacement detection [13]. However, there is a lack of research in domain adaptation for cybersecurity. Data in cybersecurity is scarce because of many reasons such as privacy concerns, the difficulty in collecting such data, and shortage of labeled data. Thus, transfer learning and domain adaptation of deep learning models are even more critical in the cybersecurity domain as compared to others. In this paper we propose to address this significant gap.

3   Methodology

In this paper we assume that the source and target domains are related, the class labels are available in both source and transfer domains, and the machine learning task is that of *classification* of network traffic as either *benign*, or "attacks". Hence this task seems to fit the *inductive transfer learning* setting. However, the feature sets of the source and target domains are different and hence this task also has characteristics of *transductive transfer learning*.

In our approach for transfer learning the model that is used to identify cyber attacks is trained on different but related tasks. This approach works for features that are general rather than specific to the source or target tasks. Because the feature sets of the source and target domains are different, we needed to learn a good "feature representation" that is transferable from the source to the target domain. In this paper we transformed the feature sets of both source and target domains into three channel images which are subsequently used to train a CNN model.

Convolutional neural networks (CNN) are feed-forward neural networks where the neural connectivity is inspired by the organization of the visual cortex in animals where the visual fields are tiled by overlapping regions. CNNs are designed to discover local patterns in images using typically small, pre-defined kernels that slide over and convolve with small regions of an input image. The results of each convolution operation is collected in an output feature map that serves as input to the next layer. From the perspective of pattern recognition, this allows CNNs to discover local patterns that are invariant to translation and recognizable in any part of the input image. Furthermore, each layer can learn spatial hierarchies of the patterns that correspond to increasingly complex, spatially hierarchical visual concepts. From a computational perspective this saves an enormous amount of computation as compared to densely connected networks that can learn only global patterns. Multiple types of patterns can be discovered using multiple channels, where each channel represents a specific type of kernel. In this paper we have used 32 channels.

CNNs may be appropriate models in cybersecurity because such models can be trained in one domain or type of attack and adapted to another type of attack. Since the feature sets for each attack types differ slightly models that are trained directly on the raw features are not transferable. Rather than using the raw features, we transform the features into 0–1 ranges using min-max normalization and reshape them into $50 \times 50 \times 3$ images with three channels, which mimic RGB images. The CNN model is then trained on these input data in one domain and subsequently re-used for detecting cyber attacks in other domains.

Input: a set of features, $f_1 \ldots f_n$;
Input: image size $img_{row} \times img_{col}$, number of channels k;
Output: set of k Channel images;
normalize $f_1 \ldots f_n$ in the range of 0-1;
$p \leftarrow floor(m \times m \times k/n)$;
for $i \leftarrow 1$ **to** p **do**
  | reshape p rows into $image_i$
end

Algorithm 1: Reshape images

The deep learning model trains a convolutional neural network from the input data as $50 \times 50 \times 3$ images that are created as shown in Algorithm 1. Corresponding to each image is a label that indicates whether it is a "normal" traffic or a malicious traffic. This requires stratifying the raw data into the classes before they are reshaped into images. The network is initialized with random weights w and bias b. Next mini-batches are created from the training data and the class label scores are calculated for each data from which the binary cross-entropy loss is calculated and the gradients of the loss are used to update the weights through back propagation. For each epoch the losses and accuracies are calculated as performance metrics. This process is repeated for a pre-defined number of epochs at which point the model is trained. Algorithm 2 shows the details of these steps.

Input: a set of images, $I = i_1 \ldots i_m$;
Input: a set of corresponding labels, $L = l_1 \ldots l_m$;
Input: learning rate ϵ;
Input: batch size k, and number of epochs p;
Output: trained network;
for $i \leftarrow 1$ **to** p **do**
  Create mini-batches of size k from I and L;
  for *each* $X \in I$ **do**
    Calculate the binary cross entropy loss using the computed labels L_c
    and L;
    Update the network weights
  end
end

Algorithm 2: Training the deep learning model

4 Experimental Results

4.1 Data

In our experiments we used the intrusion detection evaluation dataset from the *Canadian Institute for Cybersecurity* [1], that contains common attacks that resemble real-world packet capture (PCAP) data. The data resembled network traffic for a period of five days in July 2017. We excluded the data from one of the days when there were no attacks. The type of attacks included port scan, distributed denial of service (DDoS), Botnet, Web attacks, and infiltration. Our model was built using the port scan data and used to identify malicious traffic in the other four datasets. The sizes of the datasets are shown in Table 1.

Table 1. Dataset sizes

Type of attack	Benign traffic	Malicious traffic	Total
Botnet	15,125,360	157,380	15,283,640
DDoS	4,592,746	6,017,269	10,610,015
Infiltration	23,085,280	2880	23,088,160
Portscan	10,202,960	12,714,400	22,917,360
Web attacks	13,454,880	120,560	13,629,280

4.2 Attack Scenarios

We selected four types of attacks from the CICIDS2107 dataset [1]: botnet, DDoS, infiltration, and Web attacks to test the transferability of the model trained on port scans as described in Sect. 4.3. The *botnet* attacks are launched from devices connected to the Internet to establish connection with the victim device, usually with the intent of stealing data. *DDoS* attacks are launched to make machine or network resources temporarily unavailable by overwhelming the victim machines and networks with a large number of bogus requests such that legitimate requests are blocked out. Web attacks take advantage of vulnerabilities through various mechanisms such as SQL Injections, cross-site scripting, and brute force attacks over HTTP. Infiltration attacks are launched from inside a network using a computer that has been compromised via a backdoor through launching attacks such as IP sweep, full port scan, and service enumeration.

4.3 Convolutional Base

We created a four-layer 2D convolutional neural network (CNN) with one convolutional layer, stacked up by one layer to flatten the output of the convolutional layer, one dense layer with 64 units and Rectified Linear Unit (RELU) activation function, with one dense layer having one unit and the *sigmoid* activation function. The optimizer was SGD (stochastic gradient descent algorithm) and the loss function was binary cross-entropy. The convolutional layer consisted of 32 channels with a 3 × 3 kernel size and the RELU activation function. The input data was normalized between 0–1 and reshaped into 50 × 5 × 3 images. The CNN model was trained using the *port scan* data and was tested with 50% validation split and run with a batch size of 32 over 100 epochs. As can be seen from the results in Fig. 1, the slope of the validation loss approaches 0 after 60 epochs.

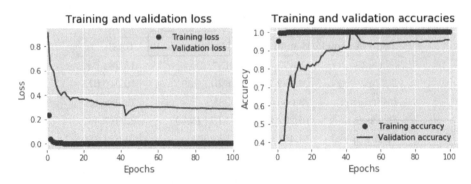

Fig. 1. Validation loss and accuracy for port scan.

4.4 Transfer Learning

As can be seen from Fig. 1 the model trained on the port scan data and tested on 50% hold-out samples was able to achieve over 95% accuracy and a loss around 0.3. However, we wanted to test whether this model can be re-used on other types of attacks with minimal additional learning. Hence we tested the model against the other four datasets we collected. The model was re-used with one additional dense layer with 32 units and the RELU activation function and one output layer with one unit and the sigmoid activation function. The models were run with the SGD optimizer and binary cross-entropy loss function with 0.2 validation split trained over 100 epochs. The validation losses are shown in Fig. 2 and the accuracies are shown in Table 2.

Table 2. Validation losses and accuracies by transfer learning

Type of attack	Validation loss	Validation accuracy
Botnet	0.3132	0.9465
DDoS	0.1371	1
Infiltration	0.0028	1
Web attacks	0.2814	0.9505

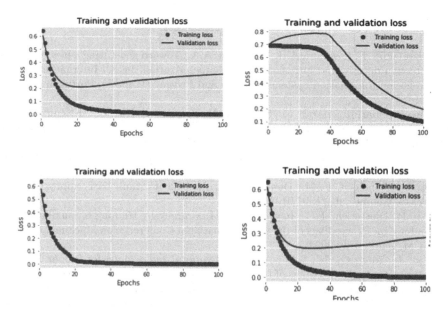

Fig. 2. Validation losses for Botnet (top left), DDoS (top right), Infiltration (bottom left), Web attacks (bottom right).

5   Conclusions and Future Directions

In this paper we have proposed a new method for domain adaptation for deep learning in the domain of cybersecurity. While transfer learning has been applied to many applications there is a critical need in cybersecurity because of lack of availability of data, let alone data with labels. Our method proposes a new representational model of cybersecurity data that is conducive to domain adaptation because the feature sets needed to detect different cyberattacks are typically different. We have demonstrated the efficacy of our proposed methods using datasets provided by the Canadian Institute for Cybersecurity, where we trained a convolutional neural networks using port scan data and applied to detect several different type of attacks including distributed denial of service, web attacks, infiltration, and botnets. The results show that it is possible to develop transfer learning models in detecting different types of cyber attacks with minimal re-training on the target domain.

Our future work in this area is in developing transfer learning models for cybersecurity that require very minimal or no re-training in the target domains. Such models can be invaluable in resource constrained environments such as edge computing. With the rapid adoption of edge computing in areas such as smart and connected communities, smart and connected health, smart manufacturing, and many other applications such methods can be very beneficial. Another are of interest is to develop domain adaptation models for malware detection with methods similar to the one discussed in this paper.

References

1. Sharafaldin, I., Laskhari, A.H., Ghorbani, A.A.: Toward generating a new intrusion detection dataset and intrusion traffic characterization. In 4th International Conference on Information Systems Security and Privacy (ICISSP), Portugal, January 2018

2. Vinayakumar, R., Alazab, M., Soman, K.P., Poornachandrac, P., Al-Nemrat, A.A., Venkataraman, S.: Deep learning approach for intelligent intrusion detection system. IEEE Access **7**, 41525–41550 (2019)

3. Pan, S.J., Yang, Q.: A survey on transfer learning. IEEE Trans. Knowl. Data Eng. **22**(10), 1345–1359 (2010)

4. Raab, C., Schleif, F.-M.: Domain adaptation via low-rank basis approximation. ArXiv, volume=abs/1907.01343 (2019)

5. Wu, P., Dietterich, T.G.: Improving SVM accuracy by training on auxiliary data sources. In: Proceedings of the 21st International Conference on Machine Learning. ACM, Banff, July 2004

6. Yin, J., Yang, Q., Ni, L.M.: Adaptive temporal radio maps for indoor location estimation. In: Proceedings of the 3rd IEEE International Conference on Pervasive Computing and Communications, Kauai Island, Hawaii, USA, March 2005

7. Pan, S.J., Kwok, J.T., Yang, Q., Pan, J.J.: Adaptive localization in a dynamic WiFi environment through multi-view learning. In: Proceedings of the 22nd AAAI Conference on Artificial Intelligence, Vancouver, British Columbia, Canada, pp. 1108–1113, July 2007

8. Zheng, V.W., Yang, Q., Xiang, W., Shen, D.: Transferring localization models over time. In: Proceedings of the 23rd AAAI Conference on Artificial Intelligence, Chicago, Illinois, USA, pp. 1421–1426, July 2008

9. Romero López, A.: Skin lesion detection from dermoscopic images using convolutional neural networks (2017)

10. Zhang, J., Li, W., Ogunbona, P., Xu, D.: Recent advances in transfer learning for cross-dataset visual recognition: a problem-oriented perspective. ACM Comput. Surv. **52**, 1–38 (2019)

11. Hao, P.: Cross-domain recommender system through tag-based models (2018)

12. Raab, C., Schleif, F.-M.: Transfer learning for the probabilistic classification vector machine. In: COPA (2018)

13. Mahdavifar, S., Ghorbani, A.A.: Application of deep learning to cybersecurity: a survey. Neurocomputing **347**(28), 149–176 (2019)

DeepNet: A Deep Learning Architecture for Network-Based Anomaly Detection

Javad Zabihi and Vandana Janeja[✉]

Information Systems Department, University of Maryland,
Baltimore County, MD, USA
{szabihil, vjaneja}@umbc.edu

Abstract. Anomaly detection has been one of the most interesting research areas in the field of cybersecurity. Supervised anomaly detection systems have not been practical and effective enough in real-world scenarios. As a result, different unsupervised anomaly detection pipelines have gained more attention due to their effectiveness. Autoencoders are one of the most powerful unsupervised approaches which can be used to analyze complex and large-scale datasets. This study proposes a method called DeepNet, which investigates the potential of adopting an unsupervised deep learning approach by proposing an autoencoder architecture to detect network intrusion. An autoencoder approach is implemented on network-based data while taking different architectures into account. We provide a comprehensive comparison of the effectiveness of different schemes. Due to the unique methodology of autoencoders, specific methods have been suggested to evaluate the performance of proposed models. The results of this study can be used as a foundation to build a robust anomaly detection system with an unsupervised approach.

Keywords: Anomaly detection · Deep learning · Autoencoder

1 Introduction

Anomaly detection has different applications and plays a significant role in preventing potential threats especially in the cybersecurity domain particularly in computer network systems. The digital world has increased the possibility of facing a wide range of cyber-attacks at an alarming rate and finding practical remedies to deal with this situation is of paramount significance. While attackers adopt complex techniques to pose a threat to network systems, researchers need to develop more advanced approaches to monitor and inspect potential threats causing serious damages. Furthermore, it is highly unlikely to have enough labeled network data available due to the rarity of these kinds of attacks and the complexity of gathering labeled datasets. Thus, it is necessary to adopt an effective unsupervised strategy, such as anomaly detection to be able to overcome the complexity of attacks and identify their patterns effectively.

Anomaly detection has been a popular area of research due to its wide range of application and is applied on different types of data [4–10]. The most researched outlier detection techniques have been around classification and clustering methods.

© Springer Nature Switzerland AG 2020
C. Debruyne et al. (Eds.): OTM 2019 Workshops, LNCS 11878, pp. 229–238, 2020.
https://doi.org/10.1007/978-3-030-40907-4_25

The first technique which is a supervised approach, trains the classifier on the labeled data and then evaluates the trained classifier on the test data and predicts the label for each observation in the test set [11, 12].

The second approach is an unsupervised technique that clusters similar data points in one group based on their characteristics and similarities [13, 14].

Recently, there has been a significant increase in adopting different deep learning approaches to detect anomalies. Hawkins et al. [15] used the neural nets for anomaly detection by calculating the reconstruction error. Sakurada et al. [16] used autoencoders as a one-class technique to detect anomalies and examined the features learned in hidden layer after adopting PCA techniques. Erfani et al. [17] proposed a model consisting of Deep Belief Network (DBN) and SVM for high-dimensional data to detect anomalies.

In this paper, we propose *DeepNet*, a deep learning approach to detect intrusion attacks inside the complex and high-dimensional network data. We utilize UNSW-NB15 dataset with more than two million records and 49 features. The proposed DeepNet, autoencoder model is first trained on the pure dataset, which contains only normal observations. The model learns hidden patterns of normal observations and reconstructs the input. Then the trained model is tested on the test set, which consists of a combination of normal and attack observations to detect potential anomalies. Based on the calculated reconstruction error and a defined threshold, the observations are classified as either normal or intrusion. We implement the same approach on the dataset after doing a comprehensive feature engineering to pick just the most important features with the aim of reducing the dimensionality of the data.

We utilize UNSW-NB15 dataset [1] which is a comprehensive data source to evaluate our methods for detecting network intrusion. There has been a lot of research on adopting different machine learning techniques based on this dataset including AdaBoost ensemble learning method [2], and Gaussian Mixture Model [3]. We discuss promising results with our methods on this dataset.

The rest of the paper is organized as follows. We discuss the methodology in Sect. 2. Experimental results are discussed in Sect. 3. Finally, we conclude in Sect. 4.

2   Proposed Approach

The idea behind using autoencoders to detect anomalies is to train the model on just normal observations. By this, we mean that we train the autoencoder on the training set containing only normal observations, and then use the test set which contains both normal and attack observations for prediction. We expect that the model, which is trained on normal observations will recreate the normal records in the test set more accurately and reproduce attack observations in the test set with higher error. We use root mean squared error as our error measure to calculate the difference between actual record and the reconstructed one. This is the key intuition behind our approach.

Figure 1 displays the steps of our proposed *DeepNet* approach to train our model, test it on the test set, calculate the error, and finally detect outliers based on the magnitude of the reconstruction error.

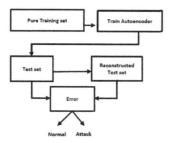

Fig. 1. DeepNet model. We use the pure training set to make the model to learn patterns of normal observations. Then we use the trained model to predict records in the test set. The magnitude of error which is the difference between prediction and actual records helps to label the predictions as either normal or anomaly.

Our proposed DeepNet approach uses a multilayer under-complete autoencoder architecture which is trained on the dataset consisting of only normal observations. We call this as pure training set. So, we need to divide out dataset to training and test sets. The dataset has more than 2 million observations and we choose 98% of the dataset for the training part and the rest for the test set. Then we remove all the attack observations from the training set. After training the model on the pure data, we use the test set to predict the anomalies. By defining a threshold for the error which is the mean square difference between the prediction and the actual test set, we label the records as either anomaly or normal.

First, the encoder part in autoencoder architecture maps data to a lower dimension which is called bottleneck with 8 dimensions by using a stack of feed-forward neural nets. Then, the decoder part starts to recreate the input from bottleneck by increasing the dimension of the latent representation. Finally, the output will be a set of observations which have the same number of dimensions as the input data.

We analyzed different combinations for the number of hidden units in each layer and finally reached to the chosen hidden dimensionalities that are shown in Fig. 2. The encoder compresses the input layer in four steps and after that the decoder part of the architecture starts to rebuild the input layer from the compressed representation.

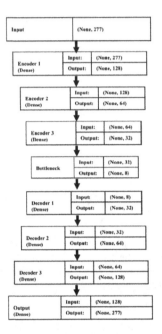

Fig. 2. The autoencoder architecture. After four dense layers, the encoder reaches to the bottleneck. Then the decoder uses four dense layers to reconstruct the training set.

We perform data cleaning and feature engineering on the original dataset and reached a dataset with 277 features that is used to build the model and evaluate it. For the training part, we create a training set which has only normal observations. We train the autoencoder model on the pure training set. Then, create our test set which is a combination of normal and attack records and use the trained autoencoder to reconstruct the test observations. To detect anomalies, we need to calculate the reconstruction error which is defined as the difference between the actual test set and the reconstructed test set. After calculating the reconstruction error, we need to define a threshold to identify the outliers. In other words, the threshold is the line that separates normal records from attack ones.

By defining a threshold, we will be able to classify observations as either normal or intrusion. If the reconstruction error for a record is greater than the threshold, it will be identified as an anomaly and if the error is lower than the threshold, the record will be normal.

Here, we are faced with the precision-recall trade-off. For precision, we want to find out how many of our attack predictions were actually anomalies. So, here we need to have lower false positives (incorrect attack predictions) to increase the precision. For recall, we want to identify the number of true attack predictions out of all actual anomalies in the test set. It is obvious that a decrease in false negatives (incorrect normal predictions) will lead to an increase in recall. As a result, we need to understand the importance of false negatives and false positives in our analysis and decide, which one is more important for us. Clearly, we would like to minimize both types of error as much as possible, but we do care more about reducing false negatives to be able to detect positive class that is the anomalies more accurately. To conclude, recall is the measure we want to maximize, and this will happen with a decrease in threshold and precision. Thus, we need to look for a threshold to give us a high recall but also not very low precision

As the final step, we need to measure the performance of our model. The dataset has labels, but we remove them from the dataset before building our model and after prediction, we can use those labels to find out how accurately the model predicted the test records.

3 Experiments

3.1 Dataset

The autoencoder approach is an unsupervised technique which means we do not need to have access to the labels. In this work, we choose UNSW-NB12 network data which consists of normal activities and nine types of attacks with 49 features defining each observation. The independent attributes contain different measurements and descriptions of the flow between hosts and the network packets. There is also a label column in the dataset which indicates whether an observation is normal or attack. We utilize this to evaluate the effectiveness of our approach.

To build our model, we need to split the dataset into training and test set. In the end, to evaluate our model we use the labels in the dataset to measure the accuracy of the model in detecting anomalies.

The test set contains 22168 normal observations and 3230 attack records which means only around 13 percent of test set belongs to anomalies. We are dealing with an imbalanced dataset and it is better to take recall and precision into account as the criteria for calculating the performance of our model. Here the positive class is the attack and negative class belongs to normal observations. The goal is to recognize the positive class more accurately. So, we are more eager to avoid false negatives rather than false positives. In other words, predicting actual normal observations as attack class is not as bad as predicting some attack observations as normal ones. As a result, having a higher recall would be more important than having high precision in detecting attacks.

3.2 Results and Discussion

We next discuss the results of our experiment on the dataset and evaluation of the DeepNet model based on different measures of performance. As we mentioned in the previous section, we need to define a threshold to measure the performance of the model. For this reason, precision and recall scores are displayed in Figs. 3 and 4 for different thresholds.

According to the plot, the higher threshold leads to higher precision and recall. We need to choose a threshold small enough to maximize recall score but also large enough to not make precision score too small.

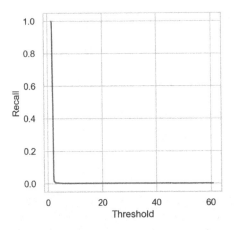

Fig. 3. The recall score for different thresholds. The recall score calculates the percentage of correctly predicted anomalies out of all actual anomalies in the test set. We aim to maximize this score.

Fig. 4. The precision score for different thresholds. The precision score gives the percentage of accurately predicted anomalies out of observations that predicted as anomalies.

Figure 5 shows both precision and recall for different thresholds in a graph to understand how they change with respect to the threshold. The Precision-Recall curve in Fig. 8 makes it even more clear how the precision-recall trade-off affects the performance of the model. For instance, take the two extremes into account. First, if we pick a threshold that gives us a precision very close to 1, the points around the vertical line on the left-hand side of Fig. 6, recall score will be very close to zero. Second, if we choose a threshold to get a recall close to 1, the points close to right-hand side of Fig. 8, the precision score will not become greater than 0.82. Another measure of performance is the Receiver Operating Characteristic curve (ROC curve) and the area under this curve (AUC) which is shown in Fig. 7. The area under the ROC curve is very close to 1 which indicates the model works well on finding anomalies in the test set.

If we choose a threshold equals to 1, based on the precision-recall trade-off, we can create a confusion matrix to find out about the number of true predictions and also the number of false predictions for positive and negative classes. Figure 8 shows the confusion matrix for this threshold. According to this graph, the DeepNet model was able to identify all attack observations correctly but misclassified some normal observations as anomalies. Figure 9 displays the performance of the model after choosing a threshold equal to 1.0 graphically. This plot shows reconstruction error for all data points in the test set and also the horizontal line which is the chosen threshold.

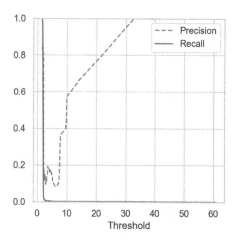

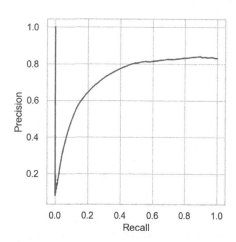

Fig. 5. Precision and Recall scores for different thresholds. This shows a range of threshold we need to pick.

Fig. 6. The precision-recall curve. The precision-recall trade-off is visible in this graph. A very high precision leads to a very small recall. A very high recall will not give a precision more than .82.

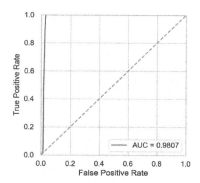

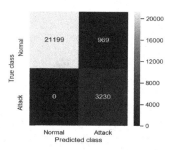

Fig. 7. ROC curve. By plotting the true positive rates against the false positive rates for various thresholds, we reach to the roc curve. By calculating the area under this curve, we can measure the performance of our model. The closer the area under the curve to 1, the more accurate is the model.

Fig. 8. Confusion matrix for threshold = 1.0. The model was able to predict all the attack observations correctly but misclassified 969 normal observations as anomalies. This is due to precision-recall trade-off which leads to a higher number of false positives when we want to minimize the number of false negatives.

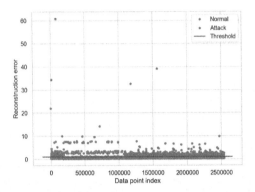

Fig. 9. Reconstruction error for threshold = 1.0. The red points and blue points are the actual attack records and the actual normal observations in the test set respectively. The orange line is the threshold. All the observations with a reconstruction error more than 1 will be above the threshold line. (Color figure online)

To visualize the effect of applying autoencoder on the test set, we can use T-distributed Stochastic Neighbor Embedding plot (TSNE plot). TSNE plot adopts dimensionality reduction technique to create a dataset with a smaller set of dimensions when preserving the most useful information. This approach makes it easier to visualize high-dimensional datasets without losing too much information.

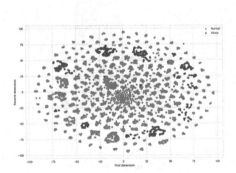

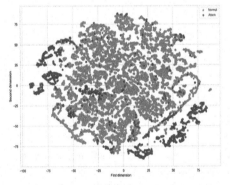

Fig. 10. T-SNE of the original test set. By reducing the dimensions of the original test set, we can visualize the spread of normal and attack observations. The green points are the normal observations and the red points are the anomalies. It is almost impossible to draw a boundary that divides the normal and the attack records. (Color figure online)

Fig. 11. T-SNE of the reconstructed test set. The new plot of the test set after learning the latent representation seems more separable. Here, by drawing a circle we can approximately create a boundary that separates normal observations from anomalies.

Here we map our test dataset with 277 dimensions to 2-dimensional dataset by adopting this approach to be able to understand how normal and attack observations spread in the dataset. Figure 10 shows the result of this transformation by representing green points as normal records and red points as attack observations. It is clear that there are not two separate clusters to classify two classes easily. In other words, it is difficult to draw a line to separate normal records from the anomalies.

Next, we train the autoencoder model on the training set and add the weights of the encoder part which learned latent representations of the training set to a new neural network. By adding these weights to a new network and predict their effects on the test set, we generate a latent representation for the test set. In fact, we predict the effects of latent representation learned by the autoencoder on the test set. Finally, we use the new test set which represents the latent representation of the original test set to create another TSNE plot and visualize the effects of the autoencoder. Figure 11 shows that there are approximately two separate clusters after this transformation. A circle can separate normal and attack observations with high accuracy. So, it is clear that learning latent representation can help to separate two classes in the dataset.

4 Conclusion and Future Work

In this paper, we have completed a thorough analysis of a network-related dataset to detect anomalies by adopting a deep learning approach in the DeepNet model. We proposed an autoencoder architecture to cluster normal and attack observations of an unbalanced dataset. By compressing the training set, the model learned some useful hidden representations. Then reconstruction the training set lead to building a model that captures the patterns inside normal observations exact enough to distinguish between normal and attack records. The experimental results indicate that the model works well on predicting the attack records. We have faced some misclassifications for normal observations due to the effect of precision-recall trade-off. It is important to have enough domain knowledge when choosing a threshold.

We plan to apply our model on additional practical applications to measure the effectiveness of using a deep autoencoder architecture. We also want to work on the architecture of the model to make it more robust in capturing the hidden patterns inside high-dimensional datasets.

References

1. The UNSW-NB12 dataset. https://www.unsw.adfa.edu.au/unsw-canberra-cyber/cybersecuri ty/ADFA-NB15-Datasets/
2. Moustafa, N., Turnbull, B., Choo, K.R.: An ensemble intrusion detection technique based on proposed statistical flow features for protecting network traffic of internet of things. IEEE Internet Things J. **6**, 4815–4830 (2018)
3. Moustafa, N., Misra, G., Slay, J.: Generalized outlier gaussian mixture technique based on automated association features for simulating and detecting web application attacks. IEEE Trans. Sustain. Comput. (2018)

4. Liu, G., Yi, Z., Yang, S.: A hierarchical intrusion detection model based on the PCA neural networks. Neurocomputing **70**(7-9), 1561–1568 (2007)
5. Sharma, A., Panigrahi, P.K.: A review of financial accounting fraud detection based on data mining techniques. Int. J. Comput. Appl. **39**(1), 37–47 (2012)
6. Nadeem, A., Howarth, M.P.: A survey of MANET intrusion detection amp; prevention approaches for network layer attacks. IEEE Commun. Surv. Tutor. **15**(4), 2027–2045 (2013)
7. Hodge, V.J., Austin, J.: A survey of outlier detection methodologies. Artif. Intell. Rev. **22**, 85–126 (2004)
8. Wang, Y., Li, D., Du, Y., Pan, Z.: Anomaly detection in traffic using l1-norm minimization extreme learning machine. Neurocomputing **149, Part A**, 415–425 (2015)
9. Xu, D., Song, R., Wu, X., Li, N., Feng, W., Qian, H.: Video anomaly detection based on a hierarchical activity discovery within spatio-temporal contexts. Neuro-Computing **143**, 144–152 (2014)
10. Wang, J., Xu, Z.: Crowd anomaly detection for automated video surveillance. In: Proceedings of the ICDP, pp. 1–6 (2015)
11. Cui, X., Liu, Q., Gao, M., Metaxas, D.N.: Abnormal detection using interaction energy potentials. In: Proceedings of the IEEE Conference on Computer Vision and Pattern Recognition (CVPR), pp. 3161–3167. IEEE (2011)
12. Li, X., Bowers, C.P., Schnier, T.: Classification of energy consumption in buildings with outlier detection. IEEE Trans. Ind. Electron. **57**(11), 3639–3644 (2010)
13. MacQueen, J.: Some methods for classification and analysis of multivariate observations. In: Proceedings of the Fifth Berkeley Symposium on Mathematical Statistics and Probability, Volume 1: Statistics, pp. 281–297 (1967)
14. Ester, M., Kriegel, H.-P., Sander, J., Xu, X.: A density-based algorithm for discovering clusters in large spatial databases with noise, pp. 226–231. AAAI Press (1996)
15. Hawkins, S., He, H., Williams, G., Baxter, R.: Outlier detection using replicator neural networks. In: Kambayashi, Y., Winiwarter, W., Arikawa, M. (eds.) DaWaK 2002. LNCS, vol. 2454, pp. 170–180. Springer, Heidelberg (2002). https://doi.org/10.1007/3-540-46145-0_17
16. Sakurada, M., Yairi, T.: Anomaly detection using autoencoders with nonlinear dimensionality reduction. In: Proceedings of the MLSDA 2014 2nd Workshop on Machine Learning for Sensory Data Analysis, p. 4. ACM (2014)
17. Erfani, S.M., Rajasegarar, S., Karunasekera, S., Leckie, C.: High-dimensional and large-scale anomaly detection using a linear one-class SVM with deep learning. Pattern Recogn. **58**, 121–134 (2016)

A Contextual Driven Approach to Risk Event Tagging

Shawn Johnson[(⊠)] and George Karabatis

Information Systems Department, University of Maryland,
Baltimore County (UMBC), Baltimore, MD 21250, USA
{yv74924,georgek}@umbc.edu

Abstract. Current methods of tagging events in a particular context, when deciding which ones pose a security risk on an enterprise network are inadequate. For example, changes in an environment, such as a larger number of HIPAA violations by certain user roles, can pose a risk to specific organizational functions or cyber infrastructure. To compound the problem, different information owners typically specify different user contexts based on differing organizational or individual needs. To address this problem, we developed an approach that utilizes semantic annotations, a technique that can aid in the understanding of how an event may affect knowledge of information in a domain. In this approach, semantic annotations are used to enable the tagging of events in accordance with differing organizational goals and user preferences. This work can be used to flag possible security violations and assist in their prevention.

Keywords: Ontology · Context · Risk · Security

1 Introduction

Context awareness has long been proposed to enable the characterization of cyber risk but current methods for utilizing context to determine which events pose a risk to an enterprise network are inadequate. This problem is even further exacerbated when trying to utilize multiple sets of user preferences in the characterization of context of an environment of varying needs of an organization or person. To address this problem, we have developed an approach that utilizes semantic annotations. We dynamically generate a local ontology from a set of events in different partitions, where each partition is intended for a separate user. We then enable a user to select entities to tag resources based on the preferences retrieved from DBpedia [23]. We also tag events according to an additional set of preferences added to an ontology after it was generated. Then a final set of semantic annotations is added, selected by the user to each event that matched the user-specified preferences. Our work makes the following key contributions: (1) We enable a user (or multiple users) to choose from a set of customizable semantically relevant annotations with robust semantics (with the same semantic meaning) from multiple data sources, rather than having to label each complaint. For example, Bob, a HIPAA compliance investigator, is investigating a potential HIPAA compliance violation due to improper disclosure of records. Multiple departments within Bob's company have different labels for improper disclosure of records

© Springer Nature Switzerland AG 2020
C. Debruyne et al. (Eds.): OTM 2019 Workshops, LNCS 11878, pp. 239–248, 2020.
https://doi.org/10.1007/978-3-030-40907-4_26

violations. Using our approach, all reports of the same violation from different departments will use the same organizational policy to report and assign meaning to an improper disclosure of HIPAA records.

(2) Our approach is highly parallelizable, allowing large numbers of users to tag large numbers of events according to their specified preferences, at the same time.

(3) The resulting ontology is dynamically generated from each user's assigned partition, rather than being forced to utilize the same taxonomy for all users in a given system.

(4) We have developed a prototype and validated our approach by conducting experiments and have evaluated the initial results using precision and recall metrics.

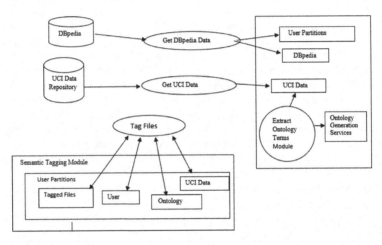

Fig. 1. Components and processes of semantic annotations architecture

Figure 1 provides an overview of the modules comprising our system. We describe the architecture of these components below:

(1) The Data Repository is used as our thesaurus to request UCI datasets to build and test our approach and ontology.

(2) DBpedia is used to request any semantic information necessary to build our ontologies. We add the retrieved semantic information to events matching selected user preferences.

(3) An extracted ontology terms module contains data pulled from the UCI Repository and DBpedia for each user partition. The ontology-generation services are software modules that use the available data files and semantically rich information retrieved from DBpedia to build the ontology.

(4) The semantic tagging module extracts the saved user preferences from the ontology, tagging any events matching the preferences and adding semantically rich tags to the matched events.

2 Approach

User partitions are generated based on the number of users in the system, and each partition has a separate taxonomy generated within it for each user. In each partition, a user can select a set of custom annotations by first dynamically generating an ontology from a corpus of available events using the Organik Framework, as each user will have different events to tag in each partition [1]. The Organik Framework creates a taxonomy with several entities generated from an existing corpus. By simply opening the previously generated taxonomy in Protégé [24], we can open the saved .owl files in Apache Jena for editing. The previously generated ontology can also be edited to specify additional preferences about the events in a corpus that can be selected by a user, such as the event owner or group. Users can also select preferences based on a list of entities that, using the ontology, can tag events. The selected entity (with accompanying URL in the taxonomy) is then sent to DBpedia, and a list of matching English attributes is returned to the user. The user selects the final set of preferences for tagging the events within a corpus, and these are added to all matching events within that corpus. A final set of matching events is then tagged based on user-selected preferences and returned to the user. Figure 2 below depicts a sample process flow detailing how events are semantically tagged. Semantic annotations are required so that semantically driven trees can characterize occurrences generated from the ontologies. We model our ontology based on "The Operational Definition of Context" [2], with five separate contextual categories.

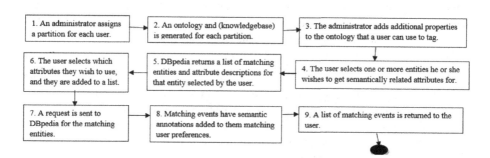

Fig. 2. Semantic annotation process flow

3 Experiments and Evaluation

3.1 Experiment Setup for Semantic Annotations

For our work with semantic annotations we elected to use a system with 16 GB of RAM, 700 GB of HardDisk and an I7 Processor with a clock speed of 4.8 Ghz. To test our framework, we created a series of virtual machines, each with approximately

10 GB of hard disk space, 4 GB of RAM, and 1 Ghz of clock speed. We wrote our code in Java, as this is the language typically used for work with Hadoop. We chose an RDF/OWL for our model because these models provide both sufficient expressivity necessary to ensure our user preferences are expressed correctly and for the mature software packages available. We chose Apache Jena because we found it to be the most mature library available for use with RDF and OWL models. Apache Jena's rich API allows us to access different parts of the ontology with ease. We chose the Organik Framework because it is one of the few publicly available robust tools capable of generating an ontology with strong semantics. In addition, to enable parallelizable generation of taxonomies and semantic tagging of different sets of files, we used Apache Spark [23], whose API is more user-friendly and more stable than MapReduce.

3.2   Semantic Annotations: Data Sources and Experimentation Settings

In the next stage of our research, we ran experiments using different corpuses from the UCI Machine Learning Repository. We conducted our experiments using the Open-Rank Data Set [3] NSF Award Research Abstracts and Reuters 50/50 Data Set [4] from the UCI Machine Learning Repository website. We also used a dataset from UCR Data Repository. The user-selected entities and attributes and matching description pairs were added to sets of events with ASCII Text in varying formats.

Sample Scenario for the Semantic Annotations Experiments: Robert wishes to tag any event concerning HIPAA-related crime. He wants to apply a set of consistent labels to ensure different events have the same applied meaning using a common set of entities found within a corpus. In this case, he applies the following attributes: thefts of laptops containing PII, from cars, occurring between 9 a.m. and 11 a.m., in 2003. Scenarios 2–5 showing in Fig. 3 are variants of Scenario 1.

We ran three sets of experiments as follows:

1. *No context and no ontologies:* These experiments were executed by searching for exact matches with specified user preferences in the document corpus.
2. *Ontologies and no context:* These experiments were executed using files tagged using the ontologies generated from the Organik Framework. The files were tagged using those ontologies but with no user preferences for the entities or their attributes added to any of the semantically annotated files.
3. *Ontologies and context:* These experiments were executed with the files tagged using both the ontologies, but also with the saved user preferences parsed from the ontologies. The tagged files were processed using Apache Spark.

3.3   Evaluation

Obtaining Ground Truth for Semantic Annotation Experiments
We obtained ground truth using the following method:

1. We manually calculated the number of events with no ontologies and no context. The no ontologies and no context experiments served as our baseline.

2. We also manually checked the events for "ontologies and no context" and "ontologies and context."
3. We then applied the measurement of precision and recall to all three sets.
4. We then compared the results of the baseline experiment with the two other sets.

We used three well-known metrics to validate our approach: precision, recall, and F-measure. Recall is defined as the fraction of the retrieved records that are relevant to the query:

$$\text{Recall} = |\{\text{relevant records}\} / |\{\text{relevant records}\} \cap \{\text{retrieved records}\}|$$

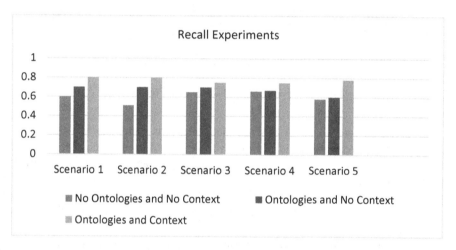

Fig. 3. Experiment results measuring recall for semantic annotations methodology

In the above sets of experiments (as in Scenario 1), the recall for "no ontologies and no context" is low because exact keyword searches were used. In "ontologies and no context," the recall is higher because terms in the dynamically generated ontology matched one or more of the search terms. "Ontologies and context" has the highest recall because the tagged events match both the terms in the dynamically generated ontology and in the user-specified preferences (Fig. 4).

Precision is defined as the fraction of the retrieved records that are relevant to the search:

$$\text{Precision} = |\{\text{retrieved records}\}| / |\{\text{relevant records}\} \cap \{\text{retrieved records}\}|$$

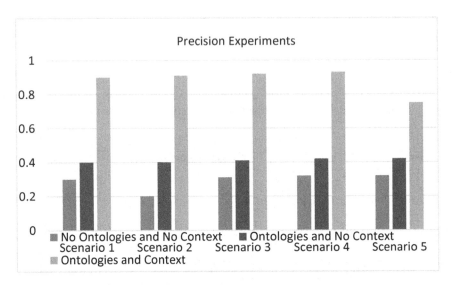

Fig. 4. Experiment results measuring precision

The precision for "no ontologies and no context" is extremely low because the majority of the search results did not match the intended user search preferences, as exact keywords were used for each search. "Ontologies and no context" returned a higher number of files because these matched the semantic constraints specified in the ontology. "Ontologies and context" returned the highest number of files, as it included those that matched both constraints specified in the ontology and the chosen user preferences (Fig. 5).

The F-measure, or F_1, is used to measure the accuracy of precision and recall by calculating the following:

$$F = 2 * (\text{precision} * \text{recall}) / (\text{precision} + \text{recall})$$

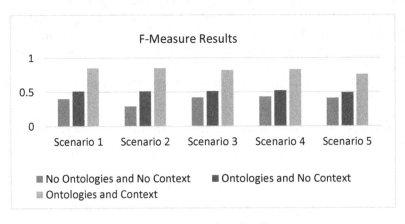

Fig. 5. Experiment results using F-measure

The *F*-scores for "no ontologies and no context" are extremely low because exact keywords were used to match the user preferences. The *F*-scores for "ontologies and no context" are higher because many of the results match the terms indexed in the ontology. "Ontologies and context" returned the highest *F*-scores because the results matched both the ontology and the semantically enriched user preferences.

Results Discussion

The empirical proof provided indicates the strong validity of our approach. We were able to illustrate real improvement in both precision and recall. In all the scenarios, recall was sustained, and precision was improved. This initial work provides the basis for a number of major contributions to this paper:

(1) We enable a user (or multiple users) to choose from a set of customizable, semantically relevant annotations with robust semantics, rather than being obliged to rely on the meaning assigned by an authoritative reference or definition in an underlying system.

(2) Our approach is highly parallelizable, allowing large numbers of users to tag large numbers of events, according to their specified preferences, at the same time.

(3) The resulting ontology is dynamically generated from each user's assigned partition, rather than being forced to utilize the same taxonomy for all users in a given system.

(4) Based on the results provided, we propose that we have developed a means of enabling user preferences to tag objects using robust semantics.

4 Relevant Work

In this section, we cover relevant background on work that has already been completed for automatically generating ontologies, and relevant work on automated and semi-automated semantic annotations as well. A large amount of work on semi-automated and automated approaches on automatically summarizing documents. (Dans and Martins conducted a survey that explains and summarizes a large body of research that has been conducted related to document summarization [6].) While both topics are similar, document summarization focuses on summarizing or paraphrasing all or parts of a document where semantic annotations focus on adding tags to a given object to provide a richer semantic association with given domain.

A large volume of research has been conducted in the automated generation of ontologies. Our literature review focused on natural language approaches from text, as well as methods that involved WordNet. Biebow at el. created TERMINAE, an ontology generation tool that assists a knowledge engineer creating a taxonomy from a corpus of texts using natural language processing methods. TERMINAE required a great degree of involvement by a knowledge engineer in assigning candidate terms and assign definitions. Organik, automatically selects which terms are most important and assigns DBpedia definitions as important references. [7] Nobecourt created an approach for iteratively creating ontology using natural language texts. This tool also required a knowledge engineer to iteratively build the model. [8] Our approach enables a user, not a knowledge engineer to select which entities and attributes he or she wants to set semantic preferences for. Melby et al. developed an approach for developing an ontology using a termbase. [9] While it was robust approach for creating ontologies there was no framework available for implementing its methodological approach. Organik offered a readily available set of libraries to implement for dynamically generating a taxonomy. Khan and Luo also developed a robust approach for automatically generating an ontology using WordNET. [10] Kong et al. [11] and Moldovan and Girju [12] also developed an approach for generating an ontology of sub-concepts using WordNet. Keitz et al., developing a semi-automated approach for generating ontologies from corporate intranets. [13] Meadache and Stab developed an automatically ontology learning framework from learning ontologies from text. While Text-2-Onto offered a framework that we could use to build ontologies from text, it was riddled with a large number of bugs vs. using the Organik Framework [14].

A large amount of work has also been conducted on looking at semi-automated and automated approaches for semantic annotations. Cimiano et al. developed an approach for automatically adding semantic annotations to semantic web resources by using a natural language processing technique that created a pattern string based off of the schema and adding a specific semantic annotation to a web resource based on that schema and the number of hits that across the web based on the same resource as well. [15] While this approach offered a unique approach for automatically tagging a web resource based on both its content and structure, our approach focuses on enabling a user to select the types of entities and attributes of those entities. Dingli et al. developed an approach for automatically semantically annotating documents by using data as seed annotations to be used in simple information extraction for boot-strap learning to be used to induce learning for additional information extraction algorithms. [16] Our work focuses on enabling a user to select which entities and attributes of entities he or she wished to semantically tag an event. Febra et al. developed a parallelizable framework for generating a semantic graph in RDF from a large collection of heterogeneous data sources. [17] Dill et al. developed an application for tagging web applications at scale using a standard ontology and tagging web pages using The Resource Description Framework Specification. [18] This work also did not involve developing user preferences at scale using ontologies. Leung et al. developed a framework for inferring semantic properties using lattice-based ontologies for model-based engineering techniques. This work also did not involve developing user preferences at scale. [19] Kiryalov et al. developed a knowledge base powered for automatically semantically indexing documents. Unlike Kiryalov et al.'s system, our system dynamically generates an ontology enabling a user to select several types of tags he and/or she may wish to tag entities with. In addition, we use a parallelizable framework for tagging annotations versus a standard knowledgebase that often requires special hardware as the size of a knowledge base grows. [1] Carneiro et al. developed a probabilistic scalable approach for automatically semantically annotating image and audio files and [20] Turnbull et al. developed a scalable system capable of semantically annotating audio files as well [21].

5 Conclusions

While we have made progress on our approach there is still considerable work to be accomplished to expand it, namely, we plan on massively expanding the experiment regime of scale related experiments including additional experiments for concurrency and latency of our approach. In addition, we plan on testing out our approach on thousands of IoT devices in parallel at the same time. Finally, we plan on researching additional techniques to be able to dynamically rebuild an ontology.

References

1. Kiryakov, A., Popov, B., Terziev, I., Manov, D., Ognyanoff, D.: Semantic annotation, indexing, and retrieval (2004). 1570-8268
2. Organik Knowledge Management: Taxonomy Learning Implementing. Organik Knowledge Management, 07 August 2015. http://organik.opendfki.de/wiki/TaxonomyLearningImplementation. Accessed 07 Oct 2015
3. Zimmermann, A., Lorenz, A., Oppermann, R.: An operational definition of context. In: Kokinov, B., Richardson, D.C., Roth-Berghofer, T.R., Vieu, L. (eds.) CONTEXT 2007. LNCS (LNAI), vol. 4635, pp. 558–571. Springer, Heidelberg (2007). https://doi.org/10.1007/978-3-540-74255-5_42
4. Ganesan, K., Zhai, C.: Opinion based entity ranking. Inf. Retr. **15**, 116–150 (2011)
5. Liu, Z.: Reuters 50/50 Data Set. National Engineering Research Center for E-Learning
6. Das, D., Martins, A.F.T.: A survey on automatic text summarization (2007)
7. Biébow, B., Szulman, S., Clément, Av.J.B.: TERMINAE: a linguistics-based tool for the building of a domain ontology. In: Fensel, D., Studer, R. (eds.) EKAW 1999. LNCS (LNAI), vol. 1621, pp. 49–66. Springer, Heidelberg (1999). https://doi.org/10.1007/3-540-48775-1_4
8. Nobecourt, J., Dagstuhl: A Method for Building Formal Ontologies From Texts. Springer, Germany (2002)
9. Lonsdale, D., Ding, Y., Embley, D.W., Melby, A.: Peppering knowledge sources with salt: boosting conceptual content for ontology generation. American Association for Artificial Intelligence (2002)
10. Khan, L., Luo, F.: ICTAI 2002, Proceedings of the 14th IEEE International Conference on Tools with Artificial Intelligence (ICTAI 2002). IEEE Computer Society (2002)
11. Kong, H., Hwang, M., Kim, P.: Design of the automatic ontology building system about the specific domain knowledge. IEEE (2006). 89-5519-129-4
12. Moldovan, D.I., Roxana, G.: Domain-Specific Knowledge Acquisition and Classification Using Wordnet. AAAI Press (2000)
13. Kietz, J., Maedche, A., Volz, R.: A method for semi-automatic ontology acquisition from a corporation intranet. Pins, France (2000)
14. Maedche, A., Staab, S.: The text-to-onto ontology learning environment (2000)
15. Cimiano, P., Ladwig, G., Staab, S.: Gimme' the context: context driven semantic annotation with CPANKOW. ACM, New York (2005). 1-59593-046-9
16. Dingli, A., Ciravegna, F., Wilks, Y.: Automatic semantic annotation using unsupervised information extraction and integration. ACM (2000)
17. Fabra, J., Hernández, S., Álvarez, P., Otero, E., Vidal, J.C., Lama, M.: A practical experience concerning the parallel semantic annotation of a large-scale data collection. ACM, New York (2013)

18. Dill, S., et al.: A case for automated large scale semantic annotation. J. Web Semant. **1**, 115–132 (2003)

19. Leung, M.-K., et al.: Scalable semantic annotation using lattice-based ontologies. In: Schürr, A., Selic, B. (eds.) MODELS 2009. LNCS, vol. 5795, pp. 393–407. Springer, Heidelberg (2009). https://doi.org/10.1007/978-3-642-04425-0_31

20. Carneiro, G., Chan, A.B., Moreno, P.J., Vasconcelos, N.: Supervised learning of semantic classes for image annotation and retrieval. IEEE Trans. Pattern Anal. Mach. Intell. **29**, 394–410 (2007)

21. Turnbull, D., Barrington, L., Torres, D., Lanckriet, G.: Semantic annotation and retrieval of music and sound effects. IEEE Trans. Audio Speech Lang. Process. **16**, 467–476 (2008). 1558-7916

22. Apache Spark. http://spark.apache.org. Accessed 07 Sept 2015

23. Yang, C.-Y., Lin, H.-Y.: An Automated semantic annotation based-on WordNet ontology. IEEE. Seoul, South Korea (2010). 978-1-4244-7671-8

24. Erdmann, M., Maedche, A., Schnurr, H.-P., Staab, S.: From manual to semi-automatic semantic annotation: about ontology-based text annotation tools. Association For Computational Linquistics (2000)

Author Index

Printed in the United States
By Bookmasters